SUFI THOUGHT
AND ACTION

SUFI THOUGHT AND ACTION

assembled by

Idries Shah

THE OCTAGON PRESS
LONDON

**Published with the aid of a subvention
from The Sufi Trust**

*Opinions expressed in the papers reproduced herein
are to be taken as those of their authors*

First published 1990
Reprinted 1993

Photoset, printed and bound in Great Britain by
Redwood Press Limited, Melksham, Wiltshire

CONTENTS

Sufi Spiritual Rituals and Beliefs

OBJECT OF SUFI TEACHING:

The object of Sufi spiritual teaching can be expressed as: to help to refine the individual's consciousness so that it may reach the Radiances of Truth, from which one is cut off by ordinary activities of the world. The term used for illuminations or radiances is *Anwar*.

MYSTICISM IS NOT MAGIC:

It is a misunderstanding, as – for instance – the book *Zia al Qulub* (among many others) emphasises, to think that a mystic either desires, or can achieve, identification with God in the sense of acquiring divine attributes or powers. Such a concept belongs to magical, not mystical, thinking.

In common parlance, as well as in the minds of many who should know better, 'mystical' is bracketted with mystery and mystification in the senses of something confusing or difficult to understand. These secondary meanings, of course, are only due to 'unconscious illiteracy'.

Sufis require the reduction of the effects of 'material attributes', those things which stand in the way of higher understanding. Many things which repetitious or over-simplified religion presents as spiritual are, when examined, found to be simply aspects of materiality. One example is emotionalism.

1

COMMON DISTORTIONS IN RELIGIOUS THOUGHT:

However widespread and familiar they may be, many presen-
tations of religion are abbreviated and distorted versions of
something of which the original is not known to current practitioners. The outlines can be discerned, more often than not, and
examples of some parts of these are given later.

A regression to primitive thinking, and the desire for order,
never far from the human mind and often (not always) useful, are
the chief culprits.

Where the primitive feeling is allied to equally primitive logic,
we get a familiar distortion: the belief that if things material are
obstacles, then 'killing or suppressing the material' should lead to
enlightenment. Yet this, far from being useful, is essentially magical thinking.

Omar Khayyam has pointed out this fallacy, when (echoing the
foolish) he writes: 'If wine is the enemy of religion, I shall devour
the enemy of religion'. Quite understandably, this phrase has
been misinterpreted, due to the narrow mentality of literalists.
They have imagined that Khayyam is himself deriding religion!
The poet is a humorist: literalists often, perhaps always, lack this
capacity.

Self-mortification, far from producing liberation from material
things, is far more likely to cause either an unhinged mind,
delusions or a masochistic taste for more suffering, experienced, of
course, as joy.

ESCAPE FROM THE INSULATION FROM TRUTH:

'Polishing the mirror', or 'removing the dust' are terms in Sufic
use, referring to the process of liberation from those elements,
natural and acquired, with which 'the world' insulates humanity
from the greater Truth.

Sufis, far from being able to build on the mentality of conditioned beliefs, generally have to help 'detoxify' the mind from
harmful, deadening or other imaginedly important illusions, fixations or emotion-based ideas.

That which is capable of perceiving objective reality is, in

Sufism, the human soul (*ruh*). Materiality is the term employed for that which weighs down the soul.

The soul is conceived of as a part of a single 'sea', a 'Sea of Peace', on the surface of which ripples, waves and storms constitute the effects of materialism, attachment to objects, and negative thought.

Speaking of the primordial unity of being, Rumi, in the first book of his *Mathnawi*, says:

> We were extensive and we were all one substance
> Without head or foot we were, all one head.
> We were all one substance, like sunshine:
> Without knots we were, and clear, like water.

PENETRATION OF PRIDE INTO RELIGION:

Materialism, attachment to things of the world, includes pride. Many religious people suffer from pride: taking pleasure or even delight in being good, or religious. In ordinary religious circles it is so common for no real distinction to be made between spiritual people and the self-deceived that a teaching such as Sufism offers on this point has been considered vital as a constant reminder and corrective. The most prideful dislike this reminder most. As a consequence, following a common pattern, they attack the Sufis, not their own problem.

Their problem is one which psychologists have long recognised; but, when subsumed in rhetoric or theology, it tends to escape analysis. Ranging from shrugging-off to deeply ingenious malevolence, its consequences reduce the likelihood of correct information circulating.

Considerable hostility can be engendered experimentally to demonstrate this malaise. I have, for example, more than once unnerved 'specialists' by telling them jokes – and delighted others of their kind by providing an appearance of what it is at the moment fashionable to call gravitas.

Everyone is familiar with sanctimonious people, suffering from the effects of materialism; and also with those who have such pride (and are therefore in Sufic terms not spiritual people at all) that they imagine that they alone are right, or that their form of belief alone is absolutely true.

In a seeming paradox dealing with intellectuals, the Sufi poet Mirza Abdul-Qadir Bedil insists that real knowledge is greater than the mechanical sort – and that even the unregenerate may eventually reach it – if they find the path:

> You are better than anything your intellect
> has understood
> And you are higher than any place your
> understanding has reached.

The Sufi affirms that he perceives the reality beyond outward form, in contrast to those who merely fix upon form. Form is useful, but it is secondary. As the great Sufi exponent Ibn al Arabi puts it, in his *Interpreter of Desires*:

> My heart has become able to take on any form
> A grazing ground for gazelles, a [Christian] monastery of
>   monks
> An idol-house [of the pagans], the [Islamic] pilgrim's
>   Mecca mosque
> The tablets of the [Jewish] Torah and the Qur'an's pages
> I follow the faith of Love: wherever its riding-mounts face,
>   that is my religion and my faith.

This passage illustrates, quite dramatically, that the mystic has a religion and a faith totally different from that professed by those wedded to externals, externals which, to the ignorant, *are* the religion.

The Sufi way is through knowledge and practice, not through intellect and talk. As Prince Dara Shikoh says, in a Persian poem:

> Do you wish to be included with the Lords of Sight?
> From speech [then] pass on to experience.
> By saying 'Unity', you do not become a monotheist;
> The mouth does not become sweet from the word 'Sugar'.

There are those who believe that the attainment of the perception of Truth can be carried out by unaided effort. They imagine that by unswerving dedication to certain practices, by adherence to rules which are laid down by experimenters or are really only fragmentary, one can complete – or get some way along – the Journey of the Soul.

But one may say something and yet not be able to do it. Try, for instance, lifting yourself up by the bootstraps.

Studying appropriate parts of some literature can provide a basis: it can be an essential prerequisite, a preparation. Beyond a certain point, however, as with every other specialisation, someone must diagnose, someone must prescribe, and the prescription must be properly carried out.

Some useful counter-thinking to the 'magical' attitude has indeed been done. If there are magical procedures, why the variety of formulations? If the path has been laid down, why the successive appearance of different teachers? Why would anyone reinvent the wheel, if everything were as cosy and sequential as primitive longing so easily convinces us?

Constant reformulation, repeatedly bringing the teaching back to its centre of gravity, is so consistent a pattern that those who have overcome greed and narcissism enough, have learnt from the pattern's existence that this is central.

It is revealing of the mentality of many would-be metaphysicians that, when faced by this statement, they so often clamour for the stage after reading or formal study, instead of applying to a Sufi to discover whether they are yet fit for further development. And whether their study has been along the right lines, or whether reading and familiarisation with certain concepts has been adequate.

Jalaluddin Rumi speaks of the 'line' *towards* Truth, leading to the 'dot' which *is* Truth, in his *Mathnawi*:

The Knowledge of the Truth is a point and the wisdom of
    the Sufi a line
From the existence of the point is the being of a line.

CONFUSION OF BOTH THE SCHOLARS AND THE POPULARISERS:

Scholars and popularisers alike, relying on observation or records of specific Sufi procedures, (and trying to assess the Sufi development 'system') have lumped these together and imagined them to be constants. But this approach is ineffective. It renders both narrative and academic materials useless. The scholars and other outward observers do not discriminate between real and impoverished procedures, between essential and local or time-centred practices or concepts. They cannot, either, see the personal element, how the student may vary from time to time, in potential or attitude.

It is easy to see how this misunderstanding has arisen. The mentality and methods of scholasticism and linear thinking have been employed to approach something which is of a completely different nature.

THE SUFI GUIDE:

The aspirant has to be guided by a mentor. The stage at which this guidance can take effect is seldom, if ever, perceptible to the learner. Those who say 'I am ready to learn', or 'I am not ready to learn' are as often mistaken as they are correct in their surmise. Yet the aspirant must try, neither thinking that he is nothing, nor 'trying to sit on a throne'. I found this couplet in the Persian text of Rumi's *Letters*:

> If you cannot sit on a throne like a king
> Seize, like a tent-pitcher, the rope of the Royal tent.

The Sufis are unanimous that a Guide (*Sheikh*) is absolutely essential, though never available on demand: 'the Sufis are not merchants'. Many Sufis are not guides. As with any other specialisation, teaching is a vocation, open only to those who are truly capable of discharging its functions.

A Sufi may be carrying out functions 'in the world' which are not perceptible to others. He (or she) may be of a higher rank than a teacher and yet have no teaching mission.

The very concept that the teacher is the highest stage of human being is taken from somewhere other than Sufism. Sufis do not exist only to lead others to enlightenment; where they have a hierarchical function, this is for purposes other than teaching. Perhaps it is the never far distant human feeling of self-importance that assumes that the Sufi teacher is the greatest human being? If the assumption is that the individual is the most important thing there is, and that no other function than his or her wellbeing exists, then we can understand this unfounded assumption.

Some hold that the Sufi way is not distinct from that of Islam, but that it follows the esoteric meaning of the Qur'an, of which the exoteric meaning is in the overt text. Hence Ghazzali or Abu Hanifa (the founder of one of the major Islamic orthodox Schools) could be both Moslems and Sufis at the same time.

Some Sufi writers draw attention to the non-timebound nature of Sufism ('before man was, we were') and none regards Sufi thought as absent from any legitimate religious framework.

There are many mystical passages in the Moslems' holy book, as well as in the Traditions of the Prophet. One is 'We are nearer to him [man] than his jugular vein'; another, 'He is with you wherever you are'; and 'He is in your own souls: you do not perceive Him'.

Those are general statements; but Sufi exponents draw attention to Sura XVIII (verses 65f) for a close analogy with Sufi teaching and teachers. In this chapter, a teacher with special knowledge (whom many call Al Khidr, the wandering guide) meets Moses and teaches him that there are meanings in life beyond appearances – a classical Sufi contention.

Moses asks to be taught the truth, but the man answers, 'You will not be able to have patience with me!' Moses, however, persists, and undertakes to obey the stranger in everything.

They start on a journey, just as the Sufis call the following of the Path 'a journey', with the compact of obedience and patience, and that Moses will ask no questions.

First they come to a boat, which the teacher scuttles. Moses asks why he should do this, since it might drown the people in it. 'Truly, thou hast done a strange thing!'

The guide replies, 'Did I not tell thee that thou canst have no patience with me?'

The text continues:

Moses said, 'Rebuke me not for forgetting, nor grieve me by raising difficulties in my case'.

Then they proceeded until, when they met a young man, he slew him. Moses said, 'Hast thou slain an innocent person who had slain none? Truly a foul thing hast thou done!'

The teacher answered, 'Did I not tell thee that thou canst have no patience with me?'

Moses again agreed to keep silent, adding that if he were to question any of his mentor's acts in future, he could cast Moses aside.

Then they proceeded: until, when they came to the inhabitants of a town, they asked them for food, but they refused them hospitality. They found there a wall on the point of falling down but he set it up straight. Moses reproached his teacher with helping those who had been unkind, for he could not contain himself.

The mysterious teacher said, 'This is the parting between me and thee. Now will I tell the interpretation of that over which thou wast unable to hold patience.'

He explained that the boat belonged to poor people. By rendering it unserviceable, sinking it below the water, he had ensured that an usurping king who was seizing all boats would not find it. When the tyrant had gone away, the poor men would be able to salvage their boat, and earn their living with it.

The youth, if spared, would have grown up to be a danger to others. 'As for the wall, it belonged to two youths, orphans, in the town. There was, beneath it, a buried treasure to which they were entitled. Their father had been a righteous man. So thy Lord desired that they should attain their age of full strength and get out their treasure ... I did it not of my own accord. Such is the interpretation of that over which thou wast unable to hold patience.'

This metaphor conveys precisely the way in which the Sufi teacher carries on his function in life. Note that the disciple, if he is unable to keep up with his master, will have to be dismissed. However much he tries, he will remain at his own level.

Theologians might argue that Moses has to be an illuminate in order to carry out a prophetic function, and pass on divine commands relating to spiritual practices and worldly behaviour, the essence of familiar religion. But such would only be those who accept mysticism. To many orthodox theologians in most religions, mysticism is anathema. As the *Akhlaq-i-Mohsini* has it:

The bird which has no knowledge of pure water
Has his beak in salt water all year round.

Pure water is a technical term, with a specific meaning among the Sufis.

When they hear or read this story, a proportion of people will always wonder, inwardly or otherwise, why they should trust a teacher to such an extent. Some will question whether they should trust at all. The Sufi's answer to this is simply that, without such trust, no learning is possible. Husain Waiz Kashifi, in the *Lights of Canopus* says:

The person who has not seen the face of trust – has seen nothing
The person who has not found contentment – has found nothing.

Some writers have gone further in explaining. The human being, whether he realises it or not, is trusting someone or something every moment of the day. He trusts the floorboards not to collapse, the train not to crash, the surgeon not to kill him, and so on.

But, one might answer, we trust these people and these things because we have reason to believe that they will not let us down. But that, say the Sufi's supporters, is exactly the position in Sufism. Only unthinking, heedless people fail to observe it.

Sufis, traditionally, dwell among those whom they teach, living good lives as people of probity, acting according to their words, fulfilling undertakings: until, as with the floorboards, the train or the surgeon, they have earned a sufficient degree of trust from those who come in contact with them. According to the nature of the individuals among whom their lot is cast, this time put in by the Sufis will vary. None of them complains if it is measured in decades – though the would-be learners may complain. The latter, like Moses, may lack patience when only this will overcome their suspiciousness. If the teacher does not dismiss them, they effectively dismiss themselves. One cannot learn from someone whom one distrusts. Yet plenty of people, again perhaps because of self-flattery, 'follow' those whom they do not entirely trust. To the Sufi, such people may be followers: they cannot, in that condition, be pupils.

NEED OF THE LEARNER TO LEARN HOW TO LEARN:

The Sufis have some striking allegories designed to indicate both the Path and the situation of humankind when ignorant of the Path. How, for instance, does the Sufi see the ordinary individual, trying to make his or her way through life?

One saga dealing with this 'view from another world' is found in a succession of short tales about Mulla Nasrudin, playing the part of the human being who makes sense of the world – as we all do – while the reality is very different:

Nasrudin is a foolish youth, whose mother sends him to market to sell a bolt of cloth which she has woven. On the way to the town, Nasrudin meets another traveller, and they are soon deep in conversation. The young man's words are so unrealistic that the other man realises that he can fool him.

'Give me that cloth, you don't need it for yourself, do you?' he says.

Nasrudin thinks that he is clever. 'Not so fast, friend. My mother told me to sell it, as she needs the money. We are poor folk, you know. It would not be a responsible act just to give it away.'

'Very well,' says the man, 'I'll give you twenty silver pieces for it. I haven't got the money on me, but you can have it next time we meet.'

Twenty pieces of silver! This seems a great opportunity to Nasrudin, for his mother has told him that three silver pieces would be the most he could hope to get.

'You can have it, then,' says Nasrudin; adding, with great cunning, 'although I am robbing myself' – something he has heard merchants say when concluding a deal.

'I'll be off then,' says the other man.

'Stop!' says Nasrudin, for another thought has occurred to him. 'I have to know your name, so that I can find you again.'

'That's easy,' says the other, 'I'm me, that's who I am...'

Nasrudin, pleased with his day's work, goes home and tells his mother what has happened. 'All I have to do is to find "Me" and he will pay me...'

'Foolish boy!' says his mother, 'everybody is called "me". You are me to yourself, I am me to me, and that man is me as well.'

'That's too complicated for me,' Nasrudin tells her. 'But I'll go out tomorrow and find Me and he'll pay me.'

The following day Nasrudin sets out again, and half way to the market he comes across a man sitting in the shade of a tree. Now, being rather dim-witted, Nasrudin has forgotten what the man who had his cloth looks like. This man, he thinks, may well be the one, so he decides to test him, to make sure.

'Who are you?' he asks the man.

The other man does not appreciate this direct approach, and waves him away. 'None of your business. Get on your way!'

Nasrudin, coached by his mother, believes that one should always give a civil answer to a question. The man is behaving badly. Nasrudin picks up a large rock and holds it over the traveller. 'Who are you? I think you are "Me"!'

'All right,' the man answers, nervously, 'If you like, I'm me!'

'I thought you were. Now, give me the twenty silver coins.'

Convinced that Nasrudin is a dangerous lunatic, the man quickly throws down twenty silver pieces and runs away, glad to escape with his life.

It is noteworthy that Nasrudin is generally ignored or deplored by scholars and heartily disliked by pompous clerics, who lack a sense of humour.

In this tale, however, the discerning reader is able to taste something of the Sufi's overview of life, thought and behaviour, as he experiences the absurdity of assumptions in action.

A word often used for the aspirant is Seeker (*salik*). Those who, though practising Sufic exercises or otherwise concerned with Sufic matters, are not at the end of the Path, cannot call themselves Sufis. 'Sufi' is the name for the Realised Human Being. In the Sufic phrase, 'He who calls himself a Sufi is not one'. Yet the world swarms with people who call themselves Sufis. They have been numerous for centuries.

THE FOUR MAJOR CONDITIONS OF HUMANITY:

There are four major conditions of humans, according to the Sufis. These stages are variously named, but the following are representative:

HUMANITY (the ordinary state)
DISCIPLESHIP (being on the Path)
REAL CAPACITY (when progress starts)
ATTUNEMENT WITH THE DIVINE (the final condition).

These conditions have also been allegorised as:

EARTH
WATER
AIR
FIRE.

The stage of Humanity is that of the ordinary man or woman, lacking flexibility, given to 'earthly' behaviour and also fixed by habit or training into certain beliefs. Hence its symbol, EARTH: a static condition. It is also known as the Condition of Law, in which people act according to almost inescapable rules. These rules may be seen as the interplay of everyone's inherited susceptibility to training and the training itself. This is the stage of most people, characterised by its relative immobility as 'Mineral'. It includes many, if not most, of the people who imagine themselves to be spiritually-minded: the heavily-conditioned ones.

WATER is the stage when the individual is taken onto the Path, and can exercise some capacities towards self-realisation. It is also the stage of potentiality. Since some growth and movement takes place at this stage, the Sufis also call it 'the Vegetable stage' – just as a vegetable, moving, grows from the earth.

AIR is the condition in which real capacity develops. Real capacity is as different from simple movement (as of a vegetable) as an animal is from a vegetable. Hence its symbol is 'Animal'.

Beyond 'Animal' comes 'Man'. The Fourth Stage is therefore dubbed 'Human', and its analogy is FIRE.

This very ancient formulation, still employed by the Sufis, is said by some to be referred to in the New Testament, with the concepts of Water, Spirit and Fire. Their understanding of the categories is very different from the interpretation generally and usually unexamined among Christian theoreticians and scholars. For them, the baptism of water is the ceremony which testifies to their potentiality for the First Experience ('Water'). A relic of this rite is said to be preserved – though in abbreviated form – in the words of John the Baptist: 'I baptise you with water...'

John continues, in the same passage, with: '... but he who comes after me shall baptise you with *pneuma* [air, the Holy Ghost] *and with fire . . .*'

That the experiences come in a necessary succession is testified in John, iii, 5: 'Except that a man be born of water and the Spirit, he cannot enter the Kingdom of God.' So the sentence, in Sufi terms, gives the names and order in which the successive initiations, corresponding to ever-improving perceptions, take place: water (purification from 'the world'), air/Holy Spirit (understanding), and fire, 'Kingdom of God' (higher consciousness, awareness of Truth).

In Sufi parlance, the four Stages are conceived as:

1 Being in contact with, and partaking of the nature and behaviour of, ordinary humanity
2 Being in harmony with a Teaching Master
3 Being in contact with the Founder of the Teaching
4 Being in harmony with Absolute Truth.

It is possibly because of the correspondence between the Sufi ideas and this conception of the meaning of Christianity that the Sufis have so often been accused of being 'secret Christians' – and perhaps also because Jesus has their high respect and is regarded as a Master of the Way. But the Sufis do not accept that there is a correlation at the low level of ritualism, approximate ideas and outward formulation.

Sufism, they say, is that which enables one to understand religion, irrespective of its current outward form.

Hindu and Jewish mystics have also claimed that they have found a similar 'internal dimension' in their own religions which corresponds with the Sufic one. This is the reason why, in the Middle Ages and afterwards, people reared in these traditions have adopted Sufic formulations in their writings.

The characteristic and sequential cast of mind of the professional scholar has caused such good people to spend much time in puzzling out the 'Sufi influences' upon various thinkers of the past, assuming culture-creep or familiar literary influences. They have succeeded better in describing their own way of thinking than in illuminating their theses.

FOUR LEVELS OF PERCEPTION:

The Four Levels of Perception, again corresponding to the above-cited Four Stages, are, in the Sufi formulation: CONCENTRATION, RENUNCIATION, PERCEPTION and ABSOLUTE KNOWLEDGE. The aspirant's description changes as he climbs the 'Ladder of Four Rungs': first he is an *Abid* [a worshipper], then a *Zahid* [renouncer], then an *Arif* [knower] and finally a *Muhibb*, [lover]. LOVE is the word used for the highest stage of development.

UNDERSTANDING AND MISUNDERSTANDING OF 'LOVE':

The use of the word 'Love' by Sufis and others has misled verbal literalists and emotionalists alike into imagining that a state of bemusement akin to romantic love, or 'being in love' is what the Sufis mean when they use the term.

The use of the technical term 'Love' in formal religion may even be, according to the Sufis, part of a 'test'. This test may become apparent when one interrogates the injunction 'Thou shalt love thy God...' It soon becomes evident (even with a little thought) that nobody can possibly love *as the result of a command.* Hence it is said that 'Love' here means something other than a command. It is believed to mean that the goal is 'Love'.

A similar 'test' is contained in the adjuration to 'Love thy neighbour as thyself'. Since it is not a particularly creditable thing to love oneself, the phrase cannot mean what its overt words convey – unless addressed to a pretty hopeless case.

Again, to do unto others what one would wish them to do unto oneself is a further example of this kind of approach. Since anyone's experience will tell, nobody can wish for anything which he or she can be certain will be the best, the command must have a different meaning. And supposing one wished to die: would one be right in wishing that upon another?

DETERIORATION OF UNDERSTANDING OF SACRED TEXTS:

Sacred texts are rich in what were formerly instructional materials intended to be thought about. They have deteriorated into mere slogans attracting righteous approval and perplexity, according to who meets them. Another such is the Judgement of Solomon, this time from Old Testament lore. In spite of this tale being taken literally, a moment's thought will tell anyone (especially any woman) that such an event could never have taken place. Is there, has there been, anyone, particularly a woman, on

earth who would hold out her skirt for half a dismembered baby?
If so, the instance, given as a universal, is surely nothing more
than an isolated incident, best consigned to morbid psychology.
The meaning is, obviously when one thinks about it, bound to be
something else.

These examples could be multiplied; but they are only offered
here as illustrations of how easily one may be indoctrinated with
the most bizarre concepts, and suspend thought about them;
accepting them as significant when, in the repetition, they are
absurd.

A Sufi explanatory text, *The Meaning of the Path*, by Qalimi,
deals with this area thus:

> The Way of initiation, in which the individual can reach, if his
> desire is pure, the status possible to him, has been called the
> *Idkhal*, the Causing to Enter (on the Way).
>
> The Way has three parts. It must begin with an individual
> who has already travelled the Way. This individual must come
> into contact with those who are at the lowest stage, in order to
> conduct them higher. He explains absurdities in formerly
> respected formulas. The lowest stage is called 'Earth', denoting
> the passivity and fixity of the stage of the participants. The
> other Stages, successively, are known as
>
>> Water
>> Air, and
>> Fire.
>
> These terms are chosen partly because they consecutively
> represent items in increasing degree of refinement or decreasing
> density. The use of them by the spiritual alchemists is too
> obvious to need comment.
>
> At the stage of 'Earth', people are still in touch with the
> grosser substances of materiality, thought and deed, as well as
> with the coarseness of one another in a manner which precludes
> much understanding. These include conventional scholars and
> others prone to petty emotions such as jealousy and other
> subjective feelings which the Sufis (for this and not only for
> social or pious reasons) deplore.

The stage of 'Water', also symbolising purification in some traditions, takes place when the Teacher is in a position to amalgamate the watery (that is, the mobile and purified) element in the postulant with 'water' in another sense. This latter 'water' is a finer substance of a spiritual kind, partaking of the nature of an energy. When this is possible, a certain kind of 'mobility' can take place. In procedural terms, it means the stage when the higher elements of the mind and individuality are connected through the intermediary of the Teacher. This is what is attempted in faiths which possess a priesthood; though the initiatory lore of this procedure is now universally lost among organised religions.

The stage of 'Air' is reached after completing the Water *daraja* [grade]. In this, the consciousness of the individual (or the group, if there is one) rises to a perception of true Reality higher than is possible at the 'Water' stage. In other words, the experiences will be such as to cancel out, supplant, make irrelevant, the earlier ones.

In all the degrees, candidates cannot proceed from one range of perceptions to the next until they are 'ready'. Readiness is a mark of worthiness, and does not depend upon minor criteria, such as the time taken or the seniority of the individual.

At the same time, Sufis select disciples in such a manner as to enable one to affect the other and make the process more effective. Hence study groups when indicated. The Sufic 'current' can also be conveyed between members of a group who do not formally meet.

'Water' cannot truly purify without the deliberate effort of the person to be cleansed. As the degrees proceed, the effort becomes greater. Although the effort may appear continuous or otherwise, the true harmonisation which is taking place at each stage requires the correct attunement of all the members of a group (*taifa, halqa*) involved.

Immature (*kham*) individuals, still suffering from too much material thinking, may be found resenting the fact that they have to wait for others to make a certain kind of progress before they can benefit from it. They have failed to note that others, too, are waiting for them to progress.

From 'Air', where the consciousness has been transferred by the Teacher from himself as a conductor to that of all substances of the 'Air' level, of all teachers and saints, the process continues to that of 'Fire'. This, highest, consciousness – gnosis – is represented in ordinary words as contact with the Divine. This is the stage referred to, also, as the 'Death before death'. Unless the Teacher has been through this 'death', as it were on behalf of his pupils, so that he is enabled to bring its possibilities to them, he cannot lead them to it.

Did they but know it, the very greatest effort and sacrifice has to be undertaken by the Teacher first of all to endure this 'death' on their behalf.

Shabistari, in *The Secret Garden*, says:

> He is the Completed Man who, from his completeness
> Performs, with his Mastership, the work of a slave.

THE PLEDGE OF DISCIPLESHIP:

The acceptance of a Seeker, in traditional Sufic circles, starts with the taking of the pledge, the *Bayat*. The Seeker places his hands between the hands of the Guide. This is the start of the Dual Pledge: the Seeker, for his part, undertakes to accept the Guide, and the latter agrees to accept the Seeker as his pupil.

Many people have a superficial, or sentimental, concept of the Pledge. It is no mere formality, not something which is entered into lightly, emotionally or on demand. The aspirant may approach a guide for acceptance: but the Guide, for his part, cannot accept the Seeker until he is sure that the Seeker is in a state to carry out his undertaking.

This state may take a long time to arrive; or it may not develop at all. The Seeker may be convinced that he can carry out any directions of a guide; but the responsibility is on the Guide to make sure that this is possible. If either party is not competent to carry out the respective undertakings, there is no contract. For the

Guide to accept the Seeker on any other terms would be improper. Worse, it would demonstrate the incompetence of the alleged guide.

Hence, the stage *before* the acceptance is most important, and may be the longest part of the novitiate. The Guide may agree to provide the would-be Seeker with opportunities of becoming a disciple. He may require him (or her) to read, to carry out exercises, to make journeys, to do various kinds of work, to give written or spoken reactions to teaching materials. Unlike the purpose of other systems, this is not a form of training. It is a means of exercising a flexibility which almost everyone has lost due to the twin effects of nature and conditioning: the effect of 'the world', sometimes called Earth Sickness.

It is during this initial period that many people fall away or lose interest, to follow more alluring ideas. People who have set up cults of their own are generally from this category. Starved of nutrition for their vanity, deprived of a sense of importance to inflate the secondary self, not allowed scope to dominate or to be dominated, most people crave one or more of these things to a greater or lesser degree.

Systems, allegedly Sufic, which plunge the aspirant straight into exercises, are either bogus or imitative. They are not Sufistic, though they are so numerous and widespread as to have created the belief (among both Eastern and Western scholars) that they represent Sufism. Orientalist and historical literature is full of accounts of them. Though their provenance is suspect or even obvious, even 'specialists' take them seriously; perhaps because their intellectual or emotional character attracts the pedantic mind subconsciously.

The Sufi has the knowledge of states, and he has to help the aspirant to harmonise with objective reality, stabilising these states. Al Muqri, quoted by Hujwiri, (in *The Revelation of the Veiled*) therefore says:

> Sufism is the maintaining of States in relation to Objective Truth.

There is no standardised series of practices among the Sufis.

The reason for this is that the teacher will prescribe exercises (or prescribe none) according to the state and nature of his pupil and the character and condition of his 'work'.

RELIGIOUS EXCITATION NOT SUFISTIC:

Congregations of supposed Sufis who simply perform spiritual practices in unison are not genuinely Sufic, though they may be practising religious excitation. In the East, they are often called Dervishes. Since this kind of activity is widely believed (in a number of faiths) to be sufficient, one cannot deny them the name 'religious'. The Latin word *religare*, 'to bind' – if this is, as some authorities believe, the origin of 'religion' – effectively portrays the non-Sufic sense of 'being conditioned by, tied to, a belief'. Such a form of religion is, on its own incompatible with the flexibility of Sufism, which breaks through the 'bind', or 'knot', as it is called in Sufic terminology.

Where conditioning, the binding force, is active, something more is occluded. Haji Bektash of Khorasan noted the following problem, and which of us has not seen it in many an instance where much lesser matters than Sufism are concerned? :

> To him who has sense, a sign is enough
> For the heedless, however, a thousand expositions are not
> enough.

INITIATION:

The Pledge or Acceptance is not to be regarded as an initiation. Initiation takes place when the Guide perceives that the aspirant is ready for it.

The teacher is called *Sheikh* in Arabic, *Pir* in Persian, both roughly approximating to 'Elder'. Other titles are: *Shah* [King, especially if the Sufi is a Sayed, descendant of the Prophet], *Murshid* [Guide] or *Hazrat* [Presence].

When the time for initiation comes, the guide takes the disciple to the *Hujra*, a room set aside for private exercises; usually an isolated apartment in a *Khanqah* [monastery] or elsewhere. None but the teacher is allowed into this room without permission. It is usual for the place to be guarded by disciples stationed outside or in an anteroom.

It is customary in some formulations, for the initiation to take place on a Thursday morning or a Friday before midday. The disciple to be admitted will have carried out the instructions and preparations already given him, which include taking a bath and freeing his mind, as far as he can, from worldly concerns, signalling, to himself and others, his intention (*Niyat*).

The individual sits facing the Master, and takes his hands. The teacher then recites a holy text, and the two in unison repeat an invocation which includes their pledge and intention.

Immediately after the ceremony, the disciple fasts for three days, taking neither food nor water from sunrise to sunset. He repeats five prayers a day, and concentrates upon the meanings of texts given him by the Master.

After the third day, the disciple presents himself before his teacher, in a similar posture, to receive the *Tawajjuh* [projection of spiritual powers into his mind]. This may take the form of an audible or silent recitation.

The process may be repeated every alternate day.

The next stage is the prescription by the teacher of a recitation by the learner of the *Zikr*, the repetition of YA HAI, YA QAYUM. These words stand for 'O Living One! O Eternal!' This is carried out in a small room, with the disciple alone, where he sits with knees folded and hands on knees, the fingers in a special posture. The forefinger and thumb of each hand are joined in a circle, with the other fingers splayed out.

The number of times of this repetition, and other matters, are stipulated by the teacher in accordance with his perception of the pupil's needs.

This process may occupy any period of time. From time to time the master will assess the disciple's progress and may prescribe fasting or other practices.

These actions may have effects upon the disciple's mentation; in the Sufi phrase, 'Gold needs bran to polish it.' Arbitrary adoption of exercises, though, without 'special measure' is alluded to thus:

> Whoever makes himself into bran will be eaten by cows.

The secondary must never be mistaken for the primary. Rumi says, of a servile imitator, 'He saw the mountain, he has not seen the mine within it.'

During this period, the disciple does not yet see the mine within the mountain. He may experience what he thinks are spiritual states, 'illumination', all kinds of thoughts, feelings, experiences. These, however, are illusory. What is happening is the 'wearing out' of the spurious imagination.

The spiritual cannot act effectively on the non-spiritual. As Saadi puts it, 'If dust ascends to the skies, it is not made more precious.'

Such states often occur in people who, lacking proper guidance, believe that they are having spiritual experiences. These illusions can happen even to people who are not in discipleship, and they account for the many reports of supposedly 'higher' experiences from those who have no specialised knowledge of these matters, and who are still 'raw'. Indeed, such experiences are relatively common among the 'raw', and rare in those who are already on the Path.

This state is equivalent to that of 'random seekers' who so often plague truly spiritual people with accounts of their 'spiritual experiences'. The Sufis see such people as displaying mainly vanity: they like to feel that they have undergone a mystical or occult experience.

FALSE EXPERIENCES:

Shabistari, among many others, warns against the false experience, which is accompanied by physical signs imagined by the subject to be significant:

> Everyone does not know the secrets of Truth
> The States of Truth are not evidential.

ACTIVATION OF THE SUBTLETIES:

The Second Stage, which can be entered into only after the disciple has shown that he has 'worn out' the imaginary experiences and no longer has them, concerns the Activation of the *Lata'if*, [Subtleties] the Special Organs of Perception.

Before considering these, we shall look at two developmental practices which may be used before the Second Stage, at the discretion of the Guide, since simply carrying out exercises without being in the corresponding condition to benefit from them is worse than useless:

CONCENTRATION:

Muraqiba is an exercise which can be called Concentration. It also stands for 'casting the head down in intense thought'. The head is held down, and the individual tries to banish from the mind all thought of anything but God.

REPETITION:

Zikr (literally meaning 'repetition') consists of the Seeker repeating, as many times as prescribed by the Guide, a word which embodies a concept. Also called *Wird*, it must not be randomly indulged in, otherwise the result will simply be obsession with that concept. In the East, one often comes across dervishes, fakirs and others such as random experimentalists, who are trapped at that stage. They may constantly repeat a single word, and are unable to do much else. Many people imagined to be Sufis in fact merely teach this obsession.

According to the Sufis, the reason why people become obsessed with single ideas (and thus actually reverse the intention of the Zikr) is that the word acting on the inadequately prepared mind will work on the superficial (emotional-intellectual) level, causing obsessions or monoideism.

The mind has to be in a condition to benefit from a Sufi exercise. Adnan Wakhani says:

> You would never put pure nectar into a filthy glass.

But you will try to put a sacred thing into your head.
The result is that you become even odder than you were
   before;
Your imaginings become worse.
You believe that you have been in touch with the Divine.
You say to me 'What! Can the performance of a pious act,
   a good attempt
Have evil as a result?'
Deluded one! Real goodness, piety and true faith never
   approach you.

More succinctly, another Sufi says 'Sufi practices can lead anyone to paradise. But such a person would have to be already innocent. When a Sufi spiritual practice is attempted by one who is still unworthy, that individual will actually suffer. The reason is that such a person cannot really practise such things. What is being attempted is not what a sincere person can practise.'

The *Latifa* is conceived of as 'a sensitive spot which may become illuminated or activated'. It is also known as the Organ of Spiritual Perception, and its plural is *Lata'if*. This is (for practical purposes only) conceived of as a physical location on the body of the Seeker. It is not regarded as having a true corporeal location, but experience has shown that the act of directing the attention, under appropriate circumstances, to certain parts of the body, helps in the attainment of states of mind which are termed 'Illumination' (*Tajalli*).

The activation of one or more of the Lata'if (there are five) is conceived of as an awareness of one of the Attributes of God, sometimes called the Ninety-Nine Names, though it is not held that there is an actual arithmetical, limited, number of such attributes. Again, the figures are a conception enabling the mind to approach the reality.

Some Sufis have been accused of apostasy, being alleged to forbid disciples to use the name of God from the beginning of their novitiate. The reason for this stricture, however, is clear and evident to those who look at the matter with sufficient reflection. So many people have a totemistic, a primitive, a superstitious attitude towards deity that when the word is mentioned, they immediately enter a psychological frame of mind which is lower, not higher, than the ordinary. To them, God is a sort of idol: the concept means for them nothing more than something to be propitiated, from whom to beg favours.

For this reason Bayazid Bistami has said 'Whoever knows God does not [any longer] say "God"'.

Another Sufi has said, 'The idolator is also found among those who cry "I worship no idol!"'

There is a story of a revered Sufi who was arrested for saying 'Your god is under my feet!'

When brought to trial, this teacher showed that he had a coin in each of his sandals. The 'god' of the people of the town which he was visiting was admitted to be Mammon – and the judges there had the good sense to acquit him, admitting that the people were materialists before anything else.

The idea of God for them had become totemistic, a barrier to understanding, and the Sufi approached the problem by shock tactics, in the manner adopted in the *Divan of Shamsi-Tabriz*, where it is said:

> Though the Kaaba [building] and the Zamzam [well in Mecca] exist; and although paradise and [the heavenly river of] Kauthar exist – because this has become a screen to the heart, it must be torn aside.

The term 'Heart' (*qalb*) stands for a theoretical site in the body conceived of as located two inches under the left nipple. A pulsation may be felt at this spot.

The activation of the Lata'if leads to Major Saintship (*walayat kubra*) in which the Sufi has not abandoned the world, but has acquired the qualities which enable him to detach from it and to operate in higher dimensions. It is at this stage that he is said to gain spiritual powers, capacities which are beyond the reach or ken of the ordinary individual.

These powers are said to include the control of certain physical phenomena. The Sufi known as a Perfect Saint (*wali kamil*) can cure disease, can influence individuals and gatherings, can transport his consciousness from one place to another, and so on. These acts are regarded by outward observers as supernatural. They are indeed such in the sense that they are not to be accounted for through conventional logic or physical laws. But they are not seen as central by real Sufis.

MIRACLES AND SAINTSHIP:

Miracles, to the Sufi, are not evidential, they are instrumental.

When she had nothing with which to make soup, a number of onions suddenly appeared, from the sky, in the kitchen of the great woman Sufi Rabia. People were astonished at this 'miracle from God'. Rabia, however, chastised them, saying, 'My Lord is not a grocer!'

This instance clearly displays the difference between Sufi thinking and the simplistic, hope-and-fear, attitudes of shallow religiosity; where lower levels are accepted as higher ones. Another account, also from Rabia, illuminates the difference between Sufic and 'religious' thinking. She prayed, 'O Lord, if I worship Thee from desire for Paradise, deny me Paradise; if I worship Thee from fear of Hell, cast me into Hell!'

An important test of a suitable Sufic disciple is if, when he performs 'miracles' or when such things happen to him, he conceals them utterly, and is not affected by them.

The sublime nature of this conception – that desire and fear, excitement and publicity exist only on a low, emotional, not a perceptively spiritual, level, is the hallmark of the Sufi work. At most, hope and fear act in the human being as a prelude, a preparation. Yet hope and fear are considered by many supposedly spiritual people as the very means of achieving salvation.

Some allegedly Sufi communities place great emphasis on the festivals and burial-places of certain saints. This is a distortion of understanding, and it is useful to recognise its origin. Initially, it was noted that concentration upon the 'being' of a saint would conduce towards perception of his nature. This practice needed, however, to be allied to a certain degree of preparation. When this practice was copied by those who did not have the necessary capacity or preparation, 'the world took over', and some people started to worship graves. Effectively, something more primitive, imagined to be less so, had supervened. Such people did not cease to be Sufis – they never were. The Sufi name for them is 'Sufists', those who try to be Sufis. Many such people will swear that they are not performing worship, but merely showing respect. The reality is that they are totemists, whatever they imagine.

This may be taken as an illustration of the action of the 'secondary self', the one which will doggedly convert real religion into idolatry. Far from being a way to enlightenment, it causes a lapse into superstition.

With regard to supposed miracles, whether associated with the living or with long-dead saints, these are most often emphasised by secondary sources or by untutored amateurs. Indeed, one of the Sufis' principles, relating to discipleship, is 'that the disciple shall conceal his Master's miracles'. How different from what passes for religion even among some of the best-respected religionists!

Shallow thinkers have wondered how Sufi spirituality can be reconciled with religion as they know it. Indeed, some Christian, Jewish and Islamic theorists have claimed – and some still do – that such reconciliation is impossible.

They ignore history and have neglected to read the works of their predecessors: for the battle was waged and won centuries ago, when inquisitors and others assailed the Sufis for being heretics, idolators or freethinkers.

Great Sufis, like Ibn al Arabi of Andalucia, were called apostates from Islam. This question was thrashed out when Al Arabi was brought before an inquisition and he easily proved, even to the satisfaction of his critics, that his writings were allegorical, and that the clerics had been too superficial to understand them.

The battle with the literalist Moslem theologians was won when, though Sufis were called heretics, the great Iranian Islamic theologian Al Ghazzali was recognised as a major Islamic reformer and authority, gaining him the title of 'The Proof of Islam' nearly a thousand years ago.

The acceptance of Sufis among Christians was assured when

for instance, a myriad Christians followed the Afghan sage Jalaluddin Rumi, when medieval Christian theologians were found to
have adopted Ghazzali's methods and ideas, and when Christian
mystics were noted to have been stimulated by various Sufi
sources. And the Hebrews, too, long ago determined the debt of
some of their mystical thinkers to Sufic origins. These facts, and
many others, are well documented in the secular, academic
literature.

That it should be necessary for Sufis to defend themselves in the
religious field against experts who could not understand the spiritual content of their work until it was delineated for them in terms
which they could understand says much about the Sufis – and
more than a little about the quality of thought of their detractors.

Nowadays, happily, the picture is becoming clearer. The accumulation of knowledge about the Sufis is greater, and they have
numerous admirers among people of all faiths, many of whom
have written extensively on them: though always with their own
bias and over-simplifications. The Sufi heritage in, especially,
monotheistic religion, is widely, if not universally, appreciated.
The ancient Sufic contribution to the knowledge of conditioning,
sociology and psychology (only now being retrieved in the West)
has made it possible for members of many faiths to see which
aspects of their beliefs and practices are superficial and unessential, and how they may be manipulated, their trained reflexes
animated, by external superficialities. As Khayyam says:

> Ringing bells are the melody of slavery
> The sacred thread and the church, and the rosary and the
>   cross:
> Truly, all of them are the mark of servitude.

It remains for Sufic insights to be drawn into non-Islamic
religions, as well as to act upon (and to penetrate beyond) the
superficiality of many Moslem enthusiasts and clerics. It also
remains for the 'lunatic fringe' of bogus or self-deceived people
who operate or belong to imitative cults miscalled Sufic, to be
ousted. In a free society, with the current rapidity of communi-

cations, both developments are not only likely, they are surely inevitable.

Due consideration for humanity is essential, but vague solicitude for the happiness of the deluded or superficial, in Sufism as in anything else, will serve no useful purpose. As the Sufi saying has it, 'Too much kindness towards the fox may mean doom for the rabbit.'

I add this because, at a recent lecture, a well-meaning but insubstantial devotee cried out at me 'Don't shoot the pianist – he's doing his best!' No assassination had, of course, been proposed. Neither, though, did my critic seem to have any concern for the need of instruction for the pianist, which might surely have shown concern for his welfare...

In other words, leave an unsatisfactory situation as it is!

But one becomes accustomed to the 'commanding self's' habit of fishing out false analogies, to protect an empty house against burglars, in the Sufic phrase.

Just as the Sufis have always claimed that their path is reconcilable with all true religion, they assert that it is not time-bound, having been represented among humanity from the earliest times.

As Ibn Al-Farid puts it:

Continuously, in commemoration of the Friend
We drank wine, even before the creation of the vine.

Just as the teaching may vary in outward aspect according to cultural differences, so it remains essentially the same in its inwardness: 'The clothes may vary, but the person is the same.'

This contention is useful in distinguishing Sufic imitators from the real thing. The deteriorated or repetitious cults purporting to be Sufic tend to use outdated or irrelevant techniques, regalia, even clothes and languages, when they drift – or are imported – from one time or culture to another. This trend itself explains the many different forms of Sufic practice (and theory) which persist, long after their applicability has ceased, to the present day.

One of the marks of the Sufi is that he dresses in the garb of the country in which he lives. The disciple should not assume rags as a sign of humility. Saadi says, in his *Rose Garden* 'Be a true renouncer, (*zahid*) and [you can even] wear satin.' The aspirant should not attract attention to himself by odd costumes, even though his 'nutrition' is other than the intake of others. Hence the motto, one of many on this subject, current with Sufi teachers:

> Eat what you desire, but dress like other people.

The exotic appurtenances of these cults usually guarantee their attraction and a plentiful recruitment, especially among the gullible of the West. It also illustrates, to others, their barrenness. Further, the reluctance of the scholar to believe that anything from long ago could be once fruitful but now superseded helps in the process. He has become confused by the archaeologist's or historian's unspoken bias: 'the older the better'. There may also be an element of cultural chauvinism.

Hence the present-day scholar unwittingly helps the cults and not the reality: the false rather than the true. Sufism is imagined by the academics, in effect if not in theory, to be an exotic, culture-based survival, not (as the Sufis have always known it) as a living entity, able to operate within any culture, in any language, and at any time.

Indeed, the developmental role of the Sufi and his Way depends upon its applicability to all times and in all circumstances. This approach is very different from trying to turn reasonably good Westerners of today into second-rate Middle Easterners of the Middle Ages.

Why second-rate? Because, even if the repetition of materials from centuries ago were able to cause any effect on students, that effect would only be successful in producing insight if it were progressed by genuine mystics. And no genuine mystic would employ such materials out of time and place in the manner advocated by the imitators. Time, and its demands, are central to Sufi capacity. As the ancient teacher Amr ibn Usman al Makki says:

> A Sufi is alive to the value of time, and is given, every moment, to what that moment demands.

It need not be contended that the contemporary imitators are frauds. But the sincerest man or woman on Earth will be quite useless if he or she substitutes mechanicality for knowledge and for harmonisation with ultimate reality.

So, with Sufi spiritual studies, the essential prerequisites are fundamental, and must be observed: even if the aspirant is as eager as Moses was; perhaps especially if he is as eager as that.

Above all, the spiritual candidate must start with right conduct. Hafiz, in one of his most beautiful passages, gives this guidance:

> *Ruzi ki az madar tu uryan*
> *Khalqan hama khandan – tu budi giryan*
> *Dar ruzi wafatat ki jan bisipari:*
> *Khalqan hama giryan – tu bashi khandan.*

Translated felicitously by Sir William Jones, the classical Persian poem says:

> On parent knees, a naked new-born child
> Weeping thou satst, when all around thee smiled;
> So live, that sinking in thy last long sleep,
> Calm thou mayst smile, when all around thee weep.

But what is 'right conduct'? Social and cultural conventions in all societies allow disguised delinquency to prevail in the 'mental gymnastics' area. Sheer intellectuality, playing games purporting to be sincere thought, can soon degenerate into dishonesty.

I was once present when a Sufi outlined the tale of the Monkey and the Cherry to a certain guru. A monkey, he said, saw a bottle with a cherry inside. Putting its hand inside the bottle, it grasped the cherry – but the fist which the monkey tried to withdraw was too big. So the monkey had the cherry but did not have it. This, the Sufi continued, was the condition of those who have the exterior of things, and cannot get out of the trap of greed and ignorance set by themselves.

This was, of course, a perfect description of the Guru himself.

But the guru's invincible vanity dealt with that one. 'Ah,' he said, 'but what if *I* myself am the cherry, and *you* are the bottle, preventing me from being extracted and enjoyed?'

That seems to me to be a good illustration of why humility has to precede instruction . . .

The guru was, in reality, moving between the first two stages of spiritual learning, called by the Sufis INSTINCT and RITUAL-ISM. Virtually all conventional religionists are still at those stages.

The four stages which constitute the whole range are as follows:

1 INSTINCT, automatic emotional or mental action
2 RITUAL, where beliefs are systematised and give people emotional stimuli according to a plan
3 PREPARATION, the first Sufic stage, when the outlook becomes flexible. Now the person can really benefit from reading and interaction with a teacher
4 EXERCISES, never applied on undeveloped people.

These are the steps which lead to 'enlightenment'.

The problem for would-be Sufis is that most people have been taught to operate only in Stages 1 and 2. Indeed, they imagine that this is all there is to religious activity.

For others, the appeal to their vanity caused by imagining that Stage 4, exercises, can operate without knowledge or preparation is a total barrier to learning.

SUMMARY:

Sufis aim to refine human consciousness. This is Sufi mysticism: not mystification or magic, but a specific Path.

Much religious teaching in the world is in reality a confused or deteriorated form, very different from its roots.

Inheritance and culture obscure people's higher capacities. Well-meant techniques such as arbitrary self-mortification, are useless.

Sufis (the name for the realised individual, not the learner or follower) are reunited with objective Reality and Unity.

Theologians, scholars and morbid religionists indulge subjective emotions or ideologies in their life and thought. Hence their religion is not perceptive but self-indulgent. Yet they lack humour.

The perception of reality beyond outward form is essentially foreign to the self-indulgers.

This Reality is the essence beyond form of all genuine religions.

Familiarisation with current Sufic presentation is essential preparation for the student, but a mentor at a certain point is absolutely necessary.

Sufi study is *instrumental*, not informative or manipulative. Hence both scholars and popularisers (often called Sufis or Sufi specialists) are useless as guides – even to convey what Sufism *is*.

Characteristics of the Sufi. Sufism and Islam; and Folklore: Nasrudin; and other formulations earth, water, air, fire; Christianity and the New Testament; Hindu and Jewish mystics.

Four levels of perception: concentration, renunciation, perception and knowledge.

Sufic understanding of 'Love'.

Deterioration of sacred texts.

Pledge and discipleship.

Irrelevance of certain exercises.

Religious excitation; the Initiation (traditional form).

False experiences; activation of the Subtleties.

Miracles, saintship and the 'Secondary Self'.

False and imagined Sufis.

The Four Stages in the light of the foregoing.

SUFI PRINCIPLES, ACTION LEARNING METHODS, IMITATORS, MEETING-PLACES – AND THE WESTERN SEEKER

by

Humayun Abbas andOthers

Trust

HUMAYUN ABBAS

Trust is not something caused, it is something developed. That is to say, what is called 'trust' when it is slowly taught to animals by men who tame them, is not trust, but reliance. Real trust is different.

Trust in God, too, is not taught to human beings by God. On the contrary, God gives men so many reasons to have lack of trust (calamities, uncertainties, loss of hope) that it could be said that God actually illustrates that trust in something or someone beneficial is not to be erected on happiness or good experiences alone.

Similarly, the Sufi master does not pose as someone worthy of trust in the sense that clerics and others make sure that their externals and their behaviour inspire the trust which is reliance. Such trust as the latter kind is only to be regarded as worthwhile if it has been tested. For this reason the Sufis have asked, 'How many friends would you have if you went from one to another asking them to conceal a dead body?'

Trust is something which the Sufi postulant must find from within himself, in spite of what the superficialities seem to indicate. This is one reason that Sufi masters have even made themselves appear ridiculous or untrustworthy to intending disciples.

No less a person than Sheikh Shibli[1] said, when approached by someone who wanted to be accepted as a student: 'Repeat: "There is no God but God, and Shibli is His Prophet"!' This in order to test whether his submission was servile or otherwise.

One of the commonest manifestations of lack of trust in a

teacher, constantly emphasized by Sufi masters, is when the disciple expects attention and instructions when he has not done what he should do as a precondition of these things. Sheikh Ajal Shirazi, as only one example of this important aspect of Sufism, spoke thus to an applicant who came in search of *Zikrs* [litanies]:

'Do not allow for others what you will not allow for yourself. Desire for others what you desire for yourself.'

Some time later this same man arrived at the Master's door, asking for recitations to be given to him, saying that, after all, he was the Sheikh's disciple.

'How can I give you the second lesson,' asked the Master, 'when you have not observed the first one?'[2]

One of the most important aspects of the conception of 'trust' is that this technical term implies an activity and a posture which, in turn, developed a capacity in the individual. Monks and others, including spiritual recluses, have spent whole lifetimes obsessed by the conception of trust, and thus been unable to pass to a further stage.

In the teachings quoted by Hujwiri (*Kashf al-Mahjub*), this problem is illustrated by the account of Hallaj instructing the eminent Ibrahim Khawwas.

When Hallaj went to Kufa, he was visited by Khawwas. Hallaj asked Khawwas:

'O Ibrahim, what have you obtained from your two decades of study of the Sufis?'

Khawwas said:

'I have concentrated upon the doctrine of Trust.'

Hallaj said:

'You have wasted time in cultivating the spiritual: where is the Annihilation in Unification?'

Hujwiri explains that *trust* signifies an attitude and a reliance. 'If a man spends his whole life in remedying his spiritual nature, he will need another life for remedying his material nature, and his life will be lost before he has found a trace or vestige of God.'[3]

The story of Sheikh Shirazi, given above, also underlines another characteristic of trust which is emphasised by the Sufi masters: people who cannot trust are themselves not trustworthy, and therefore cannot be entrusted with important things. The would-be disciple of Shirazi did not trust him to attend to the disciple's needs when they were manifested. In his turn, the intending disciple could not be trusted to exercise the attitudes which were prescribed for him at the first meeting.

The disciple who asked Shirazi for further guidance was not exercising trust, as we have seen; but he may well have thought that he was asking the Master to give him a trust, having failed to perceive that he had been given the first lesson before he could get the second.

Indeed, trust is only the fourth stage of one version of the Sufi journey. The first is repentance (*Taubat*), from objectionable things. The second is *Inabat* (returning to rightness). The third is renunciation (*Zuhd*) – and then comes trust. The Master's assessment of the applicant, put in terms of 'do not allow for others what you would not allow for yourself. Desire for others what you desire for yourself', clearly covers the practices which would constitute these first three stages.[4]

The instructions given to a student by the Master constitute the practice or practices necessary for him to complete the 'station' (*Maqam*) in which he is to 'stand'. Hence, in the words of Hujwiri, the disciple must abide by this stage, 'and his fulfilment of the obligations appertaining to that "station" and his keeping it until he comprehends its perfection so far as lies in man's power. It is not permissible that he should quit his "station" without fulfilling the obligations thereof.'

Although the intending Sufi will have to 'trust' his mentor sufficiently to accept his instructions as to the three stations which come before it, he will not be capable of real trust until he has completed the fourth. Nevertheless, there is sufficient capacity in students to exercise this limited trustworthiness.

Trust itself, as Al-Ghazzali has defined it,[5] is made up of knowledge, state and work (called in Sufi technical terms, *Ilm*, *Hal* and *Aml*). These three things constitute the attunement of the learner to that which has to be learnt. When a Sufi master is coaching disciples, whether by words, signs or actions, he is preparing them to apply the attitude which is composed of these.

The coaching of disciples, to wean them from appearances, automatism and reliance upon literalism, has a very long history among the Sufis, and may be regarded as a central requirement. Indeed, the ordinary person's certainty that 'seeing is believing' has to be replaced for the Sufi by a greater flexibility of understanding before extra dimensions of the mind may be opened up.

Sir Richard Burton[6] tells the story of the great Sufi Master Bayazid and the courtesan. Bayazid's disciples revered him so much at the expense of what he was teaching that he decided that this conditioning would have to be broken. 'Men,' as the Sufi saying has it, 'should not be respected at the expense of what they represent.' One day Bayazid was surrounded by a group of admiring followers who were wedded to the belief that piety was inseparable from appearance. Bayazid sent a message to a woman of ill-fame to 'bring him some of his clothes which he had left with her; and to send an account of the money which he owed her'. Similarly, Shamsuddin of Tabriz, teacher of Rumi, once asked a disciple, as a test, to lend him his wife.

This necessary technique has caused imitators to claim that they are Sufi masters, and encouraged such people to deceive and defraud others. But the argument, put forward in some circles, that the practice should not therefore be allowed is not valid, for at least two reasons. The first is that, over the centuries, the ill-effects of pretended Sufis have not been shown to cause intolerable havoc, any more than the impostures of other miscreants. The second is that to invoke this principle is (in the words of a modern Master) 'like forbidding free speech because villains might misuse it'.

An examination of the words and deeds of such Sufi masters as we have noted above, as well as time spent among the Sufis of the present day, abundantly show that:

1 Trust is not servility; people tend to misunderstand 'trust';
2 Trust is needed before lessons can be learnt;
3 The kind of trust which is needed is stimulated by the Master;

4 The Master may stimulate this by words or action, or writings;

5 Before this stage there are other stages, similarly stimulated;

6 Many people imagine that they seek knowledge, when in reality they only seek attention or something else which they have in the back of their minds;

7 The Sufi, knowing his would-be disciple, gives him (or her) instructions which both prepare him/her and also enable him/her and others to see whether the process is working, firstly by helping to reveal the true nature of the student's attitudes;

8 The learner comes to appreciate that the Sufi is rejecting certain kinds of approach and encouraging others, in order to help to bring the disciple's spiritual, not selfish, nature to bear on the problem of progress.

In the words of Rumi, the Master will not allow the disciple's self-conceit to operate so that he is left on the teacher's hands 'like government soap'.

It is because he can appear to 'touch defilement and yet not be defiled' (Anwari) that the Master Sufi can afford to behave in a way which society does not readily allow to others. 'Nothing,' said Abu-Turab al-Nakhshabi[7], 'can defile the Sufi, and he in fact purifies everything.'

Among the modern exponents of the Way who have made the first stages possible through speech and publishing, is the Afghan adept Idries Shah, whose works are appreciated in the East and West.

In the past, such writers as Ghazzali (10/11th Centuries) or Hujwiri (11th Century) and Rumi (13th Century) used the method of tales, arguments and discourses to provide the preliminary steps for the learner, to enable him to approach the stage of Dervish (one who is on the Path). Later Sufis, while continuing this process, have often allowed private visits, attendance at lectures and personal instruction to help to carry the study further.

The great expansion of printing and reading in the past few

centuries, which have made possible a wide distribution of the earlier classics, have not completely succeeded in teaching postulants that they should prepare themselves for what the teacher in the flesh can convey by a careful study of his written work. It is still therefore very common for people to behave in the same way as the would-be disciple of the Master Shirazi: seeking the second lesson before absorbing the first.

One of the means adopted to stratify the steps for admission and progress in a graduated succession were the Sufist 'orders', which came into being in the Middle Ages. Unfortunately, with the passage of time these have always concentrated upon a reductionist interpretation of the Way, instead of a personal and flexible one, characteristic of institutionalisation. The demise of the 'orders' as effective learning channels, however, has not abolished the teaching function, but only transferred it from the 'orders' back to the traditional Masters.

NOTES

1 Quoted in Mir Khurd Kirmani's *Siyar al-Awliyya* (Lives of the Saints) Delhi, 1302 AH = 1884–5 AD.

2 *Siyar al-Awliyya*. (Persian language).

3 *The Kashf al-Mahjub*, by Hujwiri, tr. R. A. Nicholson, London 1911, 205.

4 Hujwiri.

5 Ghazzali: *Revival of the Sciences of Religion*. Book Four (*Tauhid* and *Tawakkul*).

6 *History of Sind*, 206.

7 Died 859 AD.

Sufi Activity

EMIR ALI KHAN

'IN THE WORLD, NOT OF IT'

The members of all communities, including nations and whole civilizations, are infused with the prevailing ideologies of those communities. These, in turn, create attitudes of mind which include certain capacities and equally positively exclude others.

The ideologies may be so ancient, so deep-seated or so subtle that they are not identified as such by the people at large. In this case they are often discerned only through a method of challenging them, asking questions about them or by comparing them with other communities.

Such challenge, description or questioning, often the questioning of assumptions, is what frequently enables a culture or a number of people from that culture to think in ways that have been closed to most of their fellows.

Traditionally, the Sufis have adopted the method of 'challenge and response' to assist people to enlarge their development and increase their perceptions. Naturally, the challenge is not random (not challenge for the sake of challenge, or questioning in order to be destructive, or even description just to add to the sum total of information) but is, in its specificity, calculated to lead to an advance in the level of individual and communal knowledge.

Just as the mere adoption of Sufi externals does not help in any
higher development, so is the only way to this development
through the actual experiencing of sensations which do not resemble any others in ordinary human experience. The Sufic current, it may be added, cannot be 'mixed' with any other. Those
who attempt to do this are only trying to achieve 'mixing' on an
emotional level, which is contra-indicated in Sufi work.

It is very common for those who have not been in contact with a
legitimate Sufi School to try to amalgamate Sufi ideas, techniques
and so on with other thoughts and behaviour-patterns. This
attempt in itself is evidence of low-level understanding which
must be transcended before the School can communicate effectively with such an individual.

The chief barrier to equal contact with the Sufi experience is the
over-development or over-use of imagination. As the Sufi teacher
Rumi puts it:

'Imagination blocks you like a bolt on a door. Burn that
bar.'

The next obstacle in the harmonisation of the Sufis with those
who would participate in their experience lies in the chaotic
situation which exists in all societies when the prevailing ideology
(whether scholastic, religious or other) has removed the distinctions between the three main kinds of knowledge: general,
specialised and perceptive, as applied to human development. It
is always a sign of a legitimate Sufi School when it attempts to
restore these levels in study; just as it is a sign of a deteriorated
tradition when the levels are not fully recognised by a community.

'THE THREE KINDS OF KNOWLEDGE'

One of the most specific statements of these three levels was made
by Al-Ghazzali. Everyone, he taught, is in reality in one of three
categories in respect to knowledge. First, he is a sharer in the
general stock of knowledge and what is called knowledge by the

community in which he lives: the larger, social world of his family, tribe, nation, civilization. Second, he may enter the ranks of those who understand more, who specialise. Third, he can enter the circle of those who have a realisation of understanding through direct experience.

These three levels are found, for instance, in the general *idea* of (say) being a blacksmith; then of learning how to become a blacksmith, and finally the experience of actually being a black-smith. In the levels recognised in the Islamic spiritual-philosophical tradition, the three circles correspond with The Law (*Shariat*), The Path (*Tariqat*) and Knowledge (*Ma'arifat*).

'DIE BEFORE YOU DIE'

Sufi teaching is designed to accept the learner at Level I, and help him or her, by means of the work of Level II, to reach Level III.

Level III is that which is conceived as beyond the 'sleep' (Hakim Sanai and others) which is familiar life. It is the existence in which the human phase of being is only a part and which can be seen as an interruption or stage, as sleep may be viewed as an interruption of wakefulness.

Hence the slogan *Die Before you Die*, which means that Stage III is the experiencing, before the end of ordinary (human) life of the perennial existence which follows physical death.

'DO YOU NEED A FURNACE OR A LAMP?'

Like any other legitimate teaching, the Sufi Way gives the student not what he or she may desire, but whatever is indicated as useful, to enable the passage from Stage I to Stage III to take place. This concentration upon specificity in progress is what distinguishes the Sufis from a cult or from any other form of self-indulgence purporting to be a 'Way'.

'Seek a furnace, but it would burn you,' (says Rumi), continuing, 'you only need the flame of a lamp.' In cults and other activities designed for pleasure rather than progress, the sensation is what is sought: and the most intense one at that. The School, however, seeks enlightenment, not intensity. It is to the individual and the group which have decided to seek something through such unregenerate and ignorant ambition that Saadi speaks when he says, 'I fear you will never reach Mecca, O Nomad! For you are on the road to Turkestan...'

The common occurrence of cults which imitate some Sufi techniques, remaining at Stage I while they think that they are approaching the third stage, is thus styled by Hafiz, another major teacher: 'A man must be a Solomon before his magical ring will work.'

ORGANISATION

The Sufi method of organisation has a discernible pattern insofar as studies are concerned. This is as follows:

The Sufi teacher presides over his own Circle (the *Halqa*). Next comes the Group (the *Taifa*). This is presided over by the Deputy. Finally comes the individual membership, in which single individuals are linked to the Teaching through the Office (*Daira*). The totality of the membership is the *Tariqa*, the Path (School), often inaccurately called, in imitation of Western organisations, 'the Order'.

The important point to remember in relation to the different forms of membership is that they are all considered to be equally important. In degenerate and imitation schools, comprising people who do not understand the workings of a School, it is considered 'better' to belong to the Master's circle than to be a 'mere individual member'. Such imaginings are borrowed from the First Level area of primitive human organisation, and have no place in a School.

The Teacher (or the Society, *Jamiyyat*, authorised by him) attaches students and other members in accordance with an expert assessment, to one or other forms of relationship (individual, circle, group) which may be varied from time to time, to provide the necessary learning impulses.

Since incomers generally have only the standards of Stage I as their opinion-forming instrument, it is common for some of them to demand to enter groups or circles, or to be individual members, or not to be such. People who adopt such an attitude are taken as valuing their assumptions above the expertise of the Society, and are generally discarded by the organisation, which, in Sufi terminology, 'does not feel itself competent to deal with them'.

In a Sufi School, the only Sufis are the realised end-products. The Sufi, according to classical and legitimate definition, is the illuminate. To call oneself 'A Sufi', therefore, is incorrect. People who do so are not Sufis. People who do not, may or may not be Sufis.

Members, if they are part of self-organised groups or self-styled 'Seekers', are known as *Dervishes* ('the Poor'), and sometimes form themselves into study-groups or reading circles pending acceptance by a regular School. In some cases, such bodies of students fail to obtain recognition and their amateur 'schools' may continue to exist even for centuries; being in reality cults or amusement bodies, though undetected as such in the community at large (which is generally only aware of Level I activity). Such organisations are even considered to be 'Sufi' bodies, and scholars and others regularly study them in the mistaken belief that they constitute a part of the 'Sufi phenomenon'.

These groupings are usually identifiable because of their love of emotive names for themselves, for their dramatic ideas about truth or enlightenment, their attachment to symbols and other externals, and their excitable membership. In all these respects they tend to be the opposite of the measured and effective Sufi group.

A dervish group or individual, however, can possibly be attached usefully to a School, but generally such wide-ranging organisation is needed as to upset the pleasures of the members, and hence the likelihood of such a development is not strong. Rumi is direct in saying of them, 'Let us leave such donkeys to their pastures.'

An Appraisal of Sufi Learning Methods

BENJAMIN ELLIS FOURD

The present climate of research and interest in traditional systems of life and learning greatly favours the study of those which have been preserved for centuries by the Sufis, a body of people commonly styled 'Islamic mystics', but whose teachings, both according to them and many if not all of their commentators, reach back into the human past beyond written records.

Materials on the Sufis are contained in the books which their exponents have written, and in accounts by travellers and residents in the Middle East (where they have been chiefly located) which cover a period of approximately 1200 years under the name *Sufi*.

The materials are so miscellaneous and, for many, confusing, that it has never been possible, in spite of several intensive attempts, to provide a rationale of what the Sufis do, why and in what manner, which will embrace all the acceptedly legitimate materials available. It is not a matter of too little material, but of too much. As one commentator has said: 'If we had handed down to us only a little about the Sufis, we would have been able to effect a plausible "reconstruction" of their ideas and practices which might not have been accurate: but which would certainly have satisfied our desire for order and to "close the books". Unfortunately, we cannot do this, for the materials are too abundant.'

Passing over this sad commentary upon our methods of running the profession of learning, it soon becomes apparent that sense may sometimes be made even from such a complex manifestation as that of the Sufis, by seeking the information and interpretation from – the Sufis themselves.

This process, which the present author has followed as far as humanly possible, reveals that there are roughly speaking two ways of looking at Sufi (and – who knows – perhaps many other kinds of) manifestations:

1 From the point of view of fixed assumptions which the researcher has brought with him into the equation; and
2 In accordance with what the Sufis themselves have to say about their activity.

What follows is substantially the collection of interpretations about Sufis and Sufism which originated in extensive travels and questionings, armed with questionnaires derived from the available books on the Sufis which have been written by experts. It is not too much to say that the Sufis have been considerably surprised at the lack of information and lacklustre mentality of the average researcher.

The first obvious matter of interest is contained in the question (and its answer) 'What are the Sufis *for*; why do they exist, and what are they trying to do?' In this, happily, there seems to be no confusion on the part of the Sufis, whatever motives, history or objectives the specialists may care to father upon them.

The Sufis, according to statements which command the acceptance of their own authorities, know how to dispel those things which stand between the human being and his or her perception of human origin and destiny, setting aside as irrelevant to this 'journey' the division between life before birth, during life as we know it, and after death.

The Sufi assertion is that humanity was created for a purpose, knew what this purpose was before assuming what is characterised as the human guise, forgot what this was at the point of birth, starts to remember it under appropriate stimuli, and continues to exist after physical death in a sense which has been modified by the terrestrial phase. Although this formulation may sound, to contemporary ears, like something out of science fiction, it was well-established and widely credited in this form many centuries before the devising of the science fiction genre, with all that that implies.

Sufis deny the absolute reality of time, space and physical form. These things, they say, are both relative and local. They only appear to be absolute.

This, then, is the Sufi asssertion. What of the application of methods to encourage the 'awakening' (Sufi phrase) of 'the sleeper' (their word for man)?

The Sufi answer to this differs so dramatically from all other religio-mystical conceptions that it is perhaps not surprising that some people cannot really grasp it. And yet it does not seem, once grasped, to be incompatible with any veracity of the basic argument. They say, in brief, that when the knowledge of how past, present and future are connected is experienced by a Sufi master, it is his ability to devise the methods. Further, such methods are not only unstandardised: they *must* be so. ('There are as many paths to Truth as there are souls of men' – Sufi phrase).

The Sufis, therefore, regard systems which treat everyone alike as mechanical and degenerate. They do not deny, either, that many supposedly Sufi entities have become over-simplified to such an extent, after falling into the hands of imitators, that they have lost the power to do more than automatise their followers. This, indeed, they regard as an inevitable consequence of the effects of time itself. In other words, our desire for order and our haste to organise leads to a demand for over-simplification which causes teaching to become indoctrination, and originally mean-ingful activity to become ritual. It is difficult to reverse this process, and to reclaim flexibility because of a demand for order which is so powerful, as are many other lower-level aspirations, that it grips its victims like a disease.

The Sufi approaches his task from whatever point he is able. The first consideration, in many cases, is the observation that people in general are so habituated to making habits that every-thing presented to a human being will be warped, by him, into a habit. The answer to this, according to the Sufi, is not to break habits, because many habits are important. The solution is to guide the learner to a position in which he can both have habits and manage to operate without them. The analogy which is used by modern Sufis is of an automatic mechanism which has an 'over-ride' which enables it to be operated at will.

This, in turn, leads to one of the most baffling aspects of Sufi activity: discontinuity. The Sufi claims that, in addition to rhythm and its effects, there are phases, within the human being, which can be contacted and employed to enable him to think, to work and to exist outside of familiar time and repetitiousness. Human beings, however, have an affinity for repetition. Sufi techniques explore the switchover from continuity to discontinuity by a large number of devices, both literary, physical and mental. Many of Sufi exercises are in fact based upon this conception. It follows from this that people who are not able to switch attention from repetition to discontinuity will not be able to benefit from such techniques, even if they know what they are. It is for this reason that a Sufi teacher is always needed: unregenerate man will always automatise inputs, and only someone who is consciously outside of time as well as within it can hold the line.

The second training requirement that is marked among the Sufi teachers is based on an understanding of the tendency to accept or to reject. Most human institutions are based on the binary mode 'either-or'. Faced with almost any situation, the human being will automatically decide, as quickly as possible, whether to accept or reject it. This, say the Sufis, provides a useful tool for ordinary learning and indoctrination, but when it becomes the only mode of approach to a situation it effectively screens the individual from other perceptions, other areas of experience where this mode is absent. The attempt at introducing a middle way (indecision, evaluation, and so on) only imports an uncertainty into the situation, and does not, they aver, constitute the establishment of a third specific potentiality which they hold to be essential.

Vanity and self-assertion, which have been struggled against (one feels, generally, with little success) by virtually every religion, are also regarded by the Sufis as harmful to the realisation process. They do not, however, stress the reward and punishment aspect of too much vanity. To them, vanity is a barrier to learning.

Not to be able to learn, or to progress, is just as deadly for the Sufi as 'being damned' or 'ceasing to exist' is in other dispensations.

The initial training, among the Sufis, concentrating upon modesty and repentance is, indeed, held by them to be both the essential foundation of all human spiritual progress – and also certainly in their eyes the original teaching of which the re-ligionised versions, mere emotional or social blackmail, are degenerations.

After modesty comes symbolism. I have time and again noted that genuine Sufis are almost baffled that those who copy them are unaware that the Sufi teachings contain layer upon layer of mean-ings, and that one cannot pass to a second meaning until a primary one has been absorbed.

The consequence of the failure of the imitators to understand this, even in theory, is that, for the Sufi, no outside enquirer is able to make any progress at all in real Sufism, but remains, as it were, churning up the surface of the water like a pondfly while at the same time making journeys all over the East, teaching others because of his 'experiences', writing books, doing dervish dances and generally behaving in a manner which the Sufi himself regards as first-class evidence of incompetence and superficiality.

One of the reasons for the well-known penchant of the Sufis for discouraging admirers or applicants for knowledge is to force them to re-examine the real depth of their knowledge and sincer-ity. 'It may take,' one Sufi told me, 'five or even more approaches, covering several years, before we have been able to signal effec-tively enough to the applicant that we would be glad to help him if he would only amend his own feelings of self-importance.'

What proportion of those who are thus diverted actually return that number of times? I asked him.

'Less than one in ten. Nine will decide that we are nasty people. . . . Some even go away quite unconscious that they have been reproached, so vain are they, and start to "teach".'

But, if the foregoing special characteristics of the Sufis cause general alarm or confusion, this is nothing to the degree of mis-understanding which originates in another typical feature of Sufi practice.

I refer to the fact that there are many apparently different 'systems' of Sufi study. Not only are there reported musical and rhythmic assemblies; there are formulations which appear to show that Sufis dislike music or favour it; that they practise loud (or only silent!) vocations; that there are six, nine, ten, seventeen, and any other number of stages and stations of the way. Some people say that they work on activating sensitive perception-spots on the head and body, like the Yogic *chakras*. Others hold that the Sufi methods require repetitions, memorising, and almost any kind of spiritual or other practice which you can imagine.

How can this be?

The real answer, which is not to be found in any of the 2250 books or monographs on the subject which I have studied, comprising effectively the entire bibliography of Sufism which the world can offer, is amazingly simple. All one has to do is to ask a real Sufi. Sufis, the answer goes, will employ any method in their teachings which will actually work. They are not tied to any traditional formula whatever. The use of many different kinds of methods by various teachers has given rise to the assumption that such-and-such a method is 'the real Way', among imitators. So, if nowadays you ask one of the many thousands of imitators (or sincere but misled followers of one-time imitators) as to the facts about the standardisation of methods among the Sufis – they will give you an answer which does not originate with the Sufis at all, but with dervishes: people who have tried, usually unsuccessfully, to become Sufis.

What is interesting about the fact that Sufi teachers choose their own techniques is that the fact that this is possible at all tends to support the Sufi assertion that the Sufi actually knows 'The Way' from having trodden it. In contradistinction, the very fact that people in other systems cleave so strongly to repetition, traditionalism and rote, imitation and ritual could well be taken to mean that the actual insight as to what actually does work, is absent. This point is worth pondering.

Worth pondering, of course, it may be. Whether it will be pondered is another matter. The reason for this unlikelihood, it seems to me, is that in most human societies there is little conception that there may be a 'Way' which is open and which is known and understood by its sponsors. In the West, for instance, the reverence for authority and the attachment to fixed forms must surely stem from a subconscious belief that there is no access to truth today – only repetition of what people in the past have said one should do and believe. Similarly, in the Far East, traditionalism surely spells conviction that what was once done and believed must surely produce results today. The existence of people who say, as it were, 'forget tradition, follow experience' must be very small, otherwise we would not find it hard to keep in our minds the possibility that some may be able to do something without particular, frequent or even plausible reference to standard authorities.

Sufi teaching techniques, in their true form, depend very much upon an inter-relation between master and disciple and between these two and the whole community of mystics. The 'current' which flows between these, according to the Sufis, is the most important element in their being and progress.

Given this statement, it is possible to discern that many so-called Sufi groupings and teachers are in fact no such thing, for the element of the current is absent. The sporadic nature of the Sufi activity, when there may be a lecture or a series of exercises, there may be a lecture or distinct instruction, or there may not, from time to time in a real Sufi school, ties in with this current. The fluctuation of activity parallels the fluctuation of potentiality and the knowledge of the teacher in a way which is not to be found, so far as I am aware, in other systems. This does not necessarily prove that the Sufi system is true or superior, but it does imply a strong distinction which is not noted, so far as I am aware, in the literature.

This characteristic of fluctuation leads naturally into another of the 'strange' aspects of Sufi teaching organisation. The strangeness lies in the fact that, unlike other mystical or philosophical systems, Sufis often organise their studies around communities and enterprises which are not instantly recognisable as 'spiritual'. Everyone, for instance, in the East and West, knows what a monastery is. As a settlement or collection of people, it may well run enterprises of an economic kind: agriculture, bee-keeping, the manufacture of wines or spirits, various crafts. But these activities are always looked upon as things which help to contribute to the upkeep of the foundation. With the Sufis, however, they, 'strangely' operate all kinds of enterprises. A Sufi school may centre around a colony of tinsmiths, or a factory, shop or even the running of a large house and grounds. Even some of the repetitious and formalised groupings sometimes retain vestiges of this concept. Among the Bektashis, for instance, are to be found the relics of a family, with certain functionaries known as the Cook, the Groom, and so on. In Central Asia this tradition is perpetuated (in name though not in action) by the use of the term *khanawad*, 'family' to style a Sufi group. A very large number of ancient Sufi organisations stem from chivalry, another format; with tabards still being carried (they know not why) by wandering dervishes in Iran, and swords hanging on the walls of *tekkias*, Sufi meeting-places, as widely dispersed as Bosnia and Sinkiang.

The reason for the different formats, in addition to the fact that they signal the teacher's flexibility to teach within any framework, is that the principle of fluctuation within form must be maintained. That is to say, if the teacher has to maintain contact and a relationship with his followers while waiting (as it were) for propitious times to carry out the practices which alone bring enlightenment, he must have a form within which to maintain the coherence of the group. In deteriorated systems, that form is wholly religious: people wear special clothes, pray and meditate and so on at stated times. They have, in fact, become automatised. With the Sufis, on the other hand, the primary need is to keep the decks clear for the 'moment' when the teaching can take place. This requires that the attention should be focussed upon the teaching only when it is able to operate, while other activities are carried out in the intervening time. Seen from one perspective, of course, this all means that the Sufis are creating a socio-economic group which fulfills the function of 'being in the world but not of it'

(Sufi slogan) yet at the same time not exhausting the spiritual energy by dwelling on emotional and evocative thoughts (prayers, litanies, readings and so on) which operate on people in a conditioning manner.

It has to be admitted that the principle underlying this interesting organisation might lead one to suppose that there really is one unusual insight at work. The abandonment or absence of the principle in virtually all other spiritually-oriented societies should not blind us to the possibility that here we find a method and a knowledge that could really be almost unknown elsewhere. Is *this* the Sufi secret?

The existence of these organisations, of course, depends – according to the Sufis – upon the existence of Sufis with the necessary knowledge to set up what seem to be profane organisations but which are yet subtly related with the teaching, the disciples and the outside world. Since the reality behind seemingly non-religious entities was announced some years ago by the Sufi authority Idries Shah, some attempts have been made to set up supposedly Sufi farms, camps, businesses and so on, almost always by people who were merely imitating. As has been noted with regard to Sufis many times in the past, the compulsion to imitate is not always a sign of deceit, though it is almost invariably a sign of immaturity. Readers are warned, therefore, not to adopt just any 'Sufi' organisation because it claims to be working along the lines of worldly organisation with an inner content. All authentic Sufis are in direct contact, and there is in the world at any one moment only one Sufi entity which manipulates the totality of the Sufi activity.

The existence of such a finely-tuned instrument as a total Sufi organisation, with its own organs of communication and its own programmes founded upon direct perception of truth beyond appearances, of course, makes nonsense of almost all our attempts to study Sufis through secondary sources. Further, it makes laughable the careful examination of Sufi prayers, exercises and methods which are looked at in isolation. A Sufi, if he is working in attunement with a total operation, will never be able to indicate (any more than an observer can perceive) what the actual function of the said exercise, etc., really is, for it is nothing at all when torn from context.

Today's Sufis Comment on the Scholars

MOHANDIS EL ALOUITE

The main avenues of information from which people obtain their impressions about the Sufis, apart from those few outside the fold who happen to be acquainted with real Sufis (a tiny minority) come from the written word.

The dictionaries and encyclopaedias are in general too confused or too limited in content to offer much useful material. Next come articles in the popular and specialist (religious, philosophical and academic) Press, which almost always labour a single point of view and cannot be said to provide an adequate background. Two main kinds of books in general circulation constitute the third source of material. Of these, the first are popular works which confuse Sufism with cults, with occultism or with various systems of thought such as Yoga or Zen. This class of material has greatly multiplied recently because of the growing interest in experiential religion and psychology. These works are of very uneven quality. Again, they are seldom deeply researched and for the most part their authors rely upon the 'rehashing' technique or upon information supplied by adventurous cults. The second category of printed books are those of the self-styled 'specialists', often orientalists, whose work is (because of the university or other appointments of the writers) regarded as authoritative.

The opinions and reactions of genuine Sufis to this material seem never to have been tested, and the present writer therefore submitted questions to a number of them, from Africa, the Middle East and the Far East, to ascertain their position.

It is no secret that Sufis and professional or professed scholars have been at odds ever since records on the subject are available, which means for over a thousand years. Sufis executed in the past through scholars' testimony include the redoubtable Hallaj, the great Sufi martyr. The major teacher Ibn al Arabi (known in the East as 'the Greatest Master, Sheikh al Kabir') was hauled before an inquisition and had to satisfy scholars that his *Interpreter of Desires* was mystical and not love-poetry. He satisfied them, un-usually, thereby showing what most commentators feel to be nothing more than that he was their master in debate and in-terpretation rather than that they were especially susceptible to justice. The attitudes of the medieval scholastics, however, per-sisted in the minds of even such a recent orientalist as the highly-acclaimed Ignaz Goldziher, who, in the face of almost unanimous testimony to Arabi's importance, could call him 'a swindler', which he felt able to do without the need to adduce any evidence as to his 'swindles'.

The Sufis of today, rightly one might imagine, given the back-ground just abbreviated, regard scholars with a fair amount of suspicion.

There are two main reasons for the Sufi reservations about the academics:-

1 Scholars undoubtedly distort, misunderstand and misreport – and the Sufis have adduced numerous examples of this tendency, which effectively combats scholarly claims to objectivity in the handling of materials, for instance.
2 Scholars, through their assumption of authority, tend to make people who read them think that their materials and conclusions must be authoritative and correct.

The main remarks by contemporary Sufis, which are borne out by an examination of works in print about Sufis by scholars and 'specialists', are these:

* Many of the assertions made are contradictory; as when an 'authority' will say that Sufism is derived from Christianity,

but on another page that it is self-generated. Again, another well-known writer says both that Sufism is limited only to Moslems and also that all Christians are Sufis;

* A surprisingly large number of present-day students of Sufism confuse it with a sort of occultism and resort to amazing phrases and ideas which can find no support in the classical materials;

* Islamic scholars in the West make the most childish mistakes in references to the materials and contexts of the Sufis which betray a great ignorance of Islam and of the setting of early Sufis;

* A low level of knowledge of Persian and Arabic – the main languages used in the Sufi classics – is evidenced by several scholars in the West. These include the eminent professors Arberry and Nicholson;

* Some of them translate materials while at the same time admitting that they do not understand what the Eastern people make of them: an example is Gertrude Bell, in her translations from Hafiz;

* Many writers imagine, with Birge (for instance), that a study of a deteriorated cult using Sufi externals, such as the highly fossilised form of Bektashism still lingering in areas of the former Turkish Empire, are in fact Sufi entities;

* Such writers as John Subhan imagine that superseded formulations and practices, used in olden times for specific purposes, are integral to Sufism;

* Most of the orientalists fail to study the contemporary, living aspects and organizations of the Sufis; or else fail to amalgamate into their studies such first-hand (and often first-class) materials collected by others, as for instance Burke (*Among the Dervishes*); Lefort (*The Teachers of Gurdjieff*) and Fatemi in *Sufi Studies East & West*.

There is now a considerable bibliography of materials of this kind, almost unnoticed by the 'specialists'.

* Many orientalists (some of whom are actually converts to one or other minority religious group in Islam) try to present Sufism as some sort of aspect of the area which the writers

themselves favour. This is especially marked in certain West-
ern-Shia scholars who try to establish the Shia roots of Sufis.
This 'tribalistic' approach makes much of their work, perhaps fortunately, almost unreadable and certainly of little or
no value except as curiosities of belief.

* A surprising number of modern orientalist students regularly
  mistake the imitative cultists who are running supposedly
  Sufi groups and movements as the genuine article.

Although the genuine Sufis can easily make out an unanswer-
able case for the relative incompetence of scholars in the Sufis'
own field, this does not of course establish the authority of the
Sufis as Sufis. It only shows that the Sufis, in general, are far better
scholars than the scholars themselves!

Peculiarities and Use of the Sufi Meeting-Place

FERRUCIO AMADEO

Most of the names of the Sufi meeting-place are traditionally taken from Persian and Arabic. The most familiar ones are: *Hujra* [room]; *Zavia* [corner]; *Tekkia* [a support, a place of repose]; *daira* [a circle]; *dar al baraka* [abode of blessing].

The most ancient and legitimate usage of the meeting-place is that it shall be reserved for specific occasions. This is said to be because the configuration of the room or other place is designed to attract and to concentrate a certain subtle force (baraka) which is collected and disseminated among those who attend meetings. If, so the argument goes, too many people use the premises too often, not only will this baraka be dissipated, but the 'impress' of the negative characteristics of the people present will disturb the atmosphere and may even result in cultish or other extravagant behaviour.

This stricture, however, is not found to be obeyed in most of the communities which style themselves Sufi, and hence might well be used as a measure of deciding whether they are not, after all, no matter their prestige, really only automatic or fossil remnants.

Special meetings to concentrate energies may also be held. But the use of the Meeting-place, which therefore tends to resemble an instrument rather than anything else, depends upon the presence of a teacher who knows how the personnel and the activities will concentrate the necessary energy.

The relationship between the characters of the people present is extremely important, according to the traditional lore. No meeting-place of this kind can be formed or used unless there is a community of at least 400 people. This is said to be because this makes possible the selection of 30 at most who can both take part in the proceedings and also supply the range of 'types' which are needed to absorb and to generate the needed subtle force.

As might be expected with such an 'instrument', the size, shape and siting of the place, together with the materials employed, are thought to be most important.

The dimensions, siting, interior decor and appurtenances are all subject to the most careful arrangement and calculation. As an instance, brass and wood join ceramics and wool (sheepskins) as important in the collecting and reflecting of the 'baraka'. How they are placed and when and where and even by whom is given the most careful consideration.

The attitude of the people entering the room must be taken into account since it affects the proceedings which are held there.

Each individual, however, may be of more than one 'type', since the Sufis hold that all people are composed of numerous distinct, more or less developed, personalities, and that the grouping of such people will maximise or minimise their tendencies, to the advantage or detriment of the progress of the individuals and the group in the search for higher consciousness mediated by the teacher.

Most of these considerations, it will be observed, have fallen into disuse in the Sufi groups which are generally accessible to most researchers.

Photographs of alleged Sufi meeting-places, too, indicate that they tend to become cluttered with appurtenances of merely traditional value or sentimental significance: something which a major part of the traditional Sufi activity is devoted to avoiding wherever found.

When the meeting-place is called a *sama-khana* [hall of listening] it is often used in deteriorated groups, for all kinds of purposes, such as meetings, 'dance' and other exercises, and for the participation in the 'dance' or other movements which is a sign of the deterioration of the Teaching according to the best authorities.

Traditionally, the building or organising of the Meeting-Place is of the greatest importance. Ancient accounts of the setting up of such places seem to agree on certain principles and practices. First the Teacher will collect a number of followers; then he will provide a small or introductory meeting-place. While preparations are being made for the great or ultimate meeting-place, the existing one will be used less and less. This is said to be because it is set aside for the accumulation of the baraka which will be stored and transferred to the ultimate meeting-place when this is ready.

The collection of funds for the Great Meeting-Place is approached with considerable care and attention. First, no actual collection of funds is made because it is considered a manifestation of the working of the baraka when people donate sums of money spontaneously for the purpose. It is believed that, without prompting, the fund of the meeting-place starts to grow and snowball as the need for the place and the impression of the accumulation of the baraka seeps directly (subliminally) into the minds of the disciples. As soon as this happens, they start to accumulate funds; sometimes, as with other devotional traditions, they part with much of their property, and the resultant sums are given, always anonymously and in secret, in cash, to the Teacher.

The increased cost of property throughout the world, more particularly in the West, might be thought to have slowed down this process. But when it is realised that some meeting-places of the Sufis of the past were built and organised, or converted from existing buildings, at a cost equal to half the total possessions of the disciples, an equivalent amount today, with the relative affluence of Western societies, would be colossal, and well ahead of the present-day cost of buildings.

As with other spiritual communities, the amount of material sacrifice which the members are prepared to make is regarded as an indicator of their generosity: something which in turn affects favourably their ability to profit from the Teaching.

While such an idea might not recommend itself to those who have reservations about the Sufi (or any other) system's validity, it cannot be denied that the great Masters of the Path have always adhered to this policy, even if they were kings or others who were not themselves in need of any part of the material substance handed in for the meeting-place.

Interestingly enough, it is said among the Sufis that the building of the Egyptian pyramids was originated in the same fashion. That is, a certain number of initiates donated the colossal sums needed to produce the 'power-houses' which was the function of the pyramids of old. These, incidentally, are now held to have discharged their functions and to be incapable of functioning as attractors and stores of 'baraka'.

The octagonal shape is thought to be the most important for such a building and brass or copper will attract the baraka: though only if the specialised knowledge which is held by the teachers is brought to bear on the project.

Light, sound and something else not specified work within the building to provide the substance which is supposed to perform the Sufi 'miracle' of enlightenment.

Sufi authorities point to the undeniable fact that people all over the world have built colossal and amazing buildings as a part of their religious activities, and they add that originally these were intended to work as some sort of scientific instrument, principally working with the baraka factor.

Information on this point is hard to obtain, understandably. But there is evidence that these 'concentrators' are still being built and adapted from other suitable buildings.

Avoiding Imitators

GASHIM MIRZOEFF

During the Middle Ages the writings of such Sufi greats as Al Ghazzali and Ibn al Arabi profoundly influenced the religious and scientific thought of the West. It is not too far to go to say that Western philosophical and religious thinking, as well as much of European literature, would certainly not be what it is, in content or quality, without the Sufi influence, which has been documented by an increasing number and variety of workers in the West itself.

There seems little doubt that there has been a continuing interchange between the Sufis and the West; certainly, much recent research indicates this. This intercommunication, however, appears to have become 'naturalized' very early on: the strange men in odd headgear who chant and gyrate, mentioned with approval by Ramon Lull seven centuries ago, are more likely today to be men and women who are as at home in the West as in the East. They are likely to be people who have adapted the traditional, culture-linked ideas and practices of the East to the milieu of the West, which today, of course, includes the Americas and places as far afield as Australia and South Africa.

But there is another layer of supposedly 'sufi' activity which has invaded the West, and which is clearly based either on the excitatory (primitive and shamanistic) cults of the Middle East, or else upon the adventures of certain spurious or self-deceived 'teachers' who have regularly invaded the West since Victorian times. Let us now look at some of them.

The most numerous emanate from the Indo-Pakistani subcontinent. Few are well educated, though many have what seem to be impressive degrees from local universities. They tend to favour outlandish garb, beards and even turbans. They make trips across the world, contacting as far as possible both local Indians and Pakistanis and also certain Western people who have heard about Sufism, trying to present themselves as legitimate teachers. They tend to be ignorant and they usually try to get local people to form study groups and to raise money. Although they tell tall tales about their origins and their important spiritual teachers and ancestors, they are ignorant of the wider materials about the Sufis, and can always be detected if they are questioned from the basis of the classical Sufi books, of which they generally have only the slightest acquaintance. Real Sufi 'missionaries' always speak the language of the country in which they are working perfectly. The accented tones of the adventurers generally give them away.

The second group generally emanates from North Africa, notably Algeria and sometimes from Egypt. They are clearly to be recognized as sectarians as they stick to a limited number of excitatory techniques and rely heavily on the supposed sanctity of their 'saints', about whom they talk a great deal. Originally having made considerable inroads into certain French intellectual circles, they have now spread to several other countries. As with other secondary cults, they have succeeded in inducing some orientalists to regard them as genuine expressions of Sufism; but this reflects such scholars' poor knowledge of the phenomenon.

The third body of alleged Sufis are those who have become fascinated by the so-called 'dancing' Dervishes of Turkey. Some of them even emanate from Turkey itself, but these are in general in any case followers of a mere cult, though claiming spiritual descent from the illustrious Jalaluddin Rumi, Teacher of Konya. In fact, as is fairly well-known, Rumi himself banned 'dancing' except for certain specific cases. Furthermore, in all Sufi circles, 'dancing' and all such movements, are restricted to employees, since the effect of the movement and music is not on the participants, but upon the observers. That is why even the Mevlevi musical halls are technically termed Sama-Khana (Hall of Listening), and not 'Hall of Music' (participation) or 'Hall of (Taking part in) Dancing'. Sufis are notoriously careful in their use of words, and this point is well attested through reference to the classical masters. What has perpetuated the thirst for participation in music and dance is nothing less than the aspiration which is specifically interdicted by the real Sufis: the desire for emotional stimulation.

The 'dancers' cover a great range; from self-deluded followers and self-imagined descendants of Rumi's Way to self-apppointed teachers who have merely attended the deteriorated ceremonials of the cult.

They delight, too, in dressing up in tall hats and flowing robes.

Iran, in recent years, has given rise to a number of equally spurious sects all using the name of Sufi. None of these is regarded as legitimate by the real Sufis of the East, though their numbers are increasing so rapidly, with followers in the West as well, that they may before long become accepted by Western people as genuine.

There are also several stray Arabs who may or may not be sincere, who are carrying on supposedly Sufic activities in the West and in the East. They brandish what seem to be impressive credentials and yet most of them are extremely ignorant about the real bases and procedures of the Sufis. They will tend to amalgamate bits and pieces of Sufi activity from any source, especially from books.

Authentic Sufis go to great lengths to avoid actually meeting such people, partly to prevent them pretending that they have their blessing.

The work and writings of Idries Shah in recent years have served to highlight many of the spurious practitioners; since Shah's published materials provide a basis from which to assess at least some of the adventurers. Shah and others, too, have provided, within the Society for Sufi Studies, an umbrella organization which provides all the information and instruction necessary, so that only those who crave the spurious or the absurd need patronise the mountebanks. The others can obtain legitimate contact from the Society, whose books and monographs are published by The Octagon Press of London. Another legal and authentic Sufi body working in the East and West is, of course, The Sufi Trust, which makes available the materials and contacts which are sought, increasingly, by sincere enquirers.

This latter activity should go a long way towards clearing up the confusion which has allowed almost free rein to the adventurers and deluded cultists.

The Western Seeker seen through Eastern Eyes

ALIRIDA GHULAM SARWAR

Most of the material on Sufi and other spiritual approaches available today is either in the form of accounts of ancient encounters between Sufis and others; or else Western appraisals of Sufis and supposed Sufis in the East and working in the West. It is hardly possible to find any account of how the Sufis of the East see the seeker of the West, his strengths and weaknesses and his peculiar manner of approach.

'Peculiar' here, of course, is used in the technical sense of 'special' or 'characteristic', because the people of the West in general, sharing for the most part a common culture, will tend to approach and to view something outside of their format – as well as within it – in a manner conditioned by their own environment.

Contemporary Sufis in the East have a remarkably homogeneous attitude towards the seeker from the West. Extensive enquiries have succeeded in eliciting the following personality-picture from such teachers:

The typical Western 'seeker' is very much conditioned to names, symbols and labels. He will be impressed if something which he has thought or felt seems to chime with something which he comes across in the East or in Eastern writings, such is the influence of associations upon him. This 'associative tendency' marks him out from the Easterner, who will want to know why something strikes him so powerfully, not merely be influenced by it. The Western seeker, again, holds in his mind a wide range of assumptions and imaginings about what is spiritual and what is not. Just as his ancestors when they were pagans were scandalised because the early Christians would not give divine honours to the Roman Emperors, so his descendant is amazed when Sufis will not acknowledge that certain things, regarded as sacramental or spiritual, are inherently important in spiritual activity. One of the reasons why a lot of Eastern mumbo-jumbo which has filtered into the West is so highly esteemed there, according to today's Sufis, is through this tendency to idealise and to idolise things which in the East are considered instruments or approximations. These two characteristics in the people of the West are joined by a third, though some Eastern Sufis claim that this is the most prevalent, and least promising, characteristic. This is the habit of people from the West to both embark upon a spiritual search without any careful preparation and self-examination, and also their determination to retain whatever principles, practices and opinions they have acquired through their entire search. They do not, in sum, approach a teaching as a coherent whole with something to give, but rather in fact as something which should be at least partially amalgamated with their pre-existent beliefs. They are more than once termed 'collectors of trifles' by Sufi divines who are sometimes perplexed by this demand for teachings which not only accord with a pre-set pattern, but which also embody random parts of other teachings which happen to have caught the fancy of the 'seeker'.

Sufi diagnosticians aver that this tendency is linked with the general Western desire to retain control, or at the least, choice, over what he or she does or believes. They further point out, however, that this is a misconceived attempt to protect or to shine: since all the evidence shows that Western people are heavily and frequently indoctrinated by their own systems and also by any number of Eastern ones as well.

'The answer,' as one Sufi puts it, 'is to show these people that in seeking to prevail or to maintain their own ideas, they do not protect themselves. When they come to see this, they can come to see that it is we alone who are fighting the battle against indoctrination in spiritual matters. Even their own systems do not do that, in fact they make no bones about conditioning people very heavily. The results of this treatment they often term "highly spiritual", or "really dedicated", failing altogether to note that the product is a result of brain-engineering, not of faith.'

This contention, if true, surely deserves close attention and remedy.

One surprise came when Sufi teachers in the East were asked about the difference between those Western seekers who wanted to submit to a Master and those who adopted a cynical stance. Surely, they were asked, these represent two totally different types.

No, indeed, came the answer. 'Both types are the same. The common denominator and determinant is that both are obsessed by certainty. The first type seeks certainty, the second seeks to retain it.'

What, then, ran the further question, should the attitude of the learner be?

'Making preconditions, like the desire for or dislike of certitude, is not a posture which will lead to learning. Only those can learn who will learn what *is* there, not those who want to learn through a method which they bring as their commanding principle.'

Of course, since the questioner himself comes from a Western thought-pattern background, it was somewhat sobering to note how he had been unable to distinguish the identity of the 'two postures' until this was pointed out. This kind of difficulty may well lie at the very heart of the Western-inspired disciplines through which we try to understand other cultures.

The present writer put this question to a major Sufi theoretician in the Middle East in an attempt to elicit an opinion or guidance on this point:

'Would you say that our Western disciplines are so culture-bound that they cannot be used to approach non-Western systems such as that of the Sufis?'

The answer was unexpected:

'The Sufi systems are non-Western only in the sense that they are not very well developed in the West. There is nothing inherently "Eastern" about the Sufi methods; any more than there is really anything inherently "Western" about technology, just because it was developed in the West; having existed in the East previously, as the history of science shows.'

'If you wish to adopt Western methods, you may do so providing that you do not limit yourselves to too-narrow approaches. The most conspicuous is thinking that something which is spiritual must fit your own categories.'

Since the imposition of habit-patterns is so fiercely disliked by the Sufis, it was necessary to ask their authorities how they could hope to decondition, or, indeed, to have a human being who had not been conditioned.

The answer, again, indicated how superficially one had read the Sufi classics themselves, for it was contained in the work of, for instance, Rumi and Ghazzali, seven centuries to almost a millenium ago:-

'What is today called conditioning is what used to be called habit-patterns based on lower objectives. The Sufi method has never been to disturb these patterns, but rather to supply or make possible the development of a superior consciousness which would be able to perceive the habit and regulate its value. Once a person can really experience the value or otherwise, the relevance or otherwise, of a conditioned form of behaviour or thought, he or she will inevitably modify it. This is what we call "polishing the mirror" in one of its aspects. If you have a scowl on your face, and this scowl has become a habit, and you do not know about it, or do know and do not know how to remove it, you will be in a different state when you can see it in a mirror. Instantaneously or bit by bit the reflection will do its job: coupled with the other things which you "see in the mirror" – for within it is the vision of what you could be like, sensed in an interior fashion: not, as with your Western people, by imitating other people.'

Once again, then, the investigator finds that the Sufi regards the would-be illuminate as someone who not only needs enlightenment, but as someone from whom a great deal in the way of misconceptions has to be eliminated. This is also said to be a part of the progression by which 'veils are banished'. The 'veils' in the way of the Sufi realisation, then, may often be nothing more or less than habits which cannot be tackled, as we so often try in the West, by replacing them with other habits.

The last remark of one Sufi Master on this subject seems to shed further light on the problem:

'The person from the West has laudable and reprehensible attitudes of aspiration. THE LAUDABLE IS WHEN HE OR SHE TRIES TO SET OUT ON THE PATH AT ALL. THE REPREHENSIBLE IS WHEN HE OR SHE IMAGINES THAT THE SEEKER CAN MAKE THE RULES.'

It is not without interest that, of all the Sufis and imitators visited and queried on this subject, it was the imitators who were unable to describe the shortcomings of the Western seekers in these terms, since, obviously, they welcomed the tendency towards obsessionality which was often shown by their own Western disciples. They gave themselves away somewhat, however, by welcoming the obsessed Westerners as 'people who had seen the Truth' – and condemning the cynics as 'people not ready for enlightenment'. Similar distinctions are made by false or primitive religionists throughout history and in all parts of the world.

CURRENT SUFI ACTIVITY: WORK, LITERATURE, GROUPS AND TECHNIQUES

by
Chawan Thurlnas

A NOTE BY THE TRANSLATOR...

Out of old fields, as men see
Comes all this new corn, year by year
And out of old books, in good faith:
Comes all this new science that men learn

Chaucer: *Parlement of Fowls*

Sufi Procedures, Organisation
'In the World'

The Sufi approach to professional, vocational and business activities resembles that of other communities, but the similarity serves also to conceal certain dramatic differences. Sufi disciples will co-operate in what seem to be almost every kind of activity: ranging from the arts, through commerce to academic and other undertakings in the world of learning. A number of seekers will associate together to pursue a project, because the successful completion of a mundane activity is often regarded as an index of the necessary harmonization of the group. In other words, if the project works, the members of the group are in the kind of alignment which will enable them to profit from the subtle, spiritual impulses which the Sufi work is offering.

This kind of pattern is familiar in all groups with a common interest. Both religious and other groupings, of short or long duration, can be found working together in a wide variety of areas, throughout the world. The difference comes when one examines the theory and mechanism of the Sufi and the other groupings.

In the case of the Sufis, a project is devised and an attempt is made to carry it out. If this succeeds – that is, if the shop, factory, artistic atelier and so forth – flourishes within a reasonable period of time, the group concerned is accepted with its membership as eligible for special exercises and instructions which are believed to be able to operate through this 'organism' with extraordinary rapidity and effectiveness. The group need not be money-orientated: some groups are charitable, others devised for entertainment, still others work in the fields of planning, design, agriculture or even certain spheres of diplomacy. But, while there need not be a financial aim in the undertaking, if it is one which ordinarily yields a profit, then the index of its success always includes profit: and the entire yield is always made available to the Sufi Path. The Sufi teacher ordinarily authorizes the experiment and may give it the time-scale in which it is to succeed. If the project does not progress sufficiently well, the harmonization of its individual members is considered to be at fault, and the effort must be stopped. Many such entities fall into the hands of people who 'capture' them and milk them for their own profit. This is not only regarded as reprehensible: it also has a positive side – the entire group and the operation itself is deemed to have gone sour. The positive advantage has been that the unsuitable members have been identified. Henceforth the Work, as it is called, can insulate itself from this 'diseased' limb.

This application of the doctrine that 'the exterior is an indicator of the interior' strikingly emphasises the belief that harmony brings about coherent ('organic') growth; and, in contradistinction, that the imposition of patterns upon groups will never succeed in developing anything. From this it can be seen why so many Sufis are on record as working so vehemently against imposed structure. It also gives a clue as to why Sufis (other than those who imagine that they are Sufis) will never subject *everyone* from their communities to the same exercises, or even to the same range of ideas.

It is, however, true that the Sufi organism *as a whole*, constitutes one single body. But this unity is one which is understood and worked with only by the 'realised' Sufi. The unity is invisible at ground level, as it were.

The vast miscellany of some Sufi masters' activities, from this viewpoint, makes – if not sense – at least a distinction between repetitious and limited activity and the whole complicated structure within which the teacher works.

An important and highly-respected Sufi teacher in the Middle East, when asked his reactions to what we often think of as truly Sufi groups, with attentive disciples clustered around a teacher who gives out invocations and encourages unusual dress and talks all the time of 'unity', 'self-realization' or 'unification with the Absolute' (instead of carrying out a comprehensive programme) said: 'I constantly see such people, both here and in Europe and America. Everyone thinks that they are Sufis except the Sufis themselves. Whenever I meet these circuses I go home to have a good laugh'.

SUFI USE OF LITERATURE

Technical and instructional literature is well understood in all cultures as a source of information and education. This is no new invention: some of the oldest materials found in written form (from long-dead civilizations) are instructional ones, ranging from commercial formulae to descriptions of the correct manner of organising funerals or religious ceremonies.

It has, however, been observed that when written and oral materials have been employed for many generations they can acquire a ritualistic significance. They begin to be revered for their own sake, for their sound or for their ancient origins or repute.

Among the Sufis, it is somewhat startling, though always refreshing, to note that only in secondary or deteriorated groupings is there any sign of reverence for literature apart from its instrumental function. As an example, while spurious and imitative groupings (which are common and widespread throughout the East) will repeat litanies, ranging from shouts of '*Hu*' [He!] or '*Ya Pir*' [O Teacher!] the use of sounds and ideas in written or spoken form within the legitimate Sufi organizations is confined to the people, the times and the occasions where they are believed to have a specific – as we would in current terminology call an intended and technical – effect.

So striking is this difference between ritualism and function that it may be taken as the dividing line between ignorant quasi-Sufism and the real thing.

Ritualistic exclamations and the magical repute of words and phrases is, of course, very widespread in all religious communities. The absence of these in Sufi circles of the authentic type may be taken as an assurance of the way in which these materials are viewed by the Sufi. They are not used for arousing emotions or to try to cause an effect, but kept as a part of what the Sufi would call the science of religion (*Ilm al-Din*). In this respect, the genuine Sufi usage both dramatically departs from familiar religious usage and almost uncannily parallels (or perhaps duplicates, in its own field?) the educational and scientific activities.

CONTROLLING ONESELF AND BEING CONTROLLED

If the Sufi teacher's ability depends upon his being able to perceive a pattern invisible to others, and to 'snatch' parts of it for employment as ingredients of a teaching-system, it is also noted that this teacher himself must have unusual powers of detachment.

The most noteworthy of these appears to be that the teacher's behaviour is not occasioned by his needs, thoughts, desires. It is planned and executed according to the needs of the learner.

It is therefore often said, for example, that 'the Teacher's anger is better than the praise of any other individual: because he is angry in order to help to shape you; others are pleased because of every other reason'.

Detachment, which is regarded as a high aim of a spiritual nature in other systems, is the lowest accomplishment of the Sufi. Detachment, according to this way of thinking, frees a man or woman to make decisions, to see, to exist.

But the Sufi system requires that the Sufi is able to detach or not to detach. Other methods ignore this factor. For them, to be unable to be anything other than detached is the 'height of achievement'.

To the Sufi, this kind of detachment is not detachment at all, but, as it has been called: 'slavery to detachment'.

People in this state are neither controlled by themselves nor by anything else. This is the type generally referred to in Western literature as the 'quietist'. Among the Sufis, the type is regarded as a failure. His or her references to the high (or humble) state of experience being enjoyed is invalid.

So detachment becomes a part of cultism, instead of a stepping-stone in the path of learning.

Whether based on reality or not, this contention of the Sufis perhaps deserves close study. Certainly it has not been carefully noted by scholars, and even less by psychologists, who tend to accept or reject the validity of mystics' attitudes only by reference to current psychological doctrine. And this, in turn, is subject to constant changes in fashion.

DISCOURAGING POTENTIAL RECRUITS: 'DEFLECTION'

If the reputed wonders performed by the Sufi masters – and the extraordinary importance attained by them, unparalleled by any mystics in Western experience – attracted swarms of disciples, their policy of deflection certainly served to cause great confusion. 'Deflection' (*kaj-kardan*) would nowadays be termed in psychological jargon 'aversion treatment'. People who are on record over the centuries as being most bitterly opposed to Sufis are often found to be those who have applied for discipleship and been refused. The Sufi refusal methods, however, tend to specialise in making things unpalatable for the would-be disciple, so that he is deflected by the action of the Sufi's words or behaviour upon the applicant's cherished assumptions.

Deflection can take as many forms as the ingenuity of the Sufi's thought. Rabia of Basra infuriated narrow theologians anxious for initiation by saying, 'I am going to burn the Kaaba', the holiest place in Islam. The clerics denounced her as an apostate. She explained, however, to more discriminating people, that the burning of the Kaaba would be necessary if people took it as an idol, which some people certainly have done.

When recently asked whether it was not bad policy to alienate powerful scholars by deflection methods, a certain illustrious Sufi answered the present writer: 'No, because these people are generally so nasty that their enmity indicates to thinking people that we are not likely to be as nasty! Remember, only a small-minded person is affected by deflection methods....'

Modern Sufis deflect the myriad cultists who try to enrol with them by refusing to be vegetarians, to wear Indian scents, to don odd garb, to pronounce on vogueish causes – even to denounce all these things. This, as much as anything, has created the stark difference between genuine Sufis and those who pose as such. The latter are always visible because they compromise with what the obsessional cultists already believe. Astrology, numerology, strange beliefs, the formation of communes, random grouping of 'like-minded people', treks and expeditions, styling oneself by titles not now used by Sufis (Murshid, Qutub, Dada, Maula, Pir, Hakim are among those said to have been abandoned since they have sometimes been assumed by anyone who felt like it) are very much appreciated by the hangers-on who imagine that they are Sufis and are being taught by Sufis, when both parties are usually self-deceived.

Perhaps the most telling form of deflection is when applicants approach a Sufi entity and seek admission as 'disciples' or 'followers'. Since the Sufis, like all other educational bodies, first have to determine the suitability of the candidate, they almost always require the novice to undergo a course of study to prepare him or her by first removing misconceptions. This is no more onerous, of course, than expecting a witch-doctor who wants to study medicine first to familiarise himself with the principle of science as distinct from magic. But the applicant, almost by definition, wants to be stimulated, not to be informed and helped to develop. (We have to be wary of the use of terms here, since someone who wants illumination and sensation will often imagine that he is approaching just that by saying that he wants 'teaching'.)

Deflection takes place when the expectations of the entrant are disappointed. It is not uncommon for would-be Sufis to say that they have applied to join another path since they received no answer to their letters, or that they 'waited eight weeks' (or eight or more months) 'and nothing happened'. All that was happening was that the Sufi authority was preparing to supply the necessary teaching programmes.

Time and again, of course, in the Sufi teaching materials, we find that people missed their chance through not having enough patience. In realistic terms, this simply means that the applicant was not seeking what the Sufis supply. He (or she) wanted excitement. The Sufis are able to supply only the *right* way to knowledge.

The deflection necessity, of course, has caused the greatest possible discomfort and annoyance to those who imagine that they are being held back from secrets or are being treated with disdain: while in reality they are already partly on the path and need very badly the straightening out of their approach to learning.

THE IDEA OF ORGANIC ENTERPRISES

If activities originated by intending Sufis provide (through their success or failure) an index of the progress of the individual and the entire membership, the 'work for the work' format offers an example of the structure of the whole 'church' or 'organism'.

'Work for the Work' essentially means taking part in an enterprise laid down and controlled by the Sufi teacher. In its most common form, this involves the establishment of a *Khanqah* [monastery] or *Zavia* [place of activity] where all kinds of tasks, ranging from domestic and agricultural ones to special exercises and procedures, may be participated in. The chief difference between this (Sufi) organization and those belonging to, say, Christian, Buddhist and other denominations is that the study-course is not fixed but manipulated; the number of people attending may be large or small, (may fluctuate); there may be no apparent regularity in the activities.

The belief is that the community is an organism which is constantly changing. The experiences of the individual human unit in this must change from time to time to produce an all-round 'development' (known as maturing) and a harmonization (known as *Hamdard*, sympathy, literally 'breathing together').

An example of the inter-relation of factors in the Sufi system is seen here in the matter of constant and irregular activity. While the irregularity of the activities is held by the Sufis to mirror the rhythm of another (spiritual) dimension, the unfamiliarity of this behaviour places a strain upon those who seek constant or regular activity, leading many of them to eliminate themselves from the study course. Hence the learning process itself is employed to sift students and to dissuade those who cannot harmonize with it, without a word being said. The Sufis also make no attempt to explain what has happened; with the result that many disappointed students have always claimed that 'nothing happens among the Sufis', without refutation.

When working for a cause, the lay and religious people of other denominations may be said to be already converted, or, at least, to have faith or belief – or admiration – which causes them to be attracted to and involved in, the work which is the aim of the community. The overall concern of the enterprise may be, as an example, putting Christian charity to work by helping the poor or afflicted, the less well off. It may take the form of social or psychological action. The case of the Sufi is different.

Among the Sufis, it is the Teacher alone who knows the pattern of the work and who organizes its shape and cadence. Since its *aim* is to illuminate the seeker, this illumination cannot exist (so runs the argument) at the point at which the disciple enters the movement. He still has to learn. The Sufi activity, therefore, is more like a school, an educational activity, whose members are mainly there to follow the course which shall give them the ability to fulfil yet further functions. The participation does not provide the emotional interests or immediate rewards (or punishments) which are implicit in membership of other spiritual bodies. For this reason alone it must be admitted that the long-standing concept that 'all religious enterprises are ultimately the same' cannot be sustained after a close examination of the Sufi way.

What, then, attracts the intending Sufi to the school in the first place?

Sufis themselves will say that there can be any reason or none. They seldom or never employ the backwards reasoning which holds that the fact that the applicant wishes to join proves that he is attracted to the Real. The teacher's role, however, is to maintain a healthy relationship on some basis of co-operation with the student; and from there to direct his development along the lines which the school, the individual and the overall activity make possible.

This very conception concentrates a very considerable amount of authority and almost omniscience in the teacher. He has very broad scope and the implication is that he has knowledge which is available to few other men or women.

When the point was put by the present writer to an important Sufi teacher, the reply was, verbatim, as follows:

The importance or authority is more imagined than real when it is rendered in the terms employed by you. Looking at it in this way should enable you to see it as it really is:

If a man who has been accustomed to working in a potato field and knows little about intensive and varied cultivation comes across a farmer with wider knowledge and experience, he might well exclaim: 'Why should you have such power over these matters which I do not know about – pruning, seedlings, gathering the flowers and not the roots of the crops! Is there nobody to check you, and why do you exercise such a miscellaneous and patternless sway over this area?'

The apparently chaotic nature of the Sufi activity, continued this informant, could be given in similar terms: the newcomer would wonder why the farmer was at one moment ploughing and at another covering plants, and at a third cutting them down. He would be, of course, dealing with different crops, as he was concerned with the overall activity as well as the individual plants and specific crops.

There is a circumstance in which the disciples may be at some risk if they follow a supposed Sufi teacher who behaves in an eccentric manner. They may attribute his commands or actions to 'tests', or to 'hidden knowledge', or, again, to 'his following the Path of Blame' (deliberately incurring odium for spiritual reasons) – when in fact, due to the inevitable ravages of nature, his mind may be impaired.

Naturally enough, this condition has occurred, and may be expected to occur again, frequently in the past. How do the students know whether their Master has taken leave of his senses, is deteriorating mentally: for the brain, after all, is among other things a machine subject to decay and damage?

In all areas where Sufi operations are in train there are always imitators, casualties and – Sufi Schools. It is the task of the School to make sure that its teaching staff (whether the Master or his secondary representatives, the 'channels') are not the sole source of information as to their own condition. Hence, in the West for instance, the Society for Sufi Studies carries on that task. What is deplorable is that some students become so earnest that they 'transfer' onto the personality of the director without imagining that they should keep in direct contact with the real head of the work through the Society (in the West) and the Mu'assisa (in the East). It is a pity that other religious bodies do not provide similar safeguards.

'Work for the Work' has been observed by the present writer organised in the form of a farm, of a business, of a school and of a department of administration. It is often imitated by those who have heard of it or who have made it a study, but such attempts generally fail, for one or more of the following reasons:

1   The 'teacher' yields to pressure to provide activities to satisfy the craving of the students;
2   The activities are chosen from books or through reference to folklore;
3   The recruitment is haphazard;
4   The 'teacher' begins to employ the students to serve him, obtain things for him (perhaps including money) and/or amuses himself at their expense.

The conception of a community of people who, within the seemingly ordinary structure of a business or a house and grounds, can be working also in a harmony which activates something 'other', something spiritual but not emotional, something purposeful beyond the overt purposes of the enterprise, is startling and has far-reaching implications. Not least of the latter is the fact that the more successful a Sufi school of this kind is, the less likely will it be to resemble what people imagine a Sufi school to be. Instead of ritual, there may be activity of an apparently mundane kind; instead of unusual garb, there will be specific clothing appertaining to the task on hand; in place of hierarchy there will be co-operation; the place of chanting, symbols and various appurtenances will be taken by specifics which are directly and reasonably to all appearances connected with the surface aim of the community. It has been remarked that this may be the origin of the phrase 'work is prayer', also employed on a lower level by those who claim that work is in itself good morally – though not in the sense understood by the Sufis that within a certain kind of work, carried on in a certain manner, with specially selected people, resides the means of realizing an inner perception.

I have had the opportunity of studying several Sufi entities which operate as social units, including what in the West would be called cultural societies: involved in the study and enjoyment of literature and leisure pursuits. The striking thing about these is that the ordinary human tendency to make a means into an end is strictly excluded and strongly resisted. For example, people who waste the time of the society in discussion and minute involvement in the day-to-day running or administrative procedures (often the real mainstays of Western associations) are singled out as being opposed to the real aims of the society. It exists for them to relate to others and to harmonise with 'the Work'. If they talk too much, draw attention to themselves too much, bore or annoy other people – no matter how much work they put in for the entity – they are regarded as opposing the conditions which alone make the individual and group understanding towards which all are working possible.

Those readers who belong to societies which harbour compulsive activists and sticklers for the rules may well wish that they were subject to Sufi discipline!

It is noteworthy that the best known and therefore most 'visible' forms of Sufi organization tend to be those which are characterized by rules, outward show and ritualism: anathema to the authentic tradition. It is therefore possible that these forms, long considered to be typical of Sufi bodies, are in fact only visible because they have developed distorted, externally striking, characteristics.

Naturally, if a Sufi organization can in fact bear a resemblance to any kind of human enterprise, we are faced with the possibility – even the likelihood – that the ones known to us on the whole are not typical and less than legitimate; while the essential 'Sufi Work' continues in forms which almost by definition would be invisible to any but the most careful observer.

This ability of the Sufis to work within any framework which they find convenient may have given rise to the belief that the Sufis are, or have, a secret society; since people engaged in an activity which on the surface is – say – commercial but which is in essence spiritual are likely to be labelled as assuming a disguise. In actual fact, however, Sufi doctrine has it that any human organization may be useful spiritually as well as productive in other senses and should therefore be used, since it fulfils two functions, both of them laudable. It could well be that our assumption that, for instance, a literary society can only be used for one purpose merely betrays a relative ignorance of the potentialities of organization itself.

After all, as one Sufi put it when commenting on this proposition: 'A human being or a piece of wood – and many other things besides – are never regarded as solely for one purpose: why should a body of people be similarly limited?'

The conception may be strange, but the logic is not weak.

ENTRY INTO A SUFIC GROUP

The classical Sufi group does not closely resemble, in recruitment and operation, the traditional 'wise man's circle' image. In the forms of spiritual instruction familiar to us from the Hindu and Buddhist public projections, there is the picture of the Sage, surrounded by his disciples, speaking or not speaking, giving out instructions and exercises, and generally forming the centrepiece of what most closely resembles a family as we know it.

First of all, not all Sufis are teachers. The Sage may exist in order to exercise functions (and so runs the tradition) which are not perceptible to the public.

Secondly, the Sufi Master teaches when and as he can, not in a mechanical pattern. Unchanging groups and frequent and repeated exercises, indeed, are taken by Sufis to indicate deteriorated forms which can scarcely be called 'Sufi' at all.

This also brings up the question of 'Who is a Sufi?' The classical masters are unanimous that: (1) a Sufi does not call himself such, though others may so style him; (2) A Sufi is the product of Sufi study and development, and therefore seekers or learners cannot call themselves Sufis or even be called such, except for convenience of reference. A 'Sufi Group', therefore, is not 'A group of Sufis', but 'A group of would-be Sufis'. Those who are seeking and who are not teaching, are called *Dervishes* ['The Poor'].

In organizations which have developed into mere social or local groupings, people may be admitted by 'initiation' and take part in all or many of the activities of the group. These, numerous in the East, are regarded by authoritative Sufis as having lost their Sufic content, and to be mere power structures. It is important to be able to recognise these, whether they occur in the East or West, since they do not represent the real tradition, but a dilution of it.

Since by definition the intending Sufi does not know what it is that he is going to learn; and since he is, also by definition, unable to contribute to the activities or influence of the Sufis; and since, again by definition, he cannot claim the *right* to become a Sufi, there is no such thing as an application to join the Sufis. The situation, however, is not as vague as this may seem to imply.

The Sufis have, and apparently have had for centuries, organizations and individuals, both in the East and in the West, which exist partly for the purpose of attracting people who already feel some kind of harmony with the 'inner sense' of the Sufis. As already noted, these organizations are usually not put forward as 'spiritual schools' at all, but much more often seem to be mundane associations of people. Someone may even be a member of one or more of such bodies for years before realizing that it has an inner, spiritual core.

In countries where the actual word *Sufi* is known, and in order to offer an alternative to the cults which claim to be Sufis but which are really not such, there is always someone who represents what is known as the *Mu'assisa* (roughly translated as 'The Institution'). Quite often such an individual also has prestige in the host community. He (or she) may be a literary or legal, nowadays a scientific or an administrative, figure. There may be several organizations in any one country, all linked to the Mu'assisa, which together form the complete Sufi school, creating confusion among outside observers: which is one of the objects of this kind of arrangement.

It is widely believed among the followers of this path that 'Anyone on a straight Path is never lost' (Saadi, a classical author of the Sufis); and, conversely, that people who become attached to spurious or diluted cults or remain in them are at least themselves partly to blame. This has been known to startle people who tend to imagine that it is the disciple who is led astray by the villainous and bogus 'mystical teacher'. This contention that the learner may be at least as much to blame may well be deserving of investigation.

Sufis who feel that any individual may be a candidate for study will often contrive to get to know such people, and see whether a social as well as a more subtle harmonization is possible. In such cases, the people being approached will not necessarily be introduced to the typical Sufi literature. This, again, is because (as it is claimed) Sufis may teach within any format, amd the frameworks and literature which are generally considered to be essential to the Sufi are in fact only those which form a single facet of their activities. This contention has been constantly stressed by the classical Masters, but oddly enough no single scholar, so far as the present writer is aware, has ever given it any attention whatever.

Given that even scholars, including many world-famous 'experts' on Sufism, do not accept the statements of the authorities of the system which they are allegedly studying, there would seem to be a case for a completely fresh approach to Sufi studies this time taking note of all the Sufi materials and not just those which appear to concur with a pre-existent image of what the Sufi should be in the minds of those who do not really know and who therefore effectively concoct the Sufi Cult from a set of ideas obtained from a highly miscellaneous ragbag of information.

THE SUFIS AS A CULT

A study of the academic and popular writings on Sufis – both in the flesh and through their literature and the comments of others – clearly shows that there is a vast shortfall in accurate information.

Writers tend to copy one another, to such an extent that almost the entire chapter on Sufis and Sufism in an otherwise respectable book may be lifted from an unverified source. Borderline cults, which may have been started and operated by charlatans and ignoramuses, are treated with the same credence as typically Sufic entities which are clearly more authentic. Scholars, no less than propagandists, can be seen, again and again, to edit and to excise important information which does not fit into their version of what the Sufis are and what they do and believe.

In short, the situation as regards Sufi studies is so chaotic that most of the materials, aside from the works of the classical masters, cannot be relied upon at all.

Given this situation, it is scarcely surprising that spurious cults constantly spring up and blot out the legitimate, providing still more 'information about Sufism' which is not worth the paper on which it is written.

Much of the blame for this state of affairs must squarely be laid at the door of the scholars, throughout the world, who have lacked the means to verify their materials but have yet not shrunk from compiling vast tomes, rushing into print with articles and generally muddying the waters when their task should have been one of clarification before anything else.

Sufis, for example, have been characterized as people who induce frenzy; who carry out religious dancing; who make public displays of music; who affect strange garb. To collect, almost at random, such 'evidences' of supposedly standard and important practices is tantamount to assessing anything by means of secondary and unreliable criteria. But scholars and travellers are no less human in being affected by externals and the dramatic. The only fault herein is that they do not emphasise this. Christianity, too, could be described by exactly the same practices as have been regarded as standard ones of the Sufis. Let us list them: the induction of frenzy is found in the snake-handling and other revivalist cults, in America and elsewhere; but this behaviour, clearly deviant, is not taken as an evidence of membership in Christianity. Resuming our list, we find religious dancing in Christian churches in Lebanon; public displays of music among others with the Salvation Army; and strange garb everywhere in Christendom. Add all these up. Does this make a picture of our basic faith of Christianity – or does it mean that the Sufis are in fact Christians?

The reality is, of course, as almost any sociologist should be able to conclude, that none of these local and limited manifestations has anything much to do with the religion which is supposedly represented therein.

So, lamentably, the state of understanding of the Sufis both in the East and in the West resembles a superficial and arbitrary evaluation such as we might find if, say, railways were to be described by their 'chief features' by someone (or some people) who said that they were things which caused death, which were traversed by vehicles painted green or red, which made consignments of fish deteriorate because they were left too long in sidings, and so on. . . .

The conclusion, based on the classics and contact with a very different type of Sufi from the one dear to the cultists and commentators, is that 'The Sufis are not a cult; but there is no lack of people who wish to make them such'.

The Western literature, regarded as standard reference and descriptive works, covering supposedly Sufi activities almost never deal with legitimate groups. Their very size and the apparent authority wielded by such assemblages of people seem to have confused the writers into imagining that they are in the main line of the tradition. Among the writers who have been taken in in this way are Sir Richard Burton (in his work about the Sindh cultists); Birge, in his *Bektashi Order of Dervishes*, which is a survey of a series of contaminated cults; Brown, in *The Darvishes*, a hotchpotch of information and confusion, again relying upon secondary manifestations; and several others, some of whom have attained a certain status by means of these largely worthless books. Works by Fatemi, Shah and Shushtery also exist, these being the reliable materials which deserve close attention.

A cult may be termed a belief-system with fixed observances, which practices indoctrination. Approved cults in any society tend to be the 'official' belief-systems, the national cult (patriotism given a framework of beliefs and practices) and any other set of beliefs which either supports the local consensus or at the last does not militate against it. Scientifically speaking, therefore, it is impossible to distinguish between the Boy Scout Movement (as an example) and any other religious or nationalistic training system: even though the adherents and sympathisers of such systems would insist, in all probability, that their own organization bore no resemblance to others.

The Sufis, on the other hand, in their classics and in the work of their genuine present-day exponents, work against the formation of cults and also provide a means to distinguish the cult from the educational organization.

For this reason, it is impossible to label the Sufis as members of any cult whatever, unless one chooses so to style the entirely unrepresentative bodies which (for instance) teach a single system and maintain a single set of practices applicable upon all or most of the participants.

The Sufis' claim, therefore, to be scientific and also to be non-cult and anti-cult must be accepted by all reasonable people as verifiable in terms of the most modern methods of assessment. What has prevented the understanding of this is the fact that, at the time of writing, even advanced sociologists have often failed to absorb the information of what a cult is, and to accept as cults those bodies of thought and action which surround them. Until this understanding is diffused among the scholarly and professional community of sociology and its kindred disciplines, it will not be open to sociological and psychological thinkers to discern the real effect and contribution of the Sufis, dating from over a thousand years ago, to their very modern science. It can hardly be surprising that the members of the sociological professions find it hard (sometimes even impossible) to believe that their metier has already been pioneered by people of whom they have never heard (because their work is in the literature of the Middle East), centuries ago.

Sufism is clearly to be seen, if we examine its documents and deal with its legitimate proponents of today, to be both a means of understanding spiritual paths as well as a series of systems which have paths (methods) of their own.

Herein lies the key to the confusion among three kinds of people in respect to the Sufis. The three kinds are: the Orientalists, the sociologists, and the cultists.

The Orientalists, accustomed to dealing with the very large number of degenerate forms of Sufis, which are in fact nothing more or less than cults, imagine that all Sufism must be composed of cults. In so thinking, of course, they are undoubtedly guilty of selective study and one-sided thinking – as they fail to read the classics on this matter. The second group, the sociologists, have come to think of all human development groups as cults, and therefore hardly expect that advanced thinking on this topic existed centuries before modern sociology. The third section, the cultists, are looking for cults, like the other two categories (but in order to join, not to study, them) and therefore seize upon whatever they can in Sufism which seems to them to have cultism attitudes. They find plenty, because of the proliferation of deteriorated forms already referred to.

The contemporary notion, that the Sufis are in fact carrying on a scientific enterprise, pioneered in recent years by their spokesman, Idries Shah, is slowly but steadily percolating into the literature, and should eventually find complete recognition.

As with other discoveries, there is a tendency for the professionals to avoid admitting that they have failed to observe in identical materials something which someone else has illustrated. For this reason it is noticeable that it is the younger sociologists and others who have found it possible to look at the materials objectively. Their personal self-esteem is not bound up with the traditional way of looking at things enshrined, irretrievably, in the writings of their elders.

RELIGION, EVOLUTION AND INTERVENTION

The great religious organizations, with their churches and temples, priesthoods and liturgies, with their sacred documents and their regalia, rituals and monasteries: these are perhaps the most familiar form of spirituality to a majority of the world's peoples. They are, indeed, to almost everyone, religion itself. What they teach is regarded as literally true by most believers; their priesthoods (or the equivalent, even in systems which deny having such) command almost supernaturalist respect.

A study of the writings and words of the Sufis, however, reveals that this attitude is far from being that of the nominally Moslem, Christian or Jewish thinkers who have had their say in this area. Religious externals, according to them – and these externals include both outward acts and emotional sensations – are secondary. Primary is the experiential source of both revelation and also the verification of spiritual truth. Early and contemptuously, the massive organizations derided such attitudes as 'gnostic' – originally a word for those who know ultimate Truth by direct perception. Since 'gnostic' was turned into a sneer, anything connected with it became bad by association of ideas and by implication. The fact that some gnostic sects and communities from time to time deteriorated into magico-mystical cults did not improve their image: but the same thing has happened with the fragmentation of beliefs and the production of bizarre sects in all religions without the said faiths being regarded as totally bad.

So the religious externals are secondary. That they are subject to a process of superficialisation and dilution is evident from many beliefs and practices which are today found in all the major religions and which in fact, as certain purists are not slow to point out, sometimes even conflict with earlier sanctions.

Historical and archaeological research has, indeed, borne out many of the long-standing contentions of the Sufis in this respect.

But if the Sufis have been right in anticipating modern

researchers in emphasizing that cherished ideas of today are often of relatively recent development in world faiths, this does not mean to say that the Sufis accord with the scholars who imagine that all religion is simply an elaboration of primitive totem and taboo thinking and practice, developed over the centuries as societies become more and more sophisticated.

The Sufis have altogether a far more intriguing, and no less plausible, idea. They assert (with, for instance, Rumi) that man is evolving, and that his religious ideas start with worship of sticks and stones and then develop into something higher. They also aver that, at a certain stage, these primitive faiths evolve into a stage where they can receive the intervention of a higher impulse – the truly divine of which the primitive faith was the ground or precursor – following which the belief-system develops into a knowing – (gnostic) one, which is able, so long as its system and teaching remains intact, to refresh itself from the single source of all truth.

And the next phase; the primitive may develop into the gnostic; following which it may well deteriorate again into the hidebound, fossil, form which is found in most societies. Or it may remain true to its correct form. When temporal power, that of the State or of religious leaders who are in fact disguised power-seekers, becomes supreme, as often occurs in most communities, this inward religion, the gnostic one, has to go underground, and may remain for centuries as a parallel stream, waiting to come to the surface again. The initiatory current itself, under such unfavourable circumstances, may also degenerate, giving rise to secret societies or weird sects. This is caused by the loss of the teaching succession. Due to the natural wastage caused by death, the succession of teachers may be interrupted, and others take over the system. When this happens the organization ordinarily shrivels and becomes a kind of deposit, a compost, which may nurture the next legitimate intervention from the source of truth, sometimes called, in the Middle East, *Ornalhaq*, Lair of Truth.

The massive institutional religion, according to the Sufis, also undergoes experiences which produce, first, the fossil stage, where people have to be conditioned to belief since it can no longer supply the inner experience which is now locked within its teaching or sacraments. After this comes the period of disillusionment, which in turn leads to the post-liturgical stage, when the stream of Truth can again intervene, starting the cycle once more.

It is possible to render this process in diagrammatic terms:

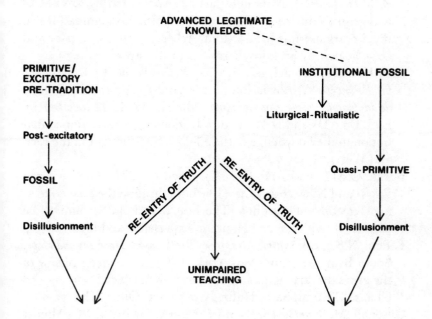

Arberry, A.J., *Muslim Saints and Mystics*. London 1966. A partial translation from Attar's major work *Tadhkirat al-Awliyya* (*Memoir of the Friends*). Although partially sponsored by UNESCO and genuflecting to the disgraced Emperor Muhammad Raza, the literary merit is hard to find. Arberry's English is poor and complicated by an idiosyncratic transliteration.

Asin Palacios, Miguel, *The Mystical Philosophy of Ibn Masarra and his Followers*. A translation of *Abenmasarra y su escuela, Origines de la filosofia hispano-musulmana*: Madrid 1914. Translated by E.H. Douglas and H.W. Yoder, Leiden, 1978. (A major contribution to the knowledge of the effect of Sufi thought in the East and West).

Burke, O.M., *Among the Dervishes*. London 1973 (The Octagon Press) and New York 1975. (Journeys through the East collecting data on Sufic groups. The best first-hand account to be published, with a nice balance of experience and theory).

Fatemi, N.S., *et al*, *Sufism: Message of Brotherhood, Harmony and Hope*. South Brunswick and New York 1976. (A balanced review of the great literary figures of the Sufis, with special reference to Ghazzali, Rumi, Sadi, Hafiz, Nizami and Omar Khayyam).

Gilsenan, M., *Saint and Sufi in Modern Egypt*. Oxford 1973. (Almost entirely devoted to the tribalized, low-level cults either derived from Sufi ones or else imitating them. Readers will recognize the degeneracy which Idries Shah has been describing in false cults since 1964).

Masud-ul-Hasan, *Hazrat Data Ganj Bakhsh – A Spiritual Biography*. Lahore. Not dated. (Badly written, poorly arranged, this is yet an excellent example of the heavily-religious projection of Sufism current among Moslems today. The psychological insights and universal viewpoint of the subject, Hujwiri, are hardly touched upon).

Nicholson, R.A., *Selected Poems from the Divani Shamsi Tabriz*. Cambridge 1898, 1952 etc. Typical of the curiosa which abound in scholastic orientalism, this translation and text is excellent in places, yet also teems with mistranslations of Persian words and sentiments, giving us, as much as anything else, a knowledge of the strengths and weaknesses of Professor Nicholson's Persian.

Ornstein, R.E., *The Psychology of Consciousness*. London 1975. (see especially 'contemporary Sufism', p.244, where the potential of the Sufis in the modern world is assessed).

Shah, I., *Learning How to Learn*. London 1978 (The Octagon Press). Teachings and descriptive material on the social anthropology of Sufis. Illuminates the material edited by Williams (below) and explains the cults studied by Gilsenan (above).

Williams, L.F. Rushbrook (and twenty-three other scholars), *Sufi Studies: East and West*. New York, 1974 and London (The Octagon Press). Deals with literature, history and present-day projections of the authentic Sufic current, as distinct from the deteriorated cults.

RITUAL, INITIATION AND SECRETS IN SUFI CIRCLES

by
Franz Heidelberger and Others

Time Spent Among Sufis

FRANZ HEIDELBERGER

The very first thing you find out when you spend time among Sufis is that most of what is written about them ceases to have any relevance. My own first objective when contacting real Sufi groups was to 'update' my knowledge, and to 'add to the available stock of information'. In fact, neither enterprise is possible. The reason is that the whole range of information about the Sufis and Sufism – and it is colossal – is heavily interlarded with all kinds of misconceptions, inventions, imagining and misinterpretations, rendering the 'overall picture' quite useless. Some of this, it is true, is due to the efforts of the Sufis themselves, who protect their own information-stock by adding materials which make the work of scholars and of intending imitators very difficult: in fact, virtually impossible.

If you concentrate upon, say, the writings of a certain era in history, to try to find out what the Sufis were doing at that specific time, you will also find that what has been committed to paper, even in those times, does not constitute the real or whole substance of the effort. In fairness it should be admitted that the Sufis have warned us of this, saying (as did Rumi) that the 'Sufi secrets are perceived, not understood by words'. Even those of them who will write for publication follow the adage that 'the Sufi is he who has been taught caution'. Ultimately the only way to know what the Sufis are doing is to join them – if they will let you.

This paper will concentrate upon ideas which seem strange to us, even those of us who are steeped in the literature known to the world of learning, but which have at least some sort of rationale: either in familiar terms or else in the special world of Sufi thought.

As for the question of appearing in another form, the 'riddle wrapped in an enigma' of Sufi reality does provide interesting examples of how the Sufi appears able to change his appearance. There are innumerable accounts of Sufis appearing taller, shorter, fatter, thinner, with or without beards – in fact, like completely different people – from one moment or one person to the next. Two or more people will be found, again and again, saying that a certain Sufi master looked like this, while others who saw him at the same time will give conflicting descriptions. The only explanation for this, which is hardly a solution at all, is that there is something 'given out' (emanated) by the Sufi which disturbs or reconstitutes the visual. I have noticed this myself. It can only be described as the effect which one would experience if the person were not really there but there was something which was able to project a complete human being and change the image, three-dimensional as it appears, together with most, but not all, of the characteristics, such as the walk, voice or clothing. I am aware that in saying this I may be thought to have put my sanity in question, but on the other hand a time may come when all this is found to have a perfectly sensible explanation.

If there is in fact a capacity to project images direct into another person's mind, this may account for the ability of Sufis, again witnessed countless times, to alter people's behaviour. This is sometimes called 'bringing out the real character' of the individual. It may show you what this person is really like. It may be better or worse than the image which you have of the individual. It is said to be used for teaching purposes, and is as if the Sufi can interrupt or disturb, and replace the working of the mind, as an electromagnetic wave might interfere with the sound from a radio or the picture from a television apparatus.

PRIEST, MAGICIAN AND SUFI

The Sufis, according to their own account, following their personal illumination, are 'here' to help others along the Path. I emphasise 'here' because, right at the beginning there is a problem of definition for the pedantic (or shall we say logical?) through the use of this word. Does 'here' mean 'on this Earth'? Or does it mean 'among the people who encounter him'? The best opinion seems to hold that the Sufi, quite literally, means that he is voluntarily on the earth in the guise of a human being as we know it, to help others . . .

This, of course, introduces the conception of there being a 'guise' (they sometimes actually call it 'garb') of humanity, and that there is an option in the matter. Could they be somewhere else and appearing in a different form if they *were* there?

Again the answer must be that they think that the answer to both of these questions is 'yes'. One Sufi said: 'If you think that this is odd, well, so do many people think you are odd in believing that man has an immortal soul. Hundreds of millions of people, in India, believe that human beings are reincarnated. Almost as many think that people can turn into Buddhas. So do not use your culture-bound attitudes to label others as unusual in their thoughts.' This method, of putting Sufi ideas into the terminology (culture-bound, etc.,) of the twentieth century is nowadays standard among the Sufi theoreticians.

This could be a reason for the Sufi use of a phrase which also rings oddly in our ears, coming from men themselves: it is 'The Sufi is the Friend of Man'.[1]

Incidentally, these 'powers' are said to be used by the Sufis also to test the stability and condition of the student. People who are subjected to such experiences, either on themselves or seeing them happen to others, are observed by the Sufi, in order to ascertain if they are emotionally moved by the experience. If they are, the training stops until it is found that they can observe rather than be impressed. This technique is, of course, the reverse of that of the charlatan, who would use it if he could to impress, not to test and select those who did not respond. Many Sufi techniques are, be it noted, based on the conception of a 'lack of response is better' theme: a direct reversal of our customary way of looking at things.

Not all Sufis are teachers (technically termed 'Directors'); but those who *are* such do need special capabilities. Nuri, the great

Central Asian Sufi born in Baghdad who died in 908 A.D., was called *Jasus al-Qalb* [Spy of the Heart] because he could read anyone's thoughts, a function which he developed through great self-discipline. This capacity is customarily exercised by Sufi masters only in their 'professional' capacity – to help them help their own disciples through extra-sensory abilities, especially telepathy. Unlike the priest, the Sufi Master is not seen as a permanent intermediary between humans and the Beyond. He is the link: but a link which has to teach others how to become links, and how to escape from a bondage which is how the world is described. The relative roles of the three major traditional spiritual types in human communities may be seen as follows:

THE PRIEST	SHAMAN/ MAGICIAN	SUFI
Sacerdotal function, including celebrating rituals, handed down by a ceremony. Specialises in working with social organizations. Employs emotion and sentiment.	Provides sporadic contact with higher invisible powers. Frenzy-induced techniques inspire fear (probably in himself as well as in others).	Special powers connecting to the Beyond exercised as part of overall educational plan. Has learnt, and teaches, by experience: opposes emotionality.

Sufi techniques vary, or appear to do so, in accordance with the individuality of the Master and the characteristics of the milieu in which he is working. Hence, as instances, Rumi (died 1273) carried on a school in what is today Turkey, with exercises and poetry. Ghazzali (died 1111) reached his audience through books, in closely-reasoned form, current from Syria to Spain. Hujwiri (died 1072) lived in India and asserted that it was important to learn through the lives of previous Masters and to know technical terms. Today, again using the means which reaches his own audience and makes use of their own preoccupations, Idries Shah, the current exponent of the Sufis, projects the Teaching in the idioms of literature, psychology and sociology. He also uses

humour and university platforms. All these have had the un-
usually powerful effect which people have come to associate with
the appearance of an authentic exponent of the Path. The Sufi
teachers themselves, perhaps we should note, never attribute such
success to themselves, but rather to the higher energies which flow
through their work. With the support of these, it is held, they
cannot fail. There is no doubt that something has given the first
three of these teachers an astonishing duration of influence – and
the last-named seems certain to gain as much prominence and
range.

The viewpoints of those who believe that they wish to learn from
Sufis, however, does not always accord with the true situation,
however clearly or appositely the materials are presented. Many
of the 'raw' (this is a Sufi technical term) appellant's desires,
including those which actually lead him to the Teaching, are
utterly unsuited to him as a good disciple. 'Just as the eggshell
protects that which is to become a chicken until it is ready to be
born, so the habits of the Seeker may enable him to reach the
Teacher. Thereafter, however, like the shell which has to be
pecked away, the neophyte must cast this casing aside,' says one
Sufi ancient. Another told me: 'The snake will die without its skin.
When the time comes to slough it, though, she will die if she tries
to hold onto it, through suffocation.'

Sufis have told me again and again how they find that seekers
who have spent perhaps years in trying to perfect themselves, or
even to improve themselves, have only 'succeeded in toughening
the shell'. This is because, as one put it, 'The baby bird will
automatically do the right thing, pecking his way out of the egg.
This is an inborn capacity. But the human being will "try to break
his shell" by adding to those things which reinforce it.' Small
wonder that Sufis are always saying that disciples are their own
worst enemies.

The Sufi explanation of the harm which the disciple does to
himself is that, unlike the baby chicken, which has a programme

and does nothing else, virtually, than to try to escape from the eggshell at the right moment, the human Seeker is already partly grown up, and full of what are at present colloquially called 'hang-ups'. These ideas and fantasies make him do all kinds of things to himself which actually hold up his progress.

The conflict of expectation with reality, when the Seeker finds out what the School expects, is his first real shock. But this is so important that it is no exaggeration to say that this point really signals the first authentic contact with that special Reality which may be called the Spiritual; and that is the point which tests the potential of the learner. Not only that: it is not too much to say that any teacher or school which does not shake the chief assumptions of the disciple is not a genuine one. At any rate, it is not an effective one, for in such a case the 'veils' (those things which stand in the way of spiritual perceptions) remain to cover and distort.

Those of us who have not experienced the Sufi contact as a teaching phenomenon cannot really begin to understand what it is, unless we make a strong effort to face something which is outside our ordinary ken. Sufi teaching, as has been noted, takes place only by an interaction between the Master and his disciple, following, in many cases, a preparatory period in which the learner has been exposed to special techniques and impacts, perhaps in a group set up by the Sufis for this purpose. The disciple can only be taught by the Master when circumstances are favourable. This means that anyone may have to wait for any space of time until the Master has judged that this time has arrived. More than a little fortitude is necessary if the pupil is to be able to endure the waiting which this involves. This is one of the reasons why Sufis teach, or have taught, their followers to distinguish between the desire to learn and the impulsion to be stimulated with thoughts and actions. It is often necessary to abstain from applying any stimuli to the learner while he or she is waiting for the Master's special *baraka* (high spiritual force) to be available under the right conditions.

But certain aspects of Sufi teachings *are* put into words, and these tell us three striking things, which can certainly be useful, especially for those who have not yet studied the classical teachings sufficiently to have absorbed the lessons from them:

1 It is impossible to eliminate, by oneself, many of the ideas and actions which disqualify intending disciples;
2 Sufi literature, in structure (but not in emotional content) helps to prepare the mind with patterns which are the vital factors underlying the stories, biographies, aphorisms and so on which are their overt side;
3 Those who do not trust the Sufis are themselves most likely to be both untrusting and untrustworthy.

These statements, indeed, were indicated centuries ago (in 1695) by the writer of *The Testament of One of Us*, Haji Yunus, for the following reasons, which contemporary Sufis declare to be still applicable:

1 One would normally not guess this and would, on the contrary, (as with all other teachings) imagine that we must be instructed how to combat our own weaknesses and that we must face them alone;
2 Nobody ever really looks at structure and pattern, only at what are in fact superficialities. Everyone craves excitement;
3 This assertion could only be made by a deceiver: or else by someone who speaks with the real authority of those who know what they say. Few deceivers, however, would dare to say it.

Today we can add, from the last century of research in psychology, that many, if not all, mistrustful people are so because they are themselves untrustworthy...

It seems quite likely that the emergence, perhaps the evolution, of the new 'languages' of the behavioural sciences have stimulated the Sufis' higher echelons, conspicuously via Idries Shah, to re-present their materials and to signal to us their continuing presence in current idioms. After all, the major literatures of the Middle East, as they emerged, were used by the Sufis to such an extent that it is almost impossible to study them fully without a knowledge of Sufism.

Again, with the Medieval upflow of learning, the Sufis put their imprint on the thought-systems (Christianity, Judaism and Islam) which lasted until the era – quite recently – of the soft sciences' emergence in the late nineteenth century.

One is almost tempted to say that an observer who had discerned the alacrity with which Sufis have for so long adopted the current idiom (whether it was alchemy, poetry, chivalry or anything else) would be likely to seek the outstanding Sufi voice among us in intercultural work and in the social sciences plus psychology in its widest sense, as well as in spiritual areas.

Now listen to the almost surprised tone (and the content) of some of our contemporary Western observers, reacting to this self-same phenomenon of people from the East using our most modern tools, as it unfolds before their eyes. They admire it, they are impressed. But one is not certain that they understand it, or that they think that they do; although one can clearly feel that they sense that it is of great importance.

Taken, in the order in which they appear, from a catalogue of books which quotes recent British and American opinion on Sufi books, we find the commentators intrigued, interested, impressed – and certain that this is something of very great importance indeed:-

'A peepshow into a world which most people do not imagine exists,' says *The Guardian*. The *American Scholar*, not celebrated as the most innovative of journals, characterises the Sufi materials as nothing less than 'a way of re-learning to use the mind'. 'Strikingly appropriate for our time and situation' is the statement of the London *Sunday Times*. The ultimate, however, comes from the opinion of the writer in *Psychology Today*: 'The work of Idries Shah must be considered a major cultural event of our time'.

Similar sentiments appear, too, in the Press and in learned journals of the Islamic East, generally considered to be hidebound and backward. They are to be found in such mass-circulation papers as the *Daily Mail* or the *Evening News*, both of London. The Sufi influence in the East and West for our time is well and truly under way. The only thing which could halt it is our own capacity of understanding.

NOTES

1 In Europe, the celebrated Cagliostro (1743-95) was also called 'The Friend of Mankind'. Although a charlatan, this colourful figure seems undoubtedly to have spent some time among Sufis, and perhaps had tasks to perform for them in the West, though probably not anything in the realm of teachership.

Sufi Orders

ROSALIE MARSHAM

I was walking through a town in Europe one day with a certain Middle Eastern dervish, when we came upon a religious procession. Its participants were duly robed, were accompanied by music, and bore aloft their religious symbol.

The Dervish stopped and started to laugh: quite quietly, it is true, but the tears came to his eyes as he stood aside to prevent other bystanders from noticing his condition.

Later, I asked him why he had been affected.

'Religion, for many people,' he explained, 'is the social form from which the function has evaporated.'

I asked him for an example. He offered this simile.

'If *you* were to travel to a distant land and found people in mechanics' overalls, singing about a sacred vehicle and extolling the virtues and blessings to be gained from a Holy Competition, and wearing as signs of their initiation polished crash-helmets while they headed for a sacred place which they still called "the Pits", haunted by a fear of the "treacherous demon Grease", who could "cause them to crash in a pool of liquid petroleum fire", you would be looking at the religionized remnants of the remote descendants of a former car-racing team or their imitators. Its own members, for their part, would of course be quite sure that their archaic and highly paraphrastic antics added up to something else – something which seemed to them to be more important. But to get the car back on the road, you would have recalled as you wiped the tears of laughter from your eyes, would need the restoration of training for mechanics before anything at all could be done.'

Those who have been in touch with a real Sufi school as well as the imitators will, of course, recognize delusive cult-behaviour in the latter: their symbols and rituals, in their use of liturgy, in their assumptions about what they are doing. This is so marked that the legitimate Sufi preceptors of today, the ones who continue the Sufi work in its pristine form, can have no spiritual contact with the 'orders'. The leaders, and even less the members, of the orders would be scandalised to hear from the current Sufi exponents that in place of ritual there must be a sentience which flows back and forth between a teacher and his student and which is in fact obstructed by the paraphernalia which outsiders love to think of as 'spiritual'.

During extensive journeys and contact with the Sufis who are to be found when one does not look at 'orders', I was able to compile a catalogue of characteristics of the worn-out bodies which the majority of people, including Western 'specialists' imagine to be Sufic.

As a general rule, the less the spiritual content, the greater the appurtenances. Tall hats, robes and music; secretiveness and high-flown titles are very common. Whole 'orders' are sustained on these nutrients. Several groups make much of their Islamic connexions, and their Western followers delight in adopting Eastern names and even titles. Among these the favourites are Sheikh, Pir, Qutub, Haji or al-Hajj, Murshid and Rais. In this, of course, they tend to follow the fantasies of their teachers. The more dilapidated the group, the more it will sink into either fanaticism or libertinism. One group which has branches all over the East has done a great deal to get the Sufis a bad name because the following almost invariable signs are found among its leaders: a fondness for distilled liquor; sexual excesses; handing out ultimatums to their followers, usually about once a year. Such is the suggestive effect of actions carried out in concert and at the behest of others, that participants almost always develop an increased sense of awe, 'awareness' or belief in the leader and the system after being subjected to such charades. This, however, is in line with contemporary psychological knowledge, although not widely understood by the general public, from which recruits to such groups continue to be attracted.

Another feature of the 'orders' which in fact constitutes a 'senile' phase of teaching, is concerned with exercises and movements. Mental and physical exercises are, of course, a well-known part of very many of the world's religious and especially esoteric movements. With the real Sufi school, however, the movements are never carried out by all members: since each movement is held to correspond with a particular characteristic and a certain stage of the individual's development. When the exercises become standardized, they lose their developmental effect, and instead serve either to automatize or else to provide a field for imagination. In legitimate Sufi tutelage, indeed, exercises are sometimes given for the purpose of ascertaining whether the learner will reject them – a sort of 'spiritual intelligence test'. All this is very far from the performances familiar to us in the more public, vitiated, forms of Sufism and other systems passing today under the name of genuine spiritual schools. Hindu observers have noted the same tendency in the meditation which has become standard practice in their circles, instead of being specifically designated for special purposes.

'Transvestism', dressing-up in clothes not of the period or of the country where the individual or group lives or operates, is regarded as a further example of the declining or impaired tradition. This behaviour is, of course, very common in almost all religious traditions. It is to be noted, however, that all such outlandish garb is imitative of the past – something which truly representative Sufis warn is an outward indication of an inner spiritual bankruptcy: and also, incidentally, regarded in a similar light by modern psychologists. People will, according to this doctrine, put on clothes as a compensation for a sense of inner emptiness. Clinical or morbid conditions, when cured, often first manifest their improved condition by the resumption of normal clothing.

It is not too much to say that, for many of the participants of such entities, the supposedly 'Sufi' orders constitute their real religion. It is for this reason that many religious authorities of Islam, for instance, have continuously opposed the Sufi 'Paths', claiming that they are in fact an opposition religion whose tenets are either surplus to, or opposed to, Islam. There is much truth in this charge, whether the members of the 'Sufi' groups realise it or not. The structure is there: the hierarchy, the liturgy, the regular meetings, the contact with the divine claimed or implicit, the reliance of the follower on the leadership, the threat and reward content, the punishment and joy – everything, in fact, that a full-blown religion usually provides.

Sufism, of course, is not a religion or a series of religions at all, though it undoubtedly can, in the wrong hands, develop (or degenerate) into this form. Sufism is instructional, and that instruction is not by any means in how to become religionistic. The instruction given by the Sufis is developmental and preparatory for something else; not in emotional experience, however 'spiritual' this is felt to be by the community at large.

A complication is introduced into this question by the reputed claim by Sufis that all religions originated with a local form of Sufism, and that what we take for religion today is the popularisation and the 'edited form' of the original school, which has only social and psychological, not developmental, value. Whatever may be the truth of this assertion – assuming that it has been authoritatively made at all – it is worth taking seriously, since there is no objective reason for disbelieving it any more than for accepting it without further analysis.

This assertion is also said sometimes to take the form of the Sufis claiming, 'After all, we started the religions, so we know all about them'. This rank heresy, sometimes regarded as blasphemy by the more fanatical clergy of all confessions or their counterparts, has – it is said – been queried by one researcher in the following interchange with a putative Sufi teacher.

'If you started all the religions, how and why is it that they have failed?'

'They have not failed. They have succeeded so far as anything of that type could have succeeded or have failed. They have succeeded, in the sense that worn-out shoes can be said to have succeeded. They have failed, much as you might consider, if you were taking a certain viewpoint, that worn-out shoes have failed, failed to last for ever!'

This rather recalls the phrase used by Rumi, the great Sufi luminary of the thirteenth century (A.D.), when he said, in his *Mathnawi*, 'We have taken the essence of the Koran, and thrown the carcase to the dogs' – a sentiment which is equal at least to some which have caused various Sufis, including some of the greatest, to be executed for apostasy from time to time.

The Orders are alleged to specialise in meditation, concentration and contemplation, the three procedures which, inseparable from one another yet each forming one part of the triangle which leads, under the correct mentorship, to Sufic enlightenment. But it would be a mistake, in this area as with so many others, to regard the Sufi forms of these techniques as being parallel to what is understood by them in other disciplines. I found that I had learnt more about meditation, for instance, in three days with veracious Sufi groups than I did in fifteen years of working with the Hindu and their derivatives like the Buddhist ways – and this in spite of the fact that the Indian meditation had, as I previously imagined, really given me bliss, calmness, the ability to work well in the world and relief from all kinds of symptoms that nothing else could cure. All these gains were in fact illusory compared to the reality of the Sufi achievements.

The key lies, as far as I can determine, in the difference between learning *about* a thing (scholastic knowledge); learning *of* it (subjective knowledge) and learning *in* it (real perception). The first two are only applied upon the person: the last-named actually and permanently transforms. There is some evidence to support this in the increasing restlessness now being shown by many of the converts to forms of Hindu meditation popularised in the East and West in the past few decades. They are reaching for something that they may glimpse, but which cannot be supplied, by their own 'schools'.

The reality of the Sufi "orders'" knowledge and their power to impart it is soon apparent to those who are in any position to ask the right questions from their often, admittedly, venerable guides. Perhaps the outstanding element here is the group's attitude towards 'secrets'. With a genuinely functional esoteric group, the 'secret' is ineffable; something which cannot be spoken or described, since this word is the technical term for the experience which can be induced only by the activities of the group. In diluted and secondary groups, this secret becomes secrecy, something prized for its own sake or else something learnt without any conception that it is a derivative formula which comes into being when the operational aspect is lost or absent.

The real Sufi is he whose 'concealment' is the fact that he does not give out anything unless it is indicated: not that he makes himself inaccessible. The secretive and elusive characters who pass for 'mystical masters' are seen, through Sufi eyes, as mere play-actors covering up a lack of knowledge or else imagining that secrecy is secretiveness because of verbal literality: they have no experience of the real thing. The phrase used by one of the real schools (the Khwajagan, Masters, from which the Naqshbandi, Designers, developed) is *Khilwat dar anjuman* [seclusion in company] which means that the real Sufi lives an open life. That which is secret is inexpressible, and only that which he cannot make public because there is no means to do so until the conditions are right.

The superficial 'understanding' of secrecy and privacy are undoubtedly distinct signs of the inadequacy of the supposedly Sufic group. The fact that these are in many places the best known of all the Sufi enterprises does not, of course, invalidate the fact that they are degenerate from the point of view of their capacity to communicate reality, though fully functional as mystification instruments.

The general mystery (and sometimes the prestige) of the 'orders' has given them an attraction capacity far beyond anything which they can deliver in the sense of teaching. This tendency has been equally marked in the Middle East, in Europe and in the Far East, where the costumes, intonations and other theatrical effects plus the continued propaganda that there is 'something important and concealed, only for the elect' have been the main props of such organizations through the ages. In this role, however, they play a no more significant part in the organism of the society in which they have their being than the primitive ritual societies found among the peoples of undeveloped territories. That is to say, they serve to attract and hold interest and to 'sell nothing more than prestige' – though they may preside over such functions as the 'rites of passage' which some communities find necessary to ensure the transition from one state of life or mentality to another.

Next to mystery, in very many of the large number of 'orders' (there are said to be over seven hundred of them, situated from the Atlantic in Morocco to China and India), the orders' theoreticians make much play of the subject of 'spiritual pedigree'. According to this, the link of living teachers runs from the present-day chief of the order right up to the founder of the order and thence, generally, in one of two lines, to Ali or Abu-Bakr, companions of Mohammed, fourteen hundred years ago. Since the Middle Ages, these *silsilahs* [chains] of baraka, impalpable spiritual force, have become a part of the mythology of virtually all the orders. There are, however, serious difficulties about this chain-system.

In the first place, the 'orders' themselves are late (medieval) developments, coming into being many centuries after the early classical Masters to whom their members still look as central figures establishing their legitimacy. In other words, the early Masters did not feel it necessary to claim a connected chain of spiritual succession from one Master to another. History shows that this innovation in Sufism came about in imitation of the scholastic habit of invoking higher authority in a succession of transmitters, for the *hadith*, the Sayings and Doings of the Prophet Mohammed. The habit of reciting the names of the alleged Masters of the Way in any particular Order is, however, so deeply ingrained that it is almost a litany, and yet it is a mark of a hidebound, often retrogressive, order to find great importance placed upon these names.

The second problem is that many of the Masters claim that they were independently illuminated: that is to say, they had no mentor who passed on the spiritual force. Among them are such as Ibn al-Arabi, who denied that he had any teacher in this form, and Hafiz.

The third problem is that virtually none of the alleged founders of 'orders' (Rumi, Gilani, Bahauddin Naqshband are examples) actually founded the order which takes his name. Originally, no doubt, the prototype of the order came into being after the founder's death, in order to stabilize his teaching. But of the actual establishment of the order itself there is no historical trace. This is all the more conclusive as to the secondary nature of the orders when one remembers how much importance is placed in these circles upon tradition and ceremony. That there should be no trace of any ceremony laid down by the founder of the order when initiating it is almost inconceivable in such a context or such a community, supposing that the putative founders really did establish the orders.

The orders, then, are not spurious: but they seem very likely to be highly organized derivations from the originally flexible teachings of the first or other early teachers of the system. Because we have the writings of Rumi, Saadi, Ghazzali, Hujwiri and others, we can see the 'orders' as nothing more than a living palimpsest.

That the present-day orders are not enlightened in the sense that the classical masters were is evidenced in a hundred different ways. Just to take a random example or two:

The classical writings of such great Sufis as Ghazzali plainly warn against indoctrination and conditioning, centuries before these dangerous procedures were rediscovered in the West. Today there is no 'order' in existence in the East or West which does not in some measure use these methods. As early as the time of Rabia, the woman Sufi saint of Baghdad, (born about A.D.717, died 801) the Sufis were warning against totemism and the use of the threat-and-promise mechanism. Today, in the orders which supposedly follow the teachings of the accepted legitimate early masters, these items are much in evidence. Few, if any, modern Sufi heads of 'orders' would stand for half a day the interrogation of modern psychologists. They could never defend their techniques effectively against the discoveries of contemporary behaviourists. Yet, if we examine the writings of the pre-order Sufi greats, we find that they can hardly be faulted in regard to their knowledge of fundamental aspects of human psychology and behaviour.

Beyond the orders, however, the Sufi activity continues, and in the past few decades there are many signs that the original school is making its presence and reality felt. In order to carry on the teaching, however, those behind this operation have often chosen to reach over the heads of the 'orders', addressing the public in general and even frustrating all the efforts of members of the orders and other esotericists to partake of their teaching. But why cut anyone off from a source of learning – surely everyone is entitled to it?

The essence of the operation is not to cut anyone off: 'They do that themselves,' as one exponent told me, continuing, 'there is a large number of people, both within cults and outside them, who have such fixed ideas about what Sufism is or should be that they have made themselves inaccessible to real teaching. A recent example was when several Western esoteric groups spent years in trying to get Idries Shah and others who work with the real tradition, to enter their own fold, even to lead it. This failed because the Sufis made it too hard for the mere accumulations of people to join them.'

I asked what a 'mere accumulation' meant.

'All genuine esoteric or spiritual groups work by collecting a certain number of types of individuals, who have the maximum potential, and grouping them in such a way as to establish a strong base of perceptiveness, so that others and yet others and so on in gradually increasing concentric rings of potential can be associated with them. People who do not know how to do this cannot construct their "body of the faithful" as an instrument which will resonate to the higher impulses (divine grace) in any real way. The result is the latter's development into a clan: they become a "mere accumulation of people" which is even less susceptible to teaching than any randomly collected group, since they have decided that each and every one of them should partici-pate all the time in the studies or rituals.'

The salient features of the authentic group are clearly set out here, while the misteaching's entrappment of the naive esotericist is equally patent. The distinctive, specified, nature of both the learners and the teachings seems impenetrable only to those who have been misinstructed.

The religious and secular authorities alike in those Eastern lands where self-styled Sufi Orders flourish, often oppose them for their pretensions that hierarchy and tradition are more important than function. In being able to do this, the authorities are on surer ground than those in the West who seek to avoid the excesses of such organizations. The reason for this is that the classical Sufi literature is accessible in local languages and can be employed there as a check on the 'orders'.

In one Near Eastern country recently, for instance, the chiefs of the Rifai, Mevlevi and other Orders were somewhat crushed to note that the local authorities, in pointing out their worthlessness and duping of the public, quoted nothing less than the scriptures of the Mevlevi order, *The Mathnawi* (which is even called 'The Holy Mathnawi') to the following devastating effect:

There were once three animals, a sheep, an ox and a camel, travelling together. Someone had abandoned a bale of fodder by the roadside, and they all wanted to eat it.

The sheep, however, pointed out that there was only enough for one of them. He suggested that whoever was the most ancient should have the prize. He added that it was rightfully his: for he had been alive at the time when Abraham offered his son as a sacrifice.

But the ox could not agree. 'I am one of those oxen whom Adam himself used in his ploughing: that makes me entitled, on the basis of "seniority",' he said.

When the camel heard what the others had said he was at first too astonished to speak. Then he extended his neck and picked up the food, raising it high into the air.

'Hierarchy and tradition,' he pronounced, 'can have no meaning for me – for *I* have the body and the neck to do without them!'

After the lapse of several hundred years (Rumi died in 1273) the Mevlevis ('Dancing Dervishes') who formerly claimed that action was better than tradition, now have turned half a circle, and themselves invoke the very traditionalism that their alleged founder worked against.

Observation of a Sufi School

HODA AZIZIAN

The school being observed is represented throughout the Middle East, Farther Asia, Europe (north and south) and the Americas. There are obviously severe limitations to the data and experiences available to the observer in any fieldwork connected with an organization such as a Sufi one. The following may be listed:

(1) Many organizations, especially those which are termed *spiritual* in some sense, welcome anthropological or other investigation. They hope for publicity or respectability through such activities, and will often woo the good graces of the investigator. They also generally hope for an increase in membership through any publications, films, and so on.

The Sufis, in contradistinction, seek publicity only for such materials as they believe to have a teaching function. Their 'respectability' is such that no body of people in any comparable area can match their repute. In very many communities, and in several cultures (Persian, Arabian, Turkish, Central Asian, Indo-Pakistani are some of them) Sufis are regarded as the *crème de la crème*. They have no need of image-building. As for recruitment, all reputable Sufi organizations have for centuries been so inundated with requests for membership that they all maintain a filtration system to admit only the most promising candidates.

(2) No legitimate Sufi has so far been found who will concern himself with liturgy, history, literature or personalities either alone or to such an extent as to be styled as a specialist in these areas of the Sufi phenomenon. Hence, no outside investigator will be able to contact a Sufi specialist to give him direct information of

the biographies, doings, theories and practices and so on of the Sufis. There is no equivalent to the tendency among other spiritual systems to develop schools of thought or of teaching which specialise in various aspects of the system or its congruent factors.

The reason for this state of affairs becomes very clear once a certain principle is grasped. The difficulty is that the grasping of the principle is difficult for the scholar himself: perhaps because it runs counter to his need for the organization of thought and materials. Briefly, the Sufis may be seen to be working with 'any materials which serve their purpose' (quoted from an outstanding modern Sufi teacher). This means that a Sufi will speak or write of the thoughts and doings of a number of Sufi saints, shall we say, *only insofar as these bear upon the teaching in which he is involved at the time.*

This very important technique means that the factual content of the materials being used by a Sufi may be of interest to a student of the Sufis, whereas the materials are being used for another purpose. As an example, it is almost as if we went to church to listen to the Parable of the Talents and, since we might be economists, we would want to know more about 'talents': while the voice from the pulpit would be trying to arouse in us an entirely different set of sensations. To put it briefly: the Sufi is teaching his disciples and his effect is measured by their reactions to his teaching. The observer of Sufis is trying to assess the Sufi materials within conventional categories. It is not necesary to accept the Sufis' own estimation of what they are doing to see that their *technique* is as has been described.

(3) The best-known and most often studied 'Sufi' groups and organizations must be described, from this viewpoint, as secondary or imitative. This is because the teachers or other mentors of the community concentrate upon deepening the sense of belief of the members, make sure that the rituals are carried out at stated intervals, associate every scrap of information and effort with the movement's stability and progress. In short, here we always have a recognizable cult-group, generally invisible to the researcher as such because the investigator himself most often comes from a society where such cult-groups are not regarded (as the Sufis

would regard them) as secondary, diluted or distorted in their ideas and practices.

The analogy here might be if, let us say, an expert on the entertainment industry, or the arts, were to try to assess the workings, ideas and motivations of a scholarly enterprise such as a university college. He (or she) might look for certain indications and might have little patience with others – even if the latter were emphasised to him (or her) as being central to the scholarly process.

All this is not to say that the Sufis themselves are unaware of the problems which we encounter in trying to make sense of what they think and do. On the contrary, since Sufis often have to deal with scholars or other people from conventional backgrounds of thinking, some at least of their materials are devoted to explaining how they approach things and how not to approach them if one is interested in participation. The main difficulty here, of course, is that such materials are not addressed to the 'outward assessor'; they are aimed directly at the would-be learner, and are therefore of limited use to research.

Here is a document emanating from a contemporary Sufi activity, outlining the emphases (attunement, materials and energy and focus) which the School requires.

SUFI LEARNING SYSTEM

The difficulty of outside people trying to study the Sufi system is due to two main factors:

1 They select materials according to existing prejudices and do not know which are superseded or even spurious;

2 Sufi learning is a comprehensive process (which has been called both 'holistic' and 'organic'). It cannot be studied from the outside at all without distortion.

Within the Sufi system, however, we can isolate three areas which have to be represented and in balance. These are:-

1 The *Learner has to be attuned* to the Teacher and the Teaching. This involves his achieving a balanced attitude: neither rejecting nor servile;

2 The *Materials have to be present* and 'sprinkled' (the technique known as *scatter* has to be employed). They must
by-pass excess emotional or intellectual activity;

3 The *energy and focus* of the teaching must be right. This
requires allowance for the cyclical nature of the avail-
ability of the necessary energy and of the recipient's abilities to absorb it.

While lip-service to some of these factors is often found in
supposed systems of enlightenment, it is noteworthy that in general only one or two of them are attemptedly operated, and
generally by people who are not attuned to the factors at all. The
result is, of course, fossilization and cultishness.

Sufi activity is therefore an overall operation which has to be
orchestrated in accordance with the 'times' (the sensitivity) of the
learner harmonized with the other factors.

Without this constant activity, correctly carried out, higher
development is so rare as to be discounted.

(4) There seems to be a distinct possibility that the 'outside
observer' will either reject the entire Sufi projection, since it does
not fit in with the way in which he likes to see spiritual matters
expressed; or else that he will wholeheartedly accept the Sufi
projection and abandon his former framework of conceptual-
izations. Each of these attitudes, of course, is equally immature:
but both have been found among those who have tried to study the
Sufis. Based as they are on the acceptance or rejection tendency in
the human mind, they are always characterized by Sufis as symp-
tomatic of a need for the 'ripening' of the consciousness of the
individual: indeed, Sufis go so far as to say that such behaviour
should be a useful 'indicator of the frailness and need for real
study on the part of the victim' (literal quotation from a present-
day Sufi master).

In orientalist and other specialist literature, to be sure, we
can find, as if suspended in amber, many signs of these two
postures on the part of the researcher; although one may add
another which the Sufis do not seem to refer to much: that of
qualified support or partial opposition. The Sufis would, perhaps,

simply categorize this as 'the academic's hedging his bets'.

When all is said and done, however, there are certain outstanding characteristics of the Sufi operations which can be seen as registered in the classical books and also in full manifestation in the 'school'.

First of all must surely come the combating of the assumptions of the student if these are based on his own tradition as distinct from inward perceptions. 'The most frequent type of this assumption,' says a modern Sufi, 'may be caricatured for emphasis in the words: "I have been waiting here since Wednesday – where is my share of illumination?"'

Next we may list what contemporary psychology calls *rationalization*, but which the Sufis term 'building on sand'. This may be manifested by those who come to Sufis and see in them associations which 'prove' the rightness of the candidate's choice of the Sufis as true teachers. According to the Sufis, as any reader of their books will know, such understanding does not, cannot, come at such an early stage.

The Sufi (but not the dervish) system of learning requires that the learner must avoid what nowadays would be called mechanicality, which they term 'habit training'. This is evidenced when the student 'mistakes the container for the content' (traditional Sufi phrase), and when Sufi instructional materials or processes arouse emotions or cause actions in him which may be described as standard or invariable. Dervishes in the past have been known to change habit-patterns from those of the ordinary community to certain simplified ones used in their orders – so that, in turn, these patterns may be eliminated. This could be called, in modern parlance, deconditioning.

According to the most reputable sources (which means legitimately Sufic ones) this range of practices has not been used by Sufi schools since about the fourteenth century (of the Christian Era) when it was introduced as a temporary measure which was applicable in the light of prevailing conditions. It is interesting to note, however, that such is the persistence capacity of this kind of 'mechanicality' that the externals of the outworn system have continued to capture human minds ever since, and continue to do so. Examples are the highly-organized 'dervish orders' which persist to this day, whether in Egypt, elsewhere in Africa, occasionally in Turkey, increasingly in Iran, and sporadically in Afghanistan, Pakistan, India and farther East – where Indonesia and Malaysia are examples.

It is, incidentally, rumoured that many of these 'dervish orders' (several hundred have been listed, and they continue to be founded) were instituted as 'nurseries'. The contention is that an organization is founded by a Sufi as a means both to associate together people interested in the Way and also to give them great social visibility, for the purpose of selecting from among their ranks those who might be able to profit from real Sufi teaching. This seems, on the face of it, highly unlikely, if one takes into account the deep conditioning which the members of the orders undergo. It would appear that this process is the very contrary of what the Sufis intended and continue to intend.

The problems of studying the Sufis are, in a way, paralleled by the problems of studying *with* the Sufis. A contemporary Sufi who is also a distinguished psychologist reports that 'show or no' progress is almost always entirely due to the hampering effect of habits of mind:

(A) Most people constantly switch back to almost automatic ways of looking at things or of approaching problems, because they have been automatized by their worldly training;

(B) Sufi attitudes, as taught by the Sufis and captured in their literature, have to be practised in order to provide an alternative capacity to the familiar ones like, say, concentration or associativeness or reacting;

(C) the systematic approach to life and to learning, which is undeniably valuable in many areas, acts as a disabling factor in others;

(D) the average man or woman is much more of an automaton than is generally understood. Just as a pedestrian has to change attitudes and actions when travelling in a vehicle, and the focus and action would have again to change if one were driving it, so does the Sufi aspirant need to acquire a different kind of experience than that of the conventionally-trained individual.

I suggested that all this seems very difficult, and unlikely to attract the mystically-minded, the people who do not, in general, want to trouble themselves with many words and complicated formulae.

The reaction is perhaps a good example of Sufi thinking.

'The purpose of the Sufis is not to attract those who style themselves, or who are categorized by some, as "mystically-minded". Indeed, the Sufis as mystics regularly come across people who are thought to be "mystically-minded" but who are merely vacant, lazy or self-deluded: which must happen in all kinds of human endeavour. Our experience shows that what the Sufis say and do – and are – does indeed attract those who have the ability to become Sufis, as well as attracting many other types. Someone who does not want to trouble himself is someone who may be just as automatized as "someone who does want to trouble himself". We do not find that people with such postures constitute the norm or that they influence the Sufi activity in any way.'

Observations at a Sufi school certainly do show that when many of the preoccupations with what one considers to be 'oneself' have fallen away, certain dramatic changes do take place in the individual. What are these changes, and how do they compare with the changes reported in Sufis from classical times?

For those of us who are unused to direct perception of change in people (what is generally referred to as 'spiritual development' and so on) the changes are perceived negatively. Those who formerly had loud voices do not now have low ones: they have voices which are under some kind of control. One can note that some expansion of capacity in outward behaviour in this respect has taken place. People who formerly placed great importance upon how they presented themselves in public now seem able to do so without the painful self-consciousness which one can descry beyond the supposedly comfortable exterior of even the most social people. I am in no doubt that a large degree of extra-sensory perception is in operation. People anticipate one's questions and even one's actions. For instance, several times when I wanted a glass of water, someone brought me one; when I wanted to post a letter, stamps were brought; when I was thinking of a book, it was produced for me. But there is one striking factor which cannot be categorized in the present state of knowledge: *people who 'read one's mind' only did so when one was not expecting it.* Again and again, if I thought of something deliberately, to see whether it would communicate to someone else in the community, this simply did not work. But, as soon as I stopped trying, especially if I had 'real thoughts' (as distinct from thoughts only designed to test ESP) – the 'mind-reading' would commence again.

Many of the changes in behaviour among Sufis are directly opposed to the changes which are ordinarily associated with 'mystics' or the like. As people became more perceptive, they dropped habits of behaviour, dress and attitude which had previously seemed characteristic of them. It is only partly that they became less demanding, less flamboyant in dress, less inclined to talk about Sufism. It was literally as if, to quote how an advanced Sufi put it, 'They do not need those habits now. They were, you see, only forms of behaviour which these people adopted because there was nothing *real* in them. In the ordinary world, you are surely familiar with the man who shouts to cover up his own lack of certainty. Among the Sufis, when someone knows who and what he is, he or she will not need outside manifestations. This is all because most of the things which you take as indications of what people are really like inwardly are not such at all. They are only roles which people assume, because they have no fixed individuality within at all.'

But not all forms of outward behaviour are taken by the Sufis to indicate the lack of anything inside the individual. Other activities and manifestations do, in fact, signal 'inward realities' as they are termed.

One conspicuous example is when someone does something which is held to be an indicator of his attunement with 'the Path'. I was constantly surprised to find that even mundane successes were taken, from time to time, with great joy, by Sufi teachers, as indications that this individual was at last attuned to Reality.

Questioning, whenever it was permitted, the Sufi students, had some advantages. From this one learnt, among other things:

'The Sufic experience is not like any other. If you feel that it is what you have hitherto called "religious"; even if you feel that it gives you satisfaction, or anything else which you can name, including "I realise that this is right for me", you have not yet felt it. When you do it is unmistakable.'

'The Sufi current protects itself from those who are unreliable. Ask yourself: "Can I be relied upon?" If the answer is "No", you will have to make yourself reliable. The fact is, most people enjoy being unreliable. This is because they think that a variety of reactions makes them free or masters of their fate. It does not.'

'If you do not read Sufi books, especially those designed for the present day; and if you do not avoid those which are essentially spurious, being written by self-styled mystics, you will not, under today's conditions, reach real understanding. To say, "I do not want to read, I want to know", and similar things, is a mark of incompetence, however it may appeal to some.'

'Sufism is so easy that it is amazing that so many people find it difficult. All you need to do is to stop being false; though you have to practise this first of all in the interchange with the Sufi Teaching.'

'There are certain "tests" which occur while you are being prepared for enlightenment. If the negative side of these appeals to you, you will remain one of the "people of the world", or the "people with Earth-sickness". THE TESTS ARE NOT SE-CRET, SINCE YOU CANNOT CAMOUFLAGE YOUR RE-ACTIONS TO THEM. They include:

1 Being given an ultimatum, or being asked to choose between two people or two courses of study or two forms of behaviour. Whoever asks you to choose between him and others is the false 'Teacher'.

2 If you are given anything to say or do in a language foreign

to you (in the West this means such things as phrases in Persian or Arabic to repeat), this is done by a false teacher.

3 No true Sufi meetings are held more than once a week.

4 If you are told, or if it is hinted to you, that 'something important is going to happen soon', know that you should abandon that group and seek the alternative.

5 Any supposed Sufi wearing clothes or other apparel foreign to the country in which he is living, or which he visits, means that you should avoid such a man.

6 Any alleged Sufi teacher who claims or implies that he is 'on the Path of Blame' (deliberately courting unpopularity) is false. This is never claimed by real Sufis, since the Path of Blame must be anonymously trod.

7 Anyone who says or does anything in your presence implying that he has influence in affairs of the world and is exercising it, is not a Sufi teacher; unless he is on the Path of Blame, in which case he is not an instructor but is only there to signal that you, too, must shun him, and approach the legitimate source of the Teaching which is always present under such circumstances.

8 No real Sufi will claim or imply supreme Mastership, or being a *Qutub*, or Concealed Teacher; though former dervishes (representatives for limited purposes) of Sufis may do so, if they have succumbed to the temptation of exercising power.

9 Similarly, the assumption of military, clerical or official rank is a sign of the deterioration of faculties (earth-sickness) which can attack anyone, and which is often found among *channels* (i.e., people who, though not Sufis, may be related to some of them and employed for low-level and preparatory or 'test' work).

10 The following signs are common when Sufi teachership is claimed by those not entitled to it: assumption of importance; loss of physical co-ordination; convincing others (as a major characteristic) that one is taking a deep interest in them, especially when they are ill or in distress; mysteriousness and hinting; tolerating the deluded; confusing

friendship with teaching; organizing inconsequential journeys; allowing one's hand to be kissed; appearing on platforms with "other mystics"; believing that Sufi teaching is
a matter of individual opinion, not of inevitability in techniques; allowing exercises (*Zikr*) to be carried out without
supervisors to intervene at appropriate moments.'

I sought elucidation of the foregoing statement from an authoritative Sufi source because of the problem raised by its method of
phrasing. Reference is made both to 'testing' and also to 'falsity'.
Which were we dealing with, I wanted to know: false schools or
genuine schools which wanted to test actual or potential
members?

The answer to this illuminated a further dimension of Sufi
understanding:

'There are three conditions under which any or all of the
considerations referred to may exist. These are: (a) the false Sufi
school or the deluded one (former school now in decay); (b) the
legitimate school applying tests; (c) the representative(s) of a Sufi
school who have developed 'Earth-sickness' (though not themselves Sufis, have through vanity arrogated to themselves the rank
of Sufi, generally adopting high pretensions.)

'In reality, though not in appearance, all these "work
together", just as, say, fire and water "work together" to produce
steam.'

I then asked what the observer, or individual desirous of approaching or remaining in a Sufi school, should do if he or she
were confronted with any of the phenomena of 'Earth-sickness' in
supposed teachers.

'This condition,' I was told on high authority, 'never occurs
unless the authentic Teaching is also accessible. The individual or
group should turn to the legitimate Teacher who will always be
standing by. The commonest form is form (c), when the low-level
'messenger' of the Sufis decides to present himself as a teacher
instead of a conduit. He will have been chosen as a secondary-
ranking individual precisely because he will still have had such
negative characteristics as vanity and the desire for power too

strong in him. Such people are generally given these roles as a possible way of eliminating their bad characteristics. They tend, however, to fail in the attempt, and to choose the path of "false Sufism". It is these who are described in the (Sufi traditional) phrase, "The channel transmits the water but does not itself drink".'

As to why the errant 'channel' should develop such precise characteristics as 'loss of physical co-ordination, organising of inconsequential journeys, the assumption of military, clerical or official rank' and so on, the only answer obtainable from high Sufi sources was: 'All these tendencies are well-established symptoms of the result of the triumph of environmental influences on the weak mentation of those who have preferred power to enlightenment. To detail why this happens in this way would be unproductive. As with any illness, the areas attacked weaken first'.

But could this kind of malaise assail people of otherwise great achievements or of reputable Sufi connexions?

'All Sufi connexions are reputable. All human beings are vulnerable to "Earth-sickness". There cannot be any exceptions.'

'How is the ordinary individual to know when his (or her) "Sufi" teacher is afflicted in this way?' I asked.

'By applying the assessments of common sense to the problem, just as one does with anything else. It is not necessary for the Sufi to behave in an absurd fashion in order to carry out his mission. But it *is* likely that a false, deluded or maimed one will.'

'If such is the case with Sufi teachers, does it apply too to those of other persuasions?' was my next question.

The answer:

'The Sufis are not a persuasion, they are people who have seen something beyond ordinary perception and who therefore know how to act to make this perceptible to others. But if you mean by this question, "are people who are involved in spiritual matters susceptible to deterioration?" the answer is, "Yes, all of them, as you will see from the abnormal behaviour of supposed teachers, from time to time, in all religious fields".'

'How, then, should the person interested in the Sufis, or in any

other spiritual group, defend himself (herself) against false, deluded or disabled "teachers"?' I wanted to know.

'If there is anything about such a "teacher" which is regarded
as abnormal, repulsive or objectionable by a majority of ordinary
(non spiritually-minded) people, especially when they are
informed of all the facts about this individual known to the
followers of the "teacher", then you will know that he is undesirable. This is, again, because, although the true Sufi teacher is
other-worldly, he has as a major task the need to present himself
as thoroughly acceptable in every way, in every action, in all
respects, as acceptable to the ordinary members of the wider
community in which his work is set.'

'Does that mean that the unregenerate individual may well be
better fitted to judge the Sufi teacher than the disciple?'

'No. It means that the unregenerate is better fitted to see
through the false "Sufi" than the self-deluded. This is why real
Sufis seek their disciples from among *normal* people, often those
who have no background of metaphysics. Remember that those
who stay with the false or untrue "Sufi" are almost always people
who had a background of bizarre "spirituality" before they met
him. He makes little progress with normal people, just as the
legitimate Sufi makes real progress with virtually nobody else.'

I have dwelt on this subject because one can find so little
featured on it in spiritual writings in general. It is felt that this
fresh information, even though it is supported by traditional Sufi
writings and other teachings, is neglected, and therefore contributes to the general knowledge of the subject, and adds to the
information-stock available to researchers.

Other Works

CONTEMPORARY TRAVELS AND RESIDENCE AMONG
DERVISHES IN ASIA AND AFRICA:

AMONG THE DERVISHES by O.M. Burke, London 1973 (The
Octagon Press)

SUFI CLASSIC IN A MODERN TRANSLATION:

THE WALLED GARDEN OF TRUTH (of Hakim Sanai of
Ghazna). Translation of part by David Pendlebury, London 1974
(The Octagon Press) and New York 1976

DEVOTIONAL SUFI CLASSIC:

ORIENTAL MYSTICISM ('The Remotest Aim' by Aziz Nafasi)
translated by Professor E.H. Palmer, London 1974 (The Octagon
Press)

BIOGRAPHY AND WORK OF A MAJOR ANCIENT SUFI
MASTER:

THE LIFE, PERSONALITY AND WRITINGS OF AL-JUNAYD
(of Baghdad) by Dr Ali H.Abdel-Kader,Al-Azhar University,
London 1976

SURVEY OF SUFI LITERARY CLASSICS:

SUFISM by Professor N.S. Fatemi and others, New York and London 1976

LINKAGE OF SUFI TEACHERS WITH ANCIENT AND MEDIEVAL HISTORY:

THE MASTERS OF WISDOM by J.G. Bennett, London 1977

EXPLANATION OF HIS BELIEFS BY AN IMPRISONED SUFI:

A SUFI MARTYR (translation of the *Complaint of a Stranger Exiled from Home* by Al-Hamadani) by Professor A.J.Arberry, London 1969

TEACHINGS OF THE MASTER OF A DERVISH ORDER (THE SHADHILIYYA):

IBN ATA'ILLAH'S SUFI APHORISMS translated by V. Danner, Leiden 1973

THE MAGNUM OPUS OF THE SUFI WHO 'REVIVED ISLAM':

IMAM GAZZALI'S IHYA ULUM-ID-DIN (Revivification of Religious Sciences) translated, in four volumes, by Maulana Fazul-ul-Karim, Lahore, N.D.

APPLICATION OF SUFI LEARNING CONCEPTS TO CONTEMPORARY PROBLEMS:

LEARNING HOW TO LEARN by (The Sayed) Idries Shah, London 1978 (The Octagon Press)

THEORIES, PRACTICES AND TRAINING-SYSTEMS OF A SUFI SCHOOL

by
*Canon W H T Gairdner**

*Originally published as *'The Way'* of a Mohammedan Mystic, in *Muslim World* 2 (1912) pp 171–181.

Theories, Practices and Training-Systems of a Sufi School

The Sufis are the Mystics of Islam, and Sufism is, historically, the mystical side of Mohammedanism. Originally, it was a mere protest against the worldliness and irreligiousness which material success had imported into Islam, and consisted in little more than an insistence on and a multiplication of religious exercises, with a view to drawing near unto Allah. Later on, as the connexion between Islam and the Middle East became more and more important, and Christian, Persian and Indian mystical influences sought admission to the world of Moslem thought, it was the Sufis who mainly opened to them the door, and, through the natural affinity of the mystically minded all the world over, afforded a home to the new ideas. Under their influence, Mohammedan Mysticism became more doctrinal and systematic, and, in part, more esoteric. Its tenets, its methods, and its ritual became alike more elaborate, and its consistency with the Sunnite system of theology and practice became for a time open to question.

To two men, more than any other, el-Qushairi and el-Ghazzali, Islam owes the standardising of Sufism in its relation to Sunnite orthodoxy. They in the first place gave it, for good and all, a distinct *locus standi* in Islam, and by precept and example showed how far it could go without slipping into Pantheism and becoming a mere esoteric Gnosticism or Theosophy within the Islamic community.

It may, however, be asserted with some confidence that both before and after the era of these men there was an Extreme Left in Sufism, which did, unconsciously or perhaps consciously, tremble

141

on the line or slip over it, – men for whom the gnostic and theosophical influences, which were existent in the early days of Islam not less than they were in the days before and after the birth of Christianity, proved too strong. But it would always have been very difficult to distinguish this Left-wing from the Left-centre, and next to impossible to draw a line separating the two; the fact being that most of those who were nearest that line would have been wholly unable to define their own position, while those who were aware that they had passed beyond it would keep the fact entirely to themselves.

And such, it may be hazarded, is still the case. Sufism today also has its left, its Centre, and its Right. But the Left-wing is not the typical group. That is the important thing to remember.

The object of this paper, however, is by no means to give a history of, or to write an essay on Sufism. For that we must wait for Dr. Nicholson's forthcoming history of Sufism, which all orientalists are awaiting with so much interest. The object of the present paper is merely to contribute a piece of living material to the study of Sufism, in the shape of a true record of certain conversations held by the writer with two Sufis of a very advanced type. And the purpose of the foregoing remarks has been merely to warn the reader that the following narrative is not necessarily to be taken as typical of all Sufism, nor even (for aught we know) of the Sufism of all Rifa'ite darwishes [dervishes], though one of these two men had been the sheikh, or superior, of a Rifa'ite monastery, in Bulgarian-speaking Turkey. It may, on the contrary, be hazarded that here we have an esoteric Sufism of an extreme type. Only further research can show how far these doctrines are typical of all Left-wing Sufism; also, how far they are a real part of advanced Rifa'ism: that is to say, whether they represent an unessential and untypical development of that 'Way', or whether we have here an unveiling of the advanced doctrine of that 'Way', a doctrine of which the lower grades are entirely ignorant; just as, it is said, modern Freemasonry carries its initiates in its higher grades to ideas of which novices, and still more outsiders, have no notion whatever.

The strange history of the two brothers, who supplied the writer with this material, cannot be given in detail here. One of them, Mohammed Nasimi, had developed along the line of study and reading rather than through the praxis of Mysticism. But the elder brother, Ahmad Kashshaf, had been a 'practising' dervish of an advanced type. It must suffice to say here that they were Sufis and sons of a Sufi; that they were disciplined to 'the Way' from very childhood; that they entered its novitiate at an early age, and that the elder brother at least, passed rapidly through its degrees and stages, so that for years he was head of a Sufi monastery[1] in Turkey, a dervish and the spiritual director of dervishes, and a man widely known in those regions as a saint, and one possessed of a saint's virtues and powers; that his levelling Mysticism caused him to pass, with his younger brother, beyond Islam altogether, and to seek in some other way a place where the soul is free. In the course of many conversations with the writer, those reminiscences were communicated. They are far from being complete, still further from being exhaustive. They are even fragmentary. But they are authentic, and possibly their very fragmentariness may suggest the living, personal experience which lay behind them, and thus impart to them an interest and vividness which are often somewhat to seek in more systematized accounts.[2]

WHAT LEADS TO THE MYSTIC LIFE

Sufis are recruited in various ways; for a man is not born, but becomes, a Sufi. In the great el-Ghazzali's case, for example, the determining cause was the temporary collapse of his traditional faith and his dissatisfaction with his own moral condition. These two things drove him to search where a credible faith and a personal religious experience could be found; and Mysticism supplied both demands. He became, in fact, a dervish. Others, said Sheikh Ahmad, the Dervish-become Christian who has already been mentioned, enter the Sufi life through disappointment in love. Passion for a woman awakes in them the desire to love Allah, with a love which having the Infinite for its object, will receive real satisfaction. Sometimes this earthly love is lawful, sometimes sinful. It matters not, for in both cases the same longing is aroused which drives to Allah. Sometimes, too, it may be a passionate love for a youth.

In Ahmad's case it was none of these things but rather the circumstance that he was the son of a Sufi father, and was from infancy trained, as a matter of course, in the Sufistic life. That all this, however, need not necessarily have led to his becoming a professed Sufi is shown by the fact that his younger brother, Nasimi, developed on rather different lines, as has already been mentioned.[3] Even as children of four years they were taught to practise the incessant 'making mention' of the Name of Allah. They seem never to have played childhood's games: all their lives passed either in study or in 'mentioning' the Name of Allah. When the neighbours rebuked the father, and said: 'It is not good for such young children to be given up to these things,' he replied: 'No harm can come from exceeding in the mentioning of Allah' (el-ifrat fi dhikri-llah).

FIRST STEPS

When a man aspires to enter the profession of regular Sufism, he presents himself to the sheikh, or superior, of one of the many dervish orders, who examines his spiritual condition and attainments, satisfies himself of his sincerity, and gives him preliminary counsel and advice. 'You are the corpse,' he says, 'and I the washer of the corpse. You are a garden, I the gardener.' He thus undertakes to yield himself wholly and blindly to the spiritual direction of the sheikh, and with him as guide to enter on the Mystic Way. He enters the monastery, and lives a life according to rule: for he needs three things, 'Time, Place, Brethren.'[4]

Some of those preliminary directions are of the following sort:

'Keep the commands of Allah and abstain from the things prohibited.'
'Leave all that differs from the Law and the Way.'
'Be constant in religion and keep Allah's covenant' ('ahd).
'In the Way and the Law become learned.'
'Look not on the faults of others.'

'Supply the needs of the needy with justice and mercy.'

'Leave all evil and blameable ways.'

'Obey the directions and commands of the sheikh.'

'Tell the truth ever and do not lie.'

'Think of nought but the Law, the Way, the Knowledge, and the Reality.'[5]

And thus the aspirant enters on the Way of the order he has chosen. In the case of Ahmad it was the Way of the Rifa'iya dervishes – one of the most famous of all the orders.

It is a Way with sevenfold Halts or stages[6]. The passing from stage to stage is entirely at the discretion of the superior, who judges of the aspirant's aptitude and progress by what he observes of his conduct and experiences. As he confides all to the superior – his dreams, his experiences, his character, his faults – the sheikh is able to judge of his fitness to be, or not to be, promoted to the next Stage in the Way.

THE DISCIPLINE OF A MYSTIC

Before entering on an exposition of these Seven Stages, it will be well here to gather up some of the practice that is common to all, or at least the earlier ones.

We have already mentioned the habit of confessing all things to the sheikh. It is this that enables him both to judge of the aspirant's spiritual condition, and also to prescribe for him spiritually. The aspirants invariably have dreams[7] and these the sheikh interprets, and judges by them of their state. Sometimes they seem to be fighting with animals. This is a sign that they are still in the lower Stages, before true knowledge has come to the soul. A cat is the sign of hypocrisy; a fox of deceit. Or they see fire, or water; and these, too, have their interpretation.[8] At first the aspirant depends much on the sheikh, and calls up his image much at the *Dhikr*, so as to make a way from heart to heart. This is called 'losing the self in the sheikh': that he may thus have mediated to him the way to 'losing the self in Allah'.

In the earlier instructions given by the sheikh, his moral precepts are most detailed, and go into the smallest particulars of life.

Further, he tells them that Hell is *now* about men; and that the Sufistic life is the way whereby they may now and here enter Paradise, the Janna of the *heart*. He describes some of the ecstatic experiences and inflames their desire to know them: the seeing of the coloured lights, ecstasy, self-loss in Allah.

The spiritual exercise (*riyada*) is often very severe, though not all the orders prescribe this severity. Some sheikhs prescribe fasting, little sleep, silence.

Sometimes he will prescribe the exceptional, or occasional, exercise of the Forty Days, the Retreat. The aspirant is ordered to a tiny cell, which is quite dark, and which is so small that one can neither stand nor lie at length in it. In this cell he sits for forty days and forty nights, coming forth only to take part in the spiritual exercises of the community. At night he does not lie down but sleeps as he sits at prayer. His occupation during this retreat is the *Dhikr*.

THE DHIKR

At the prayer of the Order, on Friday, in the mosque of the monastery, the usual Moslem prayer prescribed by the Law is first performed. Then the Mention follows. The sheikh now comes forward and is the leader. He faces the niche that points to Mecca; behind him, in a row, stand the advanced initiates, with the standard-bearers, holding the standard of the order on their right and left. Behind this row, in a semi-circle, stand the aspirants, and in the space between the semi-circle and the row are set twelve lighted candles.

The sheikh faces round to the worshippers. The advanced initiates and the aspirants prostrate themselves and kiss the floor; and the making mention begins.

To describe a Mention is wholly impossible here. It has an elaborate ritual, long prayers with innumerable repetitions and refrains. The object is to produce ecstasy. The 'witness' *La ilaha illa-llah* is chanted perhaps three or four hundred times, accelerando to prestissimo, until, it may be, a rapture is produced: to one thus ecstasized, fire seems to stream from his mouth, coloured lights fill his vision, he forgets himself and his neighbours; Allah becomes all. This is the entranced State; Passion; Revelation[9]; Ecstasy; Losing of the Self; Union.

At such times the ecstatic, in virtue of his State, and invoking the merit of the founder, Ahmad El Rifa'i, will stab himself with a dagger, and it passes in and out without doing harm: he will handle fire, and the fire loses its heat and does no hurt. If he drinks a deadly thing, it has no effect; 'Verily to find the signs promised to believers in Mark's Gospel, in these days it is to the Sufis thou must go' (*sic* Sheikh Ahmad).

Often an excess of ecstasy produces total physical unconsciousness, for the aspirant is lost to the world and is immersed in the spiritual world and in Allah. From this State only the sheikh can, according to his merit, bring him back. This he does by having the rigid body laid before him, and addressing to it an awaking-charm. Thereupon the soul of the aspirant returns to him and he comes back to himself.

THE SEVENFOLD WAY

With regard to the Seven Stages into which the Way of a dervish in the Rifa'ite and some other orders is divided, some preliminary considerations must be noticed here. Their origin goes back, of course, far beyond Islam, – to Neo-Platonism, to Gnosticism, to those common sources of oriental Mysticism, whether Indian or Persian, from which have sprung the various Heathen, Jewish, Christian, or Mohammedan Mysticism, Mysteries, Gnosticisms, or Theosophies from before the Christian era to this day. Their source is, therefore, really one, – the dark womb of obliterating Oriental Pantheism. But their historical *manifestations*, with their several adaptations, are bafflingly numerous and intricate. In the adaptation before us, the attempt to use *Mohammedan* terminology, and make as much use of Mohammedan ideas as possible, is evident.

TRACES OF ANCIENT COSMOLOGY OR ASTROLOGY IN THE SEVENFOLD WAY

The sevenfold journey of the soul at once takes us back to the old cosmology, as old as the Babylonians and it may be older, as young as Dante and it may be younger; according to which the earth, the gross sphere of matter, is encircled by the sevenfold planetary spheres of the Moon, Mercury, Venus, Sun, Mars, Jupiter, and Saturn; beyond which are the Fixed Stars; and beyond which again the world of the absolute Real. The Seven Stages of the Way are, indeed, actually related to the Seven Spheres, in the Rifa'ite ritual, but it is only right to say that the old cosmological or astrological significance seems to have been almost entirely lost. Sheikh Ahmad, at least, seemed unable to expound the significance of the various identifications of Stage and Sphere though he was aware of course that the *order* of the said Stages corresponded to that of the Seven Planets, according to their proximity to the earth (as supposed in the pre-Copernican systems). His mental picture of the soul's progress seemed to be, not so much an upward flight through the enveloping spheres to the infinite spirit-world, beyond the Seventh Heaven, as an *inward* journey from the exile of the circumference to the communion at the centre, where the soul rests in Reality, the fourth of the four[10] main stages from which the Seven have been expanded. These four are THE LAWS, Stages 1 and 2; THE WAY, Stages 3 and 4; THE KNOWLEDGE ('Gnosis'), Stages 5 and 6; and THE RE-ALITY, Stage 7. In the diagram with which he represented these, Reality was at the *centre*, not the circumference.

The same Gnostic traits are discernible in the Doctrine of the Seventy Thousand Veils, to which the reader's attention must for a moment be directed.

TRACES OF GNOSTICISM IN THE SEVENFOLD WAY

Seventy Thousand Veils separate Allah, the One Reality, from the world of matter and of sense. And every soul passes before his birth through these seventy thousand. The inner half of these are veils of light: the outer half, veils of darkness. For every one of the veils of light passed through, in this journey towards birth, the soul puts off a divine quality: and for every one of the dark veils, it puts *on* an earthly quality. Thus the child is born *weeping*, for the soul knows its separation from Allah, the One reality. And when the child cries in its sleep, it is because the soul remembers something of what it has lost. Otherwise, the passage through the veils has brought with it forgetfulness: and for this reason man is called *insan* (which rhymes with it in Arabic). He is now, as it were, in prison in his body, separated by these thick curtains from Allah.

But the whole purpose of Sufism, the Way of the dervish, is to give to him an escape from this prison, an apocalypse of the Seventy Thousand Veils, a recovery of the original unity with The One, *while still in this body*. The body is not to be put off; it is to be refined (*talattaf*[11]), and made spiritual – a help and not a hindrance to the spirit. It is like a metal that has to be refined by fire and transmuted. And the sheikh tells the aspirant that he has the secret of this transmutation. 'We shall throw you into the fire of Spiritual Passion (*'ushq*),' he says, 'and you will emerge refined. And the fuel that feeds that flame is the *Dhikr*'.[12]

For every Stage traversed in this return journey to Allah, then, ten thousand of the Veils are apocalypted (*kashf*).

EARLY EXPERIENCES OF THE MYSTIC

But the aspirant has been warned that these early stages are the stages where patience is above all necessary; for these are the Dark Veils. The stages of The Law are verily a husk, a bitter husk that has to be broken through. It is the stage of repentance. It was at this stage (of The Law) that the Banu Isra'il (Israelites) slew themselves for very repentance, and died. So, too, must the aspirant die, die many times daily, the death of this bitterness. This death the Sufis call The Death before Death, or, The Lesser Nirvana. If he is not willing to die this death he cannot be born again. But if he is willing, his body becomes progressively refined. The light begins to come through at the time of the *Dhikr* and rapture.

This new unknown experience astounds the aspirant. If Allah dwells in his heart now, he thinks, he *is* Allah. But this thought is premature. He is only looking within. He has reached the World of Uniting; but there is a higher stage yet: the intermediary stage is not final, for he is only looking within, and after the state of Ecstasy is over he must return to the world and break up that Union and that Unity. He does not yet see Allah in all things, and all things related to himself – that is the true goal. It is owing to the weakness and agitation of the immediate stages that he often faints and loses consciousness at the *Dhikr*. Therefore, the truly advanced consider these manifestations as signs of weakness, because signs of incompleteness, and of still imperfect attainment.

We may now consider the Seven Stages in detail: they correspond to seven states of the soul, or, more accurately, to the Seven Kinds (*tawr*, *atwar*) of Soul (the Sufi's 'Seven Ages of Man'). For the sake of clearness they may be at once named:

    I. The Soul Depraved (*el-Nafsu-l-Ammara*).
    II. The Soul Accusatory (*el-Nafsu-l-Lawwama*).
    III. The Soul Inspired (*el-Nafsu-l-Mulhama*).
    IV. The Soul Tranquil (*el-Nafsu-l-Mutma'inna*).
    V. The Soul God-Satisfied (*el-Nafsu-l-Radiya*).
    VI. The Soul God-Satisfying (*el-Nafsu-l-Mardiyya*).
    VII. The Soul Clarified, Perfect (*el-Nafsu-l-Safiya wal-Kamila*).

THE FIRST STAGE

THE SOUL DEPRAVED (*el-Nafsu-l-Ammara*).

This Stage is related:
    Of the[13] *Seven Prophets*, to ADAM:
    Of the[13] *Seven Planets*, to the MOON, the ruler of the first Sphere (*falak*)[14]:
    Of the[13] *Seven Texts*[15] to 'PRAISE TO ALLAH THE LORD OF THE WORLDS.'
    Of the[13] *Seven Days*, to the FIRST DAY.
    Of the[13] *Seven Tesserads*, to AaBuJiD.[16]

This Stage is the first of The Law. As its name informs us, it has to

do with the natural, sensual, unruly soul; with man in his unregenerate state in this world, subject to The Law, still ignorant of
The Way, of The Knowledge, and of The Reality. This is the state
of all men, including ordinary Moslems. Therefore is it related to
ADAM, for he was the father of *all men*, and because he first
disobeyed Allah. So, too, it is related to the sentence in the Fatiha,
which says: 'PRAISE BE TO ALLAH, THE LORD OF (ALL)
THE WORLDS'. Also to the MOON, the *lowest* of the Spheres,
the nearest to the Earth, the son of the Earth.[17]

Each Stage has, moreover, a special *Dhikr*, that is to say, the
Word used during that Stage in those repeated ejaculations which
form the most important part of the dervish's spiritual exercises,
and which, as has already been said, are the food of the refining
fire of the soul. The *Dhikr* proper to this first stage is the fundamental Witness of Islam '*There is no god but ALLAH*'. This Word,
moreover, controls the theological teaching proper to the two
Stages of The Law (I. and II.). We shall see how seriously the
wording of this *shahada* becomes modified for the more advanced
stages; but while the Soul is still fleshly, unregenerate, 'depraved',
it is not fit to transcend the traditional wording, with its implied
separation between the Self, the World, and Allah.

He is taught, however, that the words mean:

1 There is no Agent save Allah;
2 There is no Adorand save Allah;
and
3 There is no Existent save Allah.

Before passing from this Stage, the novice must repeat this *Dhikr*
from 100,000 to 300,000 times, according as the sheikh directs.
Between each 100 times he must also repeat the '*Azima*', a prayer
which runs, as follows:

Ilahi azhir 'alayya zahiri
   Bi-sultani La ilaha illa-llah!
Wa haqqiq batini
   Bi; haqa'iqi La ilaha illa-llah
Wa 'hfazni mina-l-balaya wa-l-amrad
   Bi-haqqi La ilaha illa-llah.

> My God, shew to me my outward self
> By the authority of THERE IS NO GOD SAVE ALLAH.
> And certify my inward self
> Of the truths of THERE IS NO GOD SAVE ALLAH.
> And keep me from troubles and sicknesses
> By the truth of THERE IS NO GOD SAVE ALLAH.

Such are the means by which the first part of the regenerative process of the soul is compassed, and its passage through the first ten thousand veils secured. From the ethical point of view, this regenerative process is conceived as, successively, the cutting away of a luxuriant tree of evil qualities; the extirpating of its evil roots; the planting of a new root; and the growing of a new tree of virtues, with branches as luxuriant as the former one. This four-fold process is not completed till the seventh and last Stage, and the contribution made to it by each Stage is fixed and definite.

In this First Stage, then, the tree of the unregenerate Soul Depraved is represented as complete and flourishing from root to outermost twig. Its two *roots* are Lust and Anger. These join into the single trunk of Ignorance, with its constituents, Misbelief, Doubt, Inorthodoxy, Polytheism, and Formalism (*Taqlid*).

Then this trunk branches into the several vices of the Soul Depraved: the central one, continuing the trunk upwards, is Envy; on each side of which are the Two Extremes, whereby the Golden Mean is missed, – Excess (*ifrat*) and Defect (*tafrit*). Then, on each side, come the ramified vices. Thus we have:

Ramifications	Worldliness	Greed / Covetousness / Stinginess
	Hypocrisy	Lying / Treachery
Trunk Contd.	EXCESS ENVY DEFECT	
Ramifications	Pride	Contempt / Dishonouring
	Enmity	Striking / Vengefulness / Hatred / Murder

The clearance of these outward ramifications of evil is the work of the discipline of this First Stage (*el-takhliyatu el-kharijiya*).

THE SECOND STAGE

THE SOUL ACCUSATORY (*El Nafsu-l-lawwama*).
This Stage is related:
Of *the Seven Prophets*, to IDRIS.[18]
Of *the Seven Planets*, to MERCURY[19], the ruler of the Second Sphere.
Of *the Seven Texts* to 'THE MERCIFUL RAHMAN'.
Of *the Seven Days*, to THE SECOND DAY.
Of *the Seven Tesserads, to* HaWuZiH.

The Dhikr for this Stage is simply 'ALLAH'. Before leaving this degree for the next, the aspirant must repeat this 87,084 times, and between each 100 times the following '*azima*'s:

1 La mawjuda siwaka, wa innaka mawjudun haqiqi. There is none other than Thou existent, and verily Thou art an exist-ent that is real.
2 Ilahi! ij'al qalba 'abdika-l-da'ifi mazharan lidhatika wa manba'an li'ayatika, wa-rzuqni bithabati 'ala dhikrika, ya Allah!
     My God, make the heart of thy feeble servant a place of manifestation for Thy Essence, and a place of welling-forth for thy Signs; and grant me to be established in making mention of Thee, O Allah.

In this Stage, the aspirant weeps much; for it is the stage of the Soul Self-accusatory. Its favourite vices are being cut away, the divine love-passion ('*ushq*) is only just beginning. All, therefore, is perplexed, vexed, anguished. The discipline is so severe that the sheikh often sends the aspirant away for a time that the heart may have time to assimilate its discipline. For this discipline is now that of the Inner Clearance (*el-takhliyatu-l-batiniya*). The ramifications of outward vices have already gone, the trunk of

Ignorance is diminished, but the roots, Anger and Lust, still remain, and it is against these inner vices of the heart that the discipline of this Stage is directed.

THE THIRD STAGE

THE SOUL INSPIRED (*El Nafsu-l-Mulhama*).
This Stage is related:
Of *the Seven Prophets*, to NOAH.[20]
Of *the Seven Planets*, to VENUS.[21]
Of *the Seven Texts*, to LORD OF THE DAY OF DOOM.
Of *the Seven Days*, to the THIRD DAY.
Of *the Seven Tesserads*, to TaYuKiL.

The Stages of The LAW are past. The two Stages of The WAY are now entered upon.

The *Dhikr* of this Stage is HU. [HE!]

The *shahada* is now changed from '*There is no God but Allah*', to the second person – '*There is no God but THOU*'. The I stands face to face with the only not-I, Thou! And this the *Dhikr* teaches, for HUWA (HU) is written in Arabic with a circle – thus, does Allah encompass the soul round about.

The extirpating process (*takhliya*) is now over, and positive instruction in love and Divine Passion (*mahabba* and *'ushk*) is given. The aspirant is now taught that forbidden musical instruments and singing are lawful. He recognises that they can be used as a means to engender Spiritual Passion. Further, when he hears the sound of this music it reminds him of the Voice which before the world was asked the question: 'Am I not thy Lord?' At that time the Prophets both saw the Light and heard the Voice; the Saints heard the Voice only; the *Hypocrites* neither saw nor heard, but understood the question; the *Misbelievers* neither heard, saw nor understood. But in this Stage the soul regains that sight – the Faith of Seeing (*iman mar'awi*), as opposed to the Faith of Deductive Proof (*iman istidlali*).

THE FOURTH STAGE

THE SOUL TRANQUIL (*El-Nafsu-l-Mutma'inna*).
This Stage is related:
Of *the Seven Prophets*, to ABRAHAM.[22]
Of *the Seven Planets*, to the SUN.[23]
Of *the Seven Texts*, THEE WE WORSHIP AND OF THEE
WE ASK FOR AID.
Of *the Seven Days*, to the FOURTH DAY.
Of *the Seven Tesserads*, to MaNuSi.

In this Stage the past is finally forgotten; the last vestiges of
Anger and Lust, with Ignorance, disappear, and the first vestiges
of Patience and Temperance (*sabr* and *'iffa*), the twin-roots of the
new tree of virtue, with their stem of Knowledge (*ma'rifa*) appear.
   True virtue thus begins to live. Hence the *Dhikr*, for this Stage is
HAYY! (Living One!).
   For all these reasons the Soul now becomes 'Tranquil'; the
struggle is past. Everything it sees now leads it to Allah, and is not
accompanied by any pain of distracted longing.
   The dervish exercises of self-flagellation and the like are sometimes begun in this Stage; they are the ordeals (*barahin*) of the saint
life. 'If the *Dhikr* (HAYY! Living One!) is operative in the aspirant, no harm will come when the viper bites; the sword does not
hurt when it pierces him; the fire does not burn when it touches
him.' These are the Three Ordeals. Before he touches the fire, for
example, the aspirant says, '*Ya Nar, kuni bardan wa-salama*' (Fire,
be thou Cold and Peace!). And lo, its heat touches him not.

THE FIFTH STAGE

THE SOUL GOD-SATISFIED (*El Nafsu-l-Radiya*).
This Stage is related:
Of *the Seven Prophets*, to MOSES.
Of *the Seven Planets*, to MARS, the ruler of the Fifth Sphere.
Of *the Seven Texts*, to LEAD US IN THE STRAIGHT PATH.
Of *the Seven Days, to the FIFTH DAY.*
Of the Seven Tesserads, to FaSuQiR.

With this stage begins the third of the fourfold division of the Stages, Knowledge (*mar'rifa*). With reason, therefore, is it related to Moses, for he had true Gnosis; he heard the Voice; he saw the *Shechina*-Light. With equal reason is it related to the text, '*Lead us in the Straight Sirat*' (path, or bridge), for with this Stage begins the true bridge to perfection. All that went before was only an external bridge; but now begins the *secret* of Sufism. Now the aspirant begins to know the wiles of The Law, and the secret machinations of The Way (*hiyalu-l-Shari'a wa dasa'isu-l-Tariqa*). Now he begins, by the command of the sheikh, to abandon a part – perhaps a fourth part – of the stated prayers and facts of the Sunnis. Nay, the command of the sheikh is not necessary; the *Dhikr* itself discloses to him (*kashf*) the same secret. For the *Dhikr* for this stage is *Qayyum* (self-subsistent). He has entered upon *Gnosis*, KNOWLEDGE, which embraces this and the following Stages.

The twin roots of Patience and Temperance, with the stem of Knowledge, continue to grow during this Maqam.

This Stage is that of the Soul God-satisfied, indicating a position more stable and positive than the preceding one (the Soul Tranquil).

In the days of this Stage the soul sings to itself, saying:

'Ho, Soul, thou Soul Tranquil! Return unto thy Lord God-satisfied, God-satisfying! Then enter among my servants and enter into my Paradise.'

'*Ya ayyatuha-l-nafsu-l-mutma'inna! Irja'i ila Rabbiki radiyatan mardiyya! Fa-dkhuli fi 'ibadi, wa-dkhuli jannati.*' (Koran, Sura 89. 27).

These words, it will be noticed, link the former, the present, and the succeeding Stages together.

THE SIXTH STAGE

THE SOUL GOD-SATISFYING (*El Nafsu-l-Mardiyya*). This Stage is related:
Of *the Seven Prophets*, to 'ISA EL MASIH (Jesus Christ).[24]
Of *the Seven Planets*, to JUPITER.

Of *the Seven Texts*, to THE PATH OF THE OBJECTS OF
THY GRACE.
Of *the Seven Days*,to the DAY OF ASSEMBLY(Friday)
Of *the Seven Tesserads*, SHaTuTHiKH.

This is a higher Stage than the last, inasmuch as it is better to
realize that one is the object of Allah's satisfaction than that one is
satisfied oneself. And with this realization, the aspirant knows
that he is now free totally to abandon all religious observances,
whether Sunni prayer or Sufi *Dhikr*. He has no further need of
them. Some, however, keep on some of these practices. If he uses
the *Dhikr*, the Name commemorated in it is LATIF! (*Kind!*).

The twin-root of Patience and Temperance is perfected in this
Stage, with the stem of Knowledge. All is, therefore, ready for the
ramification into the full-branched tree of the Final Stage.

THE SEVENTH STAGE

THE SOUL CLARIFIED, PERFECT (*El Nafsu-l-Safiya wa-l-Kamila*).

This Stage is related:
    Of *the Seven Prophets*, to MOHAMMED.
    Of *the Seven Planets*, to SATURN.
    Of *the Seven Texts*, to NOT OF THE OBJECTS OF THY
HATE, NOR OF THEM WHO ARE ASTRAY.
    Of *the Seven Days*, to Saturday.
    Of *the Seven Tesserads*, to DHaDuZiGH.

The Name appropriate to the *Dhikr* of this Stage is El Qahhar (the
Subduer-by-constraint): – for Kindness (*lutf*, see preceding Maqam) is for life; but Constraint is for life's end.

With this Stage is reached THE REALITY – the last of the
four-fold steps. The aspirant has now attained. He relinquishes all
prayer, all fasting, all religious observance whatsoever, for he sees
himself the mirror in which all things are reflected. The Confes-
sion, 'There is no God save Thou,' which superseded 'There is no
God save Allah,' and has held good since the third Maqam, now
gives place to its final transformation:

THERE IS NO GOD SAVE I (*La ilaha illa Ana*).

For the Soul becomes the mirror, the measure of all things. The Permitted and Prohibited (*halal wa haram*) are now superseded and lost, because there is now no such thing for the soul as external prohibition or permission: – all springs of action are from *within*. If he any longer prays, it is not as a duty enjoined by Allah; prayer and no-prayer are one. If he does what is prohibited to others, it is not sin to him; for all things are one, all things are related to his soul and reflected in its mirror.

At the same time, those who attain this Stage do tend, according to their temperaments, either towards the old asceticism (*suhd*) or the new-found freedom and ease (*raha*). The keynote of the action of these latter is freedom of spirit, unlimited by any *legalist* consideration whatsoever, but naturally *self*-limited by what makes for happiness. This is plain when the ramifications of the Tree of Perfection are considered, every branch of which corresponds to one that was formerly destroyed.

The roots, Patience and Temperance lead (we have seen) to the stem Knowledge; from which spring:

Ramifications	Unworldliness (*Tark el Dunya*)	Contentment, Liberality,etc.
	Sincerity (*Ikhlas*)	Friendliness, etc.

Trunk Contd.	MORAL EQUILIBRIUM (*I'tidal*)
	GOODWILL (*Rida*)
	MORAL EQUILIBRIUM (*I'tidal*)

Ramifications	Humility (*Tawadu'*)	Respect, Reverence,etc.
	Love (*Mahabba*)	Gentleness, Forgiveness, etc.

The keynote is, in fact, this moral poise (*I'tidal*), the Golden Mean; just as the keynote of the Soul Depraved was Excess, whether towards Too Much or Too Little (*Ifrat wa Tafrit*). The Sufi must not give too much prominence to any one of these virtues, for that would be to trench on some other one. He does naturally what makes for his own happiness, and that of whomsoever he is dealing with. It is for this reason that *murder*, for example, has no place among his actions, though he is the mirror of all things, not because it is *haram*, or a 'sin', but because it contributes to the happiness of no one. He does not abstain from murder because of any external prohibition, 'Thou shalt do no murder'. Similarly in the case of adultery; for the Sufi the legal has no longer any place at all: therefore there is to him no such thing as marriage – for marriage is legal, and an innovation (*bid'a*) – nor (equally) any such thing as adultery. Both are transcended. The sexual act is in itself good. His relation to it is governed entirely by his own happiness, and that of his partner in the act. The very name adultery becomes entirely unmeaning. When the great Sufi, the Sheikh Junaid el Baghdadi was asked, 'Does the man of Gnosis commit adultery?' he replied, '*Wa kana amru-lla madraq maqdurna*'. 'The affair (or 'the command') of Allah stands a determined determination'.

In the same way, the man of Gnosis does not steal, for how does stealing bring happiness to the man stolen from?

And so for all the actions of life: no outward law regulates the Sufi in regard to them, whether the one way or the other; only the Golden Mean and the General Happiness. In the mirror of his soul all things in heaven and earth are reflected. All things are in him and he in all things. There is no god but he.

APPENDIX I

THE SEVEN TESSERADS

The Arabic alphabet today does not show the original order of the letters – an order which the Arabs took over from the other Semitic peoples (and which underlies, moreover, the order of our own alphabet, which came to us *via* the Romans, *via* the Hellenes, *via* the – ?).

What that order is can be seen by the non-semitist, if he turns to the divisions of the 119th Psalm which, being an acrostic psalm, is divided according to the letters of the Hebrew alphabet.

These letters, however, number 22 only; the Arabs retained this order for their first 22 letters, and strung their remaining 6 on at the end, making 28. This number, itself made up of two mystic numbers, 7 by 4, was of course too good a chance to be lost by the Arab mystic. *Seven* seemed naturally to him to point to the Planetary Spheres, and *Four* equally, of course, to the Four Elements. By writing A B G D and then ranging the remaining letters underneath in fours, he obtained seven words or tesserads, each composed of four letters severally proper to the four elements, and each attributed to one of the seven planetary spheres. Thus:

	FIRE	AIR	WATER	EARTH
El-Qamar (MOON)	A(')	B	G	D
'Utarid (MERCURY)	H	W	Z	H
Zuhra (VENUS)	T	Y	K	L
El-Shams (SUN)	M	N	S	'
Mirrikh (MARS)	F	S	Q	R
El-Mushtari (JUPITER)	SH	T	TH	KH
Zuhal (SATURN)	DH	D	Z	GH

(See Ibn Khaldun, Muqaddima, de Slane's translation, III., pps. 138, 139, with corresponding Arabic text).

The words composed of the above tesserads of consonants were sounded by means of the three vowels (a, u, i), plus the absence-of-vowel sign (·), which in Arabic is ranged with the vowels owing to the equal part it plays with them in syntax. Thus were obtained 'ABUGID·, HAWUZIH· etc.

The passage cited from Ibn Khaldun shows us that mystical[25] use was certainly made of these cabbalistic words (the science of *Simiya*, or mystic names). We may suppose that they typified to them the *fulness* of things (*kamal, pleroma*): – *all* the

Spheres, *all* the Elements, *all* the Consonants, and *all* the Vowels entering into their composition, a convincing orgy of Sevens and Fours, the numbers of heavenly and earthly perfection.

NOTES

1 Or more properly fraternity-house, for the word monastery suggests *celibacy*, which has no essential place in Sufism. Residents at a *takiya* are either unmarried or, if married, are living apart from their wives as long as they reside there.

2 Similarly, we cannot in this article touch upon the missionary aspect of this subject. The relation of Moslem Sufism to Christian evangelism is a subject which calls for a far more complete treatment than it has received.

3 The two brothers have always been inseparable. The following study owes almost as much to the one as to the other.

4 *Al-zaman wal-makan wal-ikhwan.*

5 These four terms have a special significance, which we shall see shortly.

6 The Nakshabandi Way, for example, has but four stages; and we shall see that the last three of the Rifa'ite seven are but expansions of the fourth.

7 In this, as in many other curious details, the reader is reminded that the writer is simply setting down what his Sufi informant told him.

8 See Ghazzali – *Mishkat el Anwar*, p.31,32(Cairo edition).

9 In the literal meaning – re-velation, taking away the veil.

10 *Four* is also a mystic number, signifying the Four Corners of the Earth, the Four Elements, etc. *Seven* is related to the Planet Spheres. *Twelve* to the Zodiacal signs.

11 Original meaning of *latif*, fine.

12 We have already said that *Dhikr* originally means simply the 'mentioning' or the 'commemorating' (the Name of God); hence the multifold ecstatic repetition of the same at the services of the Sufis; and hence those services themselves.

13 It may be said at the outset that the Seven Stages are all severally identified with these Hebdomads. Possibly one could find the *reasons* for all these identifications elaborated somewhere in Sufi books. But such a science does not appear to be part of the regular knowledge of the practising Sufi. The two Sheikhs,Ahmad and Nasimi, did not appear to have any strong convictions on the subject, and showed a disposition to invent reasons on the spur of the moment. Some of their ideas are reproduced in this account; but with this precaution.

APPENDIX II.

A Diagram of the Sevenfold Mystical Way.

	Ist Stage	IInd Stage	IIIrd Stage	IVth Stage	Vth Stage	VIth Stage	VIIth Stage
	El Sharīa THE LAW		*El Tarīqa* THE WAY		*El Ma'rifa* THE GNŌSIS		*El Haqīqa* THE REALITY
	El Nafsu-l-Ammāra The Soul Depraved	*El Nafsu-l-Lawwāma* The Soul Accusatory	*El Nafsu-l-Mulhama* The Soul Inspired	*El Nafau-l-Mutma' inna* The Soul Tranquil	*El Nafau-l-Rādiya* The Soul God-Satisfied	*El Nafau-l-Mardiyya* The Soul God-Satisfying	*El Nafau-l-Sāfiya wal Kāmila* The Soul Clarified, Perfect
El Dhikr The WATCHWORD	*La Ilāha ill' Allah!* There is no God save Allah!	*La Ilāha illā Hā!* There is no God but He!	*Hā!* He!	*Hayy!* Living!	*Qayyum!* Self subsistent!	*Latīf!* Kind!	*Qahhār!* Constrainer!
El Shahāda The CREED	*La ilāha illa-llāh* There is no god save Allah			*La ilāhā illa Anta* There is no god save Thou			*La ilāha illa Ana* There is no god save I
El Nabi The PROPHET	Adam	Idris	Noah	Abraham	Moses	Jesus	Mohammed
El Mathnā The TEXT	*El Hamdu lillah etc.* Praise be to Allah, etc.	*El Rahmān el Rahīm* The merciful Rahmān	*Mālik youm el Din* Lord of the Day of Doom	*Iyyaka na 'budu, etc.* Thee we worship, etc.	*Ihdinā-l-sirat, etc.* Lead us in the way, etc.	*Sirat alladhina, etc.* The way of the objects of Thy Grace	*Ghairi-l-maghdūb: etc.* Not of the objects of Thy Hate, etc.
El Falak The PLANET-SPHERE	*El Qamar* The Moon	*Utārid* Mercury	*Zuhra* Venus	*El Shams* The Sun	*Mirrīkh* Mars	*El Mushtari* Jupiter	*Zuhal* Saturn
El Youm The DAY	First-day	Second-day	Third-day	Fourth-day	Fifth-day	Assembly Day	Rest Day
El Ahruf The TESSERAD	ABUJID	HAWUZIH	TAYUKIL	MANUSI	FASUQIR	SHATUTHIKH	DHADUDZIGH
El Hujub The VEILS	Thirty-five Thousand Dark Veils				Thirty-five Thousand Light Veils		
	EXOTERIC				ESOTERIC		

14 The old cosmology of the Seven Planetary Sphere or Heavens which as *cosmology* underlay *all* ancient thought, and as *astrology* affected, apparently, most mystic thought: is prominent here, too. Until, however, the connexion of Sufism with astrological ideas is studied, it will be impossible to define the precise significance of this Hebdomad of the Spheres as one of the correlations of the Sevenfold Way. Ibn Khaldun emphatically and expressly asserts the repugnance of Sufism and astrology proper (see App.I). The two sheikhs, Ahmad and Nasimi, seemed to have no formed ideas on the subject.

15 *Mathani*, the seven clauses into which the Fatiha is divided.

16 A word made up of the first four of the (7 by 4 = 28) letters of the old Arabic alphabet, combined with the four vocal signs: see Appendix I.

17 No reason to think that we have here a lucky hit at the modern theory of the budding off of the moon from the molten earth! 'Son of' in the East only means 'specially related to.'

18 'Idris' – *Kathiru-l-dars*. There is much studying (*dars*) in this stage.

19 For Mercury is of a mixed nature, like the soul in this Stage, with the unfavourable aspect predominating.

20 For the former Stages were like a Flood of error and iniquity; and this Stage is like the Ark of rescue therefrom.

21 Because the influence of this Star is also mixed, but good (*su'ud*) predominates.

22 The Sufis believe that Abraham underwent the discipline of the Forty Days, when the Idolaters occupied the holy Kaaba at Mecca, and by that discipline's merit overcame them. Thus he obtained the Soul Tranquil.

23 For now the Light comes out full for the first time. In the course of this Middle Stage the 35,000 dark veils are left behind.

24 For Allah exhibited His Glory on him more than on Moses, insomuch as some thought that the godhead had manifested itself in him; whereas it really is manifested in all.

25 *Not* magical, he is careful to inform us, (op.cit., p.140). He laboriously demonstrates that a Cabbala is *not* the same as a Talisman.

KEY CONCEPTS IN SUFI UNDERSTANDING

edited by
Professor Hafiz Jamal

Those Astonishing Sufis

ADILBAI KHARKOVLI

The great decade of interest and experiment, featuring Eastern religions and strange practices, has come and gone, leaving a curious detritus of beliefs, myths, practices and disillusioned seekers-after-knowledge scattered from California to Kathmandu. It has fulfilled two obvious functions: things ranging from vegetarianism to mystical chants, formerly the preserve of odd local cults and weird societies of often less than balanced people, have become known to a tremendous mass of people. The new fads, like flying saucers, have been linked with the old ones, like ancient Chinese fortune-telling books; imitation Indians (both Hindu and Redskin) are still to be found; books on magic and miracles sell by the hundred thousand. And, as a perhaps beneficial spin-off, many cults have been exposed for what they are – very often groups which attract the unbalanced and unbalance those prone to such directions.

Reading the literature and talking to a wide variety of thinking people, one sees that a single facet of this explosion of interest has been the most dramatic, yet the most elusive. This is the revelation, to the people of the East and the West, of the riches of investigation and experience locked within the literature and practices of a body of people who have been called, for the past thousand and a half years, the Sufis.

Nobody knows when or where this movement started. Its foremost theoreticians give such varying answers to the question that there can now be little doubt that they deliberately confuse any effort to trace their knowledge further than they want it to go. We know the names and much about the lives and doings of an astonishing number and variety of their sages: from Spain and Morocco to India, from what is now the Soviet Union to the middle of Africa. But as soon as you try to piece together exactly what they are doing and why – and how – you come across insuperable obstacles. Theirs undeniably is a secret which is kept in the most effective of all ways: by showing themselves and then proliferating their materials to such an extent that the conventional thinker or researcher will be unable to find characteristic traces from which he can deduce a general theory.

There are many people who take this variety and depth as the evidence of the authenticity of the endeavour. Certain it is that there is no other community which has been able to operate in this way – for all others have been compelled by social and other pressures to ossify their dogmas and to declare their principles, often in so narrow a way as to proclaim their limitations to an almost laughable extent.

But experience of true Sufi groups does reveal that the things which other systems regard as primary, central are found among the Sufis as peripheral or transitory, secondary. This idea, again, is so startling and indeed so beguiling that some have found in it a proof of the legitimacy of the Sufi approach. The Sufis themselves say that all true systems started by the use, by a skilled individual, of rituals and methods which were applied as required. Almost all of them, they continue, degenerate into mimes. Among them are the majority of the spiritual systems known at the present day, as well as traditional medicine, ideologies and social institutions.

Concealment and elective operation, then, may be taken as the hallmarks of the Sufi. What have they in common which might help us to make a link? Well, if it is true that the Sufi has a skill which has to be exercised in accordance with conditions and the state of his pupil, it would seem likely that he would 'conceal' a great deal from that pupil's curiosity for information about origins and so on. If, say, a surgeon were to operate upon you, or a doctor prescribe a treatment, neither would encourage your interfering with the process by constant enquiries about the history of his skill. That this is the probable basis of much of the Sufi mystery seems probable when we look at what the Sufis themselves say about it. 'Sufism,' they say, 'is activity, not theory'.

This activity, they continue, can take almost any form.

Sufi activity familiar to a vast and growing audience is found in the form of tales told by Sufis. They may appear didactic, caution-ary or humorous, or downright mysterious. A study of these tales and what Sufis themselves say about them reveals, however, something which is seldom suspected. People try to use them in customary ways – to penetrate their meaning or to allow them to act on them, or to relate them to something already known, and so on – but their use is otherwise. The tales are there to prepare the mind for further understanding, not to give any understanding which the pupil can perceive; and they are also designed, especially in the mass, to baffle in part, so that the learner will admit that he cannot understand, and will therefore apply to the teacher for real teaching. They are, in this latter role, the goad which takes the individual to the teacher.

Thus the Sufi story is designed to help overcome unperceived assumptions. The assumption in most cases is that the learner can learn unaided.

Similarly, Sufi assignments, whether they be manual labour or working on exercises, contain the element least suspected by the student: the one whereby he comes to a realisation that perception comes *beyond* activity. When Sufis report results of enterprises, spiritual exercises, formulae or even doing gardening chores for their master, it is to be noted that these developments do not come during the activity, but invariably after it. This is underlined by hints from Sufi sources that the ordinary 'self' as experienced by most people, stands in the way of self-realization. Only a fatiguing of this secondary self makes it possible for the subtler impulses to be perceived by the primary self; and then only when this is done as a part of a programme planned and carried out by a real teaching master, not by imitation.

Sufi stories and Sufi activities, therefore, both contain the effec-tive function of blocking the working of the would-be analytical mind and the grosser self, as a preparation for higher insight.

These conceptions, the Sufis aver, lie at the root of all genuine traditions; but, as in the case of the deterioration into ritualism already noted, they have become ossified by tradition in all other systems to mere repetition, disguised entertainment and emotionality.

Sufi mystery attracts people with an over-developed taste for it, as the Sufis themselves admit. They insist, however, that the fact of mystery brings out this proclivity and enables the Sufi to diagnose it and consequently to subtract such people from his following. Read any collection of real Sufi stories and you will see how frequently this is done. Again, the instrumental function of Sufi literature, when revealed, annoys a large proportion of superficialists, and this in turn helps the Sufi to shed them by performing what is nowadays called 'aversion-therapy'. The effect of fanaticism to destroy a person's sense of humour is well known. The Sufis make use of this, too, in their insistence that those interested in their Way should study and understand jokes and humorous recitals. This causes useless people, the kind of mind which cannot really approach the Sufi truth, to shun the Sufis, thus pleasing both parties.

Self-realization is the Sufi goal. What is this self and how is it realized? First, the Sufis are operating in the field of religion: which means that they are committed to belief in a meaning for human life, the existence of a divine power and a transmission of the knowledge of that meaning, that power and certain opportunities for mankind.

It has been said that there is no human community yet known which has no religious system. Certain it is that everyone who comes across the Sufi activity in any form will relate it to what he (or she) already assumes to be religion; or, more likely, the real religion. A study of the words and doings of the Sufis, however, seems to show that they will at one point appear to be supporting the local religious expression, and at another opposing it. The confusion arises simply because the Sufis are teaching, not promoting beliefs. Where their teaching accords with local beliefs, they will appear to support these; where it deviates, it will appear to oppose the religious structure of belief.

The Sufis themselves are frequently on record as teaching in this vein: though their attitude is generally expressed in terms which were better understood in the past. As an example, the phrase 'Sufism is the inner aspect of religion' can quite easily be seen as meaning: 'Sufi teachings, over a period of time, become covered by social, emotional and other accretions which are stabilized into religions. The living tradition of the Sufis, however, continues. Viewed from the religionist's standpoint, of course, the Sufi element is the inward component, and the rest is the balance of the religion.'

Put even more succinctly, the Sufi is saying: 'Sufism is a teaching designed to re-establish a link of humanity with the divine. From time to time this is revitalised when religious systems have become too covered with accretions to operate as teaching entities and have subsided into organisations of social action, power-seeking or mere panoply.'

This emphasis is strongly to be noted in the words of a Sufi who has said: 'The harmonization of the inward part of humanity, the Real Self, with the Ultimate Truth is actually *disturbed* when the social or emotional activity becomes too strong. The coarse drives out the finer.'

Hence when the Sufi says: 'People do not want to learn, they want to feel', he is referring to this degenerative trend, the dilution of the spiritual dimension by too much sentiment, ritualism and so on.

He does not mean that people should not feel and should learn instead. He means that feeling is not learning, and that people should at some point arrive at the capacity to distinguish between them.

Seen in this way, the Sufi analysis of human confusion and lack of awareness of perception being distinct from emotion is so very modern in tone that it has both been misunderstood in the past and not even caught up with in the present. Sufis have been regarded as promoters of generosity as a virtue because they decry miserliness. But few observers have noted that the Sufi encouragement of generosity is a means to an end, not an end in itself. The end is that, in Sufi assertion, miserliness is harmful to deeper perceptions, generosity is the way leading to a development of much higher capacity. Generosity has a social and emotional value. Beyond it lies a spiritual triumph.

Introducing such a concept – reintroducing it would be a better term – among contemporary human communities where it is believed that doing good is a key to heaven, not a way of opening a path to understanding, is an uphill task and not one which is rewarded by the community or its institutions. All societies, including 'modern' and 'free' ones, have their blinkers. There is no law or secret police which prevents people from examining such options as the Sufis offer. There is an even more effective mechanism: that of the culture itself, which offers no inducement to look at things with which it has almost never concerned itself.

It cannot be denied that the Sufis have a defensible point of view when they say that the norms, customs and principles which are commonly employed to establish and to maintain human communities may have their limitations. It is a commonplace to observe the ultimately destructive effect of 'principles' carried to excess, even to extremes. As a contemporary Sufi puts it: 'The difference between a democrat and a Sufi is that the democrat says, with Winston Churchill, "Democracy is not perfect, but it is the best system which we have"; while the Sufi says, "Keep it if it works, but work your very hardest to find the perfect: otherwise you are a disguised pessimist".'

Since all other human associations depend for their ultimate effect and solidity upon the community spirit and transference of emotions from one person to another, people who join Sufi groups soon find themselves disorientated. At first they may find friends, and are then told that the purpose of the group includes not avoiding friendship, but realising its limitations so that something higher may be attained. Only too often they find this very hard to understand. Like the 'democrats', they have been taught that there *is* nothing higher than friendship. The effect of this belief (unsupported though it may be) is to regard anyone questioning it as attacking the institution itself. But the Sufi, to quote another master, is in reality saying: 'Friendship is certainly needed and wonderful. But its place in higher perceptions is another matter'.

One student who spent many years among Sufis in the East and the West has noted that members often complain that they 'never seem to get anywhere'. It was three decades before he discovered that those who do indeed 'get somewhere' always say that they have not learned anything. The reason for this is not to disturb those still waiting to be selected for special training: those not yet 'ripe'. In the past it has been assumed that Sufis say that there is nothing to be gained from Sufism to deter curiosity-mongers or to discourage unsuitable applicants. The real reason, however, is mainly to preserve the laggards from anxiety which disturbs their concentration.

There are, it is true, Sufis who go by the name of *Malamati* ('the people of blame') who deliberately incur opprobrium and bad reputations so as to avoid the invasion of hypocrites and poseurs, and sometimes, too, to have their resilience tested, but these are a different case.

Another revelation about the Sufis recently recorded by an investigator renders many outsiders' opinions and assessments of them virtually useless. This is the study, made by Alexander Dixon, of the Sufis' habit of attacking fixed ideas. People hear – and read – of Sufis opposing this opinion or that, removing or assailing beliefs and practices so that the onlookers assume that the Sufi in question is 'against' this religion or that, this person or that one, this idea or that. But a close examination of the content of the words and actions of a number of Sufis over a long period revealed that the attacks served to soften up the fixations, reduce the dependence upon prejudice and ingrained affirmation on many levels and divers directions, which themselves render minds inflexible and inefficient. Very often this technique is carried out in a 'shock' manner, when the most dearly-loved assumptions of the student are contradicted head-on. Many devices are employed to cause this effect. Sufi jokesters, conjurers and even snake-handlers 'defy reason' by applying a shock through their performances, thus liberating 'congealed attention' which has all but paralysed the effective mentation of the victims. This pro-cedure is so little known in most societies that it is in general confined by interest-groups to purveying their own contradictions of others' beliefs. The Sufis take it to the degree of a fine art. In so doing, of course, many of them have gained reputations as mis-chief-makers or irrationals. This is because someone who is op-posing a belief which is greatly cherished gets the former name, and someone who seems to contradict himself from one moment to another, the latter. Of one eminent contemporary Sufi, for instance, it is often said that he cannot make up his mind whether he likes or dislikes a certain book, whether he is for or against certain prejudices. People simply have not noticed that he is working against fixations wherever he finds them. His own opinions are not involved. For this latter reason, of course, Sufis have been called 'objective', though few people seem to realise the extent to which this objectivity is carried on.

The Sufis, then, are quite astonishing in their behaviour and supposed ideas if they are looked at from conventional, or even from unlikely, points of view. You can only understand what the Sufis are doing if you have the requisite perception or, in a smaller way, information.

To summarise, we can only examine their activities with any hope of success if we note that they are not interested in externals, and if we remember that externals are the major source of stimu-lus to most other people. Again, we have to accept that they claim that emotional stimulus has a place and that that place is not always where we, from custom and training, imagine it to be. Thirdly, our fixation on history or personalities is held by Sufis to be a barrier to understanding, if carried too far: and they show quite clearly that they hold that we *do* carry it too far, thus attenuating the chances of our own progress.

Further, the idea of elective operation: teaching people at the right time and place and in the right manner and company, with its corollary that teaching may take almost any form; these items are so far removed from the mechanical approach to religion and cults within our civilization that it may well be beyond the grasp of most people to visualise such a system without a great effort.

The question of Sufi tales and other literature as containing a preparation ingredient, and not simply being there to produce belief or disbelief, not there for cultural colouring, not there for their externals: these concepts require a good deal of digesting before even the most intelligent individual can take advantage of whatever dynamic they might contain.

The employment of certain techniques – such as frustrating the intellectual approach, or increasing bafflement to focus attention upon the teacher and his ability to point the way – these are aspects of Sufi operation which, even in a modern sophisticated society, we have not yet learned to handle. As for the contention that real, and higher, perceptions, come *after* carrying on activities, and not necessarily as part and parcel of them: this needs the most careful attention. The function of mystery to cause mystery-minded people to reveal themselves and hence make it possible for them to be dealt with is more readily understandable, and probably provides one of the paths to understanding the Sufi mentality. Similar techniques, for instance in eliciting forms of behaviour in order to study their bases, exist in modern psychology – however unexpected it may be to encounter them in 'ancient' lore like that of the Sufis.

The equation of humour with frivolity and hence lack of 'seriousness' is more difficult for us to understand. But if it is true that our culture has lost its way in labelling humour as superficial or unimportant, we shall have to understand it sooner or later. The contention about re-establishing a contact between a human 'real self' and the Divine is also easy enough for us to grasp in theory, though the realization that what we have assumed to be the major 'self' might in fact turn out to be at least in part a social artefact, might be more difficult to swallow even theoretically, for members of a culture that at least until recently has assumed that it is superior to all others precisely because it has taken such an interest in this secondary self as the primary aspect of man.

That teaching is different from promoting beliefs is a well-known concept in modern culture, and the Sufis should have little difficulty in persuading us of its importance. The only problem here is that our way of thinking, while admitting that teaching should be free from bias, inwardly insists that this does not apply in religion. This startling evidence of internalized regulation has not yet been absorbed by Western society, though it has been pointed out often enough during the past few decades.

The conception that 'Sufism is the inner component of religion', too, should be acceptable enough if it is seen from enough examples that religion is often mainly an accretion of superficialities around an ancient core which may be reclaimed; but the corollary, that 'social and emotional activity actually *disturbs* higher perceptions' is unlikely to pass unchallenged, especially by those who believe themselves to be imbibing spirituality with every prayer or operatic aria. Naturally, such people will be less likely to assail this contention than to ignore it, to the detriment of future valuable research on the subject.

The much-repeated theory (for we can see it only on that level until it is verified by experience) that 'virtues' are not keys to heaven but essential steps which clear the way to higher understanding, is perhaps the most attractive of all the Sufi statements. There has always been, both in the East and the West, an uneasiness about believing that something done from fear or hope should be rewarded by paradise; or that ordinary human duties, carried out even by the most primitive peoples, should be represented as things which a highly-evolved religious system proclaims as part of advanced religious thinking.

This involves, of course, rethinking many of the values to see whether they are not, indeed, pitched at too low a level, rather than, as fashionable theoreticians affirm, too high. 'The best that we have' in institutions may be insufficient, not a matter for self-congratulation. This applies to the various forms of human relationship which have been in the past regarded as sublime, but which research might well show to confirm the Sufi claim that they are valuable but only on a lower level.

The Sufi habit of dissimulation ('I haven't learnt anything') does take some integrating into our way of thought, even if only because the book-bound individual, the theorist and historian, will now have to re-examine his materials to determine whether something was indeed said at some time because it represented the beliefs or feelings of someone, or whether it was said for another reason. But we can only gain if we find in the end that people whom we imagined to be contradicting themselves were only shifting ground to look at things from different perspectives, or only attacking fixed ideas, which, surely, we are united in realising to be of increasing peril to the human race.

The General Principles of Sufism

SIRDAR IKBAL ALI SHAH*

He that is purified by love is pure; and he that is absorbed in the Beloved and hath abandoned all else is a Sufi.

Of the many mystical doctrines to which our mother the East has given birth, none is more beautiful in its appeal than the way of the Sufi, nor does any point to a goal of more exalted spiritual ambition. He who is versed in its tenets and practice has out-soared the shadow of doubt and the possibility of error. He is face to face with the Divine. Many esoteric systems lay claim to such a consummation, but none with more justice than Sufism; for the disciplinary and preparatory measures it entails are of a kind to induce in the devotee an understanding that the ultimate goal to which he aspires will be triumphantly achieved.

Sufism as an organised Islamic school dates from the latter part of the eleventh century, and its projection through esotericist groups was founded by a branch of that sect community in Islam known as Ismaelis headed by Hassan Sabah, who, driven from Cairo by the persecution of the orthodox, spread a modified form of the Ismaeli doctrine throughout Syria and Persia. He was, indeed, a member of the great and mystical Western Lodge of the Ismaelis at Cairo, the early history of which is one of romantic and absorbing interest. It comprised both men and women, who met in separate assemblies, and it was presided over by a *Dai al Doat*, or chief missionary, who was usually a person of importance in the State. The assemblies, called Societies of Wisdom, were held

*Previously published in the *Hibbert Journal* 20 (1921–1922) pp 524-35, revised.

twice a week, and at these gatherings all the members were clad in robes of spotless white. This organisation was under the especial patronage of the Caliph (successor of the Prophet), to whom the lectures read within its walls were invariably submitted; and it was in the reign of the Caliph Haken-bi-emr-illah that steps were first taken to enlarge its scope and institute what might be called a forward movement for the dissemination of its particular principles.

So that it should not lack suitable surroundings, the Caliph erected a stately edifice known as the *Dar al hikmat*, or House of Wisdom. Within its walls a magnificent library was installed, and writing materials and mathematical instruments were supplied for the use of all. Professors of law, mathematics, rhetoric, and medicine were appointed to instruct the faithful in the sciences. The annual income assigned to this establishment by the munificence of the Caliph was two hundred and seventy thousand ducats, worth some $150 million. A regular course of instruction in mystic lore was given to the devotees, and nine degrees had to be passed through before they were regarded as masters of the mysterious knowledge gained within the walls of the House of Wisdom. It was in the seventh of these stages that the doctrines of Sufism were more particularly taught, projected beyond ordinary education.

But Hassan, a man of great natural force and enlightenment, saw clearly that the plan of the society of Cairo was in some respects defective. His novel views did not, however, meet with the approval of the other leaders; and he retired to Persia, where he remodelled the course of instruction, reducing the number of initiatory degrees to seven, and instituting a much more rigorous system of discipline. Around the figure of Hassan cluster many legends and traditions, most of which have been highly coloured by the passage of time. The Ismaeli School deteriorated when it became a personality-cult. It still survives as a minor sect.[1]

We may now seek for some general definition of the doctrine, such as will make clear to us its purpose and significance – the message it holds for the mystic and for humanity in general. It exhibits a close connection with the Neo-Platonism of Alexandria, with which it certainly had affinities, in that it regards man as a spark of the divine essence, a 'broken light' from the great Sun of our being, the most central and excellent radiance from which all things emanate. The soul of man is seen as being in exile from its Creator, who is not only the author of its being, but also its spiritual home. The human body is the cage or prison-house of the soul, and life on earth is regarded as banishment from God. Ere this ostracism from the Divine took place, full communion with the Creator was enjoyed.

Each soul has formerly seen the face of Truth in its most real aspect, for what we regard as truth in the earth-sphere is but the shadow of that which shines above, perfect, immaculate – a mere reminiscence of the glories of a heavenly existence. To regain this lost felicity is the task of the Sufi, who, by a delicate process of mental and moral training, restores the soul from its exile, and leads it onward from stage to stage, until at last it reaches the goal of perfect knowledge. Truth and Peace – reunion with the Divine.

As an example of the Sufi doctrine of the immanence of God in creation, an ancient manuscript tells us how the Creation proceeds directly from God.

'The Creation,' it says, 'derives its existence from the splendour of God; and as at dawn the sun illuminates the earth, and the absence of its light is darkness, in a like manner all would be non-existent if there were no celestial radiance of the Creator diffused in the universe. As the light of the sun bears a relation to the temporal or the perceptible side of life, so does the splendour of God to the celestial or hidden phase of existence.'

And what words could be more eloquently illustrative of the belief that the present life is banishment of the soul from God, than those of a great Asian Sufi, who on his death-bed wrote the following lines:

'Tell my friends when bewailing that they disbelieve and discredit the Truth.
You will find my mould lying, but know it is not I. I roam far, far away, in the Sphere of Immortality. This was once my house, my covering, but not my home.

It was the cage: the bird has flown.
It was the shell: the pearl has gone.
I leave you toiling and distraught. I see you struggling as I
   journey on.
Grieve not if one is missing from amongst you.
Friends, let the house perish, let the shell decay.
Break the cage, destroy the garment, I am far away.
Call this not my death. It is the life of life, for which I
   wearied and longed.'

There are now four stages through which the Initiate must pass
on his way to perfection and reunion with the Divine Essence; four
veils that must be lifted ere his vision is purged of the grimness of
the earth-sphere and he is granted the final wonder and bliss of
coming face to face with Truth Eternal.

The first of these stages is known as *Nasut*, or Humanity. The
essential of proper observance in this phase, and the mere approach or avenue to the temple of Sufism, is the faithful observance of the tenets of Islam, its laws and ceremonies. This
preliminary course is regarded as a necessary discipline for the
weaker brethren, and as a wholesome restraint upon those who
may be constitutionally unfitted to attain the heights of divine
contemplation. Latitude in matters of discipline in the earlier
stages frequently leads to evils which cease to trouble more powerful intellects and devouter souls as they gain the higher levels, so
that in a later phase the trammels of ritual observance and symbolic recognition can be cast aside and aspiration remain
unfettered.

The second stage is called *Tariqat*, or the manner of attaining
what is known as *Jubrut* or Potentiality of Capacity. Here the
neophyte dispenses with his guide and becomes a Sufi. It is
frequently asserted that in this stage the pilgrim may, if he
chooses, lay aside all the external forms of religion, its rites and
observances, and exchange mere worship for the delights of contemplation. But more than one of the masters contests this view,
refusing to recognise the freedom of the novice from religious
forms, no matter to what degree of advancement he may have

attained. There remains, however, a certain school, the members of which, though admitting that purity can be acquired in the first instance through the constant practice of orthodox austerities alone, assert that it cannot permanently be retained unless mere forms be transcended and outgrown.

The third stage, *Araff*, signifies that a condition of assured knowledge or inspiration has been reached, which occultists might call a condition of adeptship, or Buddhists Arahatship. The eyes of the pilgrim have become opened; he has gained possession of supernatural and inward knowledge, and is the equal of angels. Edgar Allan Poe alludes in one of his most wonderful poems, 'Al Aaraaf', to a mystical star, which he calls by this name, and which he speaks of as a plane higher than this world and not nearly so material.

> Oh! nothing earthly, save the ray
> (Thrown back from flowers) of Beauty's eye,
> As in these gardens where the day
> Springs from the gems of Circassy.
> Adorn you, world, afar, afar,
> The wandering star.

Lastly – but this is remote and to be gained by the exalted in purity and holiness alone – is the stage of Haqiqat, or Truth, perfect and supreme, for the union of the soul with Divinity is now complete. It is to be won only by long-continued meditation, constant prayer, and complete severance from all things gross and earthly, for the man must be annihilated ere the saint can exist. The fire, Qalb or steps of Heart (Dil), Breath (Nafs), the Rest of Soul (Sir), Head (Ikhfa), and Crown and the Head (Khafi) have been climbed, and he who was a scholar is now qualified to become a master.

In order that this condition or state of exalted holiness may best be brought about, the life of the hermit is temporarily resorted to; and many, to attain it, retire into the gloomy solitude of the jungle or seek the quiet of desert fastnesses, or dwell in caves situated in the heart of almost inaccessible mountains. This devotion and singleness of purpose is, indeed, characteristic of Sufism. But such a life, spent in prayer and meditation, conduces to the acquisition of wisdom as well as moral exaltation, and many of the most renowned Sufis have been men of the highest erudition. Scholarship of the right kind is regarded as predisposing a man for the life of the Sufi. The philosophic temperament and the power of penetrating into the mysteries of the Divine Nature are often found in one and the same person.

A tendency towards studious things raises a man above the level of the vulgar herd and prompts him to seek the higher excellences of holiness. It has been so in all times and in all faiths. Are not the ascetics of all religions habitually studious? And whence, it may be asked, has so much light been thrown on things spiritual as from the cave of the mystic, or the desert abode of the Sufi?[2]

The poet, especially, is looked upon as the type of man who may best develop into a Sufi of great sanctity. Poetry, indeed, may lead to the very essence of Sufism. The genius of the poet is akin to religious inspiration. The long flights by which he penetrates to the highest realms beyond the imagination are of the same nature as those by which the mystic reaches the gates of the Palace of Life and Wisdom. In the throes of his rapture, the poet transports himself into the heavenly empyrean, his wings bear him into that rare atmosphere where he can see face to face with the Divine Cause and Origin of all.

Sufism has a poetry all its own – a poetry regarded by many, whether Sufis or not, as more soulful and higher in ecstatic expression than that of any other religious activity in the world. Again, the language of poetry – its metaphor, its swift and pulsing rhythm – is more akin to the speech of the mystic than the grosser language of the sons of earth. It is not restrained by convention or the fetters of idiom. It soars supreme above the faltering, stammering necessities of the earth-speech.

Hence in Central Asia, the true home of modern Sufism, as elsewhere, we find Sufi devotion often expressed through the cadences of poetry. Nor do the services of poetry to Sufi mysticism end with its provision of a more fitting medium of expression, for in Sufi verse the constant repetition of mystical allusion and religious allegory serves to conceal from the profane the hidden meaning of the experience – those deep and awful truths which it is not well that the vulgar should know (for their perceptions would distort it) and which, at all costs, must be guarded by the adept from profanation.

That the inner significance of Sufi mysticism may be the more closely shut off from possible dilution, the language of eroticism and excess is frequently employed in its strophes to conceal hidden meanings. This has, perhaps naturally, resulted in a charge of luxury being brought against the Sufi literature as a whole. Nothing could be further from the truth. Scandalised by the interpretation placed upon the sacred writings by the ignorant, the Great Mughal Aurangzeb, himself a Sufi of exalted degree and a moralist of the strictest tendencies, decreed that the poems of Hafiz and Jami should be perused only by those who were sufficiently advanced in spiritual understanding to appreciate the works of these poets at their proper worth. The great mass of people in India had misunderstood the metaphors and figures of the Persian singers; and their songs, he learned, were even regarded as provocative of immorality. Let it be admitted, too, that even Eastern supposed mystics, mere emotionalists, have misinterpreted the metaphorical expressions in which these poems abound. Speaking generally, it is the dark riddle of human life which the Sufi poet veils beneath the metaphor of physical love and the agony of parted lovers. By such means he symbolises the banishment of the human soul from its Eternal Lover. The pain of earthly parting is merely a synonym for the deep anguish of the spirit estranged from its Creator. The wine-cup, again, and the language of debauch, are metaphors which signify the rapture of the soul which is drunken with the love of God.

We must here lay stress upon the great central doctrine of Sufism that the human soul is one in essence with the Divine. The difference is one of degree and not of kind. However much men may differ from Divinity, they are, after all, particles of the Divine Being, broken lights of God, as Tennyson so beautifully says, and will ultimately be re-absorbed in the Great Cause which projected them into the darksome regions of the earth-plane. God is uni-

versal. He interpenetrates all matter, all substance. Perfect in His
truth, goodness, and beauty, they who love Him alone know the
real fullness of love. Mere physical love is an illusion, a seeming, a
snare to the feet and an enemy in the path.

The great mirror in which the Divine splendour reflects itself is
nature. From the beginning of things, ay, from the first, it has been
the task of the Supreme Goodness to diffuse happiness among
those fitted to receive it. Thousands ignore it, mistaking the
pomps and pleasures of earth for joy, rejecting the greater bliss to
their hands.

In many faiths we hear of a covenant betwixt God and man.
This is also the Sufi creed. That covenant has been broken by the
sin of the creature against his Creator. Only when man once more
finds reunion with God shall he be restored to his ancient privi-
leges of full and unalloyed fellowship with the Divine. This alone
is true happiness. The pursuit of the material is a vain thing. As
Longfellow says:

'Things are not what they seem.'

Nature, the earth, that which we see, feel, and hear, are but the
subjective visions of God, suggested to our minds by the great
Artist. Mind or Spirit alone is immanent. The fleeting phantoms
thrown by the phantasmagoria of matter we must beware of. We
must attach ourselves to none of their manifestations. God alone is
the one real existence, the only great Reality. He exists in us and
we in Him. The visions He grants us, the pictures He casts upon
the screen of our imagination, we may use as a means of approach
to the Eternal Beauty, to the consideration of the Divine. They are
what Wordsworth calls 'Intimations of Immortality'. As a great
Frenchman once said, we weep when we listen to beautiful music,
our eyes fill with tears on looking at a great picture or noble statue.
A wonderful prospect in nature affects us in like manner. Where-
fore? We weep because we feel that these things are but shadows of
the real, the imperishable beauty which we have lost, and which
we will not regain until we are once more made one with God.
That Frenchman would have found in Sufism the complement,
the ideal, of his philosophy.

The microcosmos, or small world, said the great Paracelsus, one of the most learned Europeans of the sixteenth century, who had travelled widely in the East, was but the reflection of the macrocosmos or great world above – the spiritual world, which mirrored itself in the plane below. To him the illusory and phantasmal nature of the sphere in which we dwell was very plain. Indeed, no European mystic of old could possibly have found anything at which he could have demurred in the tenets of Sufism. In my opinion, Western as well as Oriental mysticism is heavily indebted to the Sufi philosophy, and those who believe in one must naturally believe in both.

It requires a mind of the first rank to recognise the great scheme of God at first sight. Few minds succeed in doing so. With most persons, long experience is needed ere they appreciate the marvellous arch-plan of the Almighty. To a mind naturally pure and angelic this wondrous cosmic symphony is apparent from the first. It was so to Mohammed, to Boehme, to Swedenborg, to Blake. What is man, after all, but the cloak of the soul? When we say that a man is 'naturally bad', we allude to the state of his inherited mind, not to his soul. The garment may be ragged, dross may cover the gold, but it is there all the same. Our bodies are of the earth and such as our fathers leave us. Our souls are of God. O man! is there aught that, possessing the friendship of God, thou canst not compass? Doth not thy soul strain to Him as the mountains strain unto the sun and the waters of the sea unto the moon? Verily thou dost move forth in the light of His strength, in the unquenchable brilliance of His boundless majesty, as a great star, lit by the beams of a still greater sun, launches forth into the million-lamped avenues of the night. As a ship is moved by the bright waves of the morning, so art thou urged by the breath of His spirit. Verily thou art of God as a child is of its father. What then hast thou to fear, O son of such a Father?

With such a hope before us – before every one of us, if we accept it – we must turn our souls from vanity, from all that is not of God, striving to approximate to His perfection and discover the secret of our kinship with Him, until at last we reach the happy consummation of union with the Divine. The Sufi doctrine tells us that at the moment of the creation of each creature a divine voice was heard asking the question, 'Art thou not with God? Art thou not bound by solemn covenant with thy Creator?' and each created spirit replied 'Yes,' as it stood in the presence of the Almighty Himself. Hence it is that the mystic words, *Alastu*, 'Art thou not,' and *bala*, 'Yes,' occur so frequently in Sufi poetry. For example, Rumi began his celebrated Masnawi, which I have ventured to render into English verse, as follows:

THE FLUTE
'Oh! hear the flute's sad tale again:
Of Separations I complain;
E'er since it was my fate to be
Thus cut off from my parent tree,
Sweet moan I've made with pensive sigh,
While men and women join my cry.
Man's life is like this hollow rod;
One end is in the lips of God,
And from the other sweet notes fall
That to the mind the spirit call,
And join us with the All in All.'

A regular vocabulary of the terms employed by the Sufis in their mystical poetry exists. Wine, for example, signifies devotion; sleep, meditation on the divine perfection; perfume, the hope of the divine afflatus. Zephyrs signify the gift of godly grace, and kisses the transports of devotion and piety. But the terms of significance are often inverted, in order that they may not be comprehended by the profane. Thus idolaters, free-thinkers, and revellers are the terms employed to indicate those whose faith is of the purest description. The idol they adore is the Creator Himself; the tavern is the place of prayer; and the wine drunk therein is the holy beverage of love, with which they become inebriated. The keeper of the tavern is the hierophant, or spiritual leader. The term beauty is used to denote the perfection of God, and love-locks and tresses the infinitude of His glory. Down on the cheeks is symbolic of the multitudinous spirits which serve Him. Inebriation and dalliance typify that abstraction of soul which shows contempt of mundane affairs.

The following extract from Sufi poetry will serve to illustrate the use of many of these mystical terms. At first sight it would appear to be inspired by the spirit of amorous and bacchanalian frenzy, but when translated into its true terms it reveals itself as of the veritable essence of mysticism.

> Yesterday, half inebriated, I passed by the quarter where the wine-sellers dwell,
> To seek out the daughter of an Infidel, who is a vendor of wine.
> At the end of the street, a damsel, with a fairy's cheek, advanced before me.
> Who, pagan-like, wore her tresses dishevelled over her shoulders like the sacerdotal thread.
> I said, 'O thou, to the arch of whose eyebrows the new moon is a shame!
> What quarter is this, and where is thy place of abode?'
>
> 'Cast,' she replied, 'thy rosary on the ground, and lay the thread of paganism thy shoulder upon;
> Cast stones at the glass of piety; and from an o'erflowing goblet quaff the wine.
> After that draw near me, that I may whisper one word in thine ear;
> For thou wilt accomplish thy journey, if thou hearken to my words.'
>
> Abandoning my heart altogether, and in ecstasy rapt, I followed her.
> Till I came to a place where, alike, reason and religion forsook me.
> At a distance, I beheld a Company all inebriated and beside themselves,
> Who came all frenzied, and boiling with ardour from wine of love;

Without lutes, cymbals, or viols; yet all full of mirth and
    melody –
Without wine, or goblet, or flask; yet all drinking
    unceasingly.

When the thread of restraint slipped away from my hand,
I desired to ask her one question, but she said unto me,
    'Silence.
This is no square temple whose gate thou canst
    precipitately attain;
This is no mosque which thou canst reach with tumult,
    but without knowledge.
This is the banquet-house of Infidels, and all within are
    intoxicated;
All, from eternity's dawn to the day of doom, in
    astonishment lost!
Depart, then, from the cloister and towards the tavern
    bend thy steps.
Cast away the cloak of the Dervish, and don thou the
    libertine's robe.'

I obeyed: and if thou desire with me the same hue and
    colour to acquire,
Imitate me, and both this and the next world sell for a
    drop of pure wine.

One of the most celebrated exponents of Sufi doctrine is Jami,
the author of *Laila and Majnun*. His name is venerated throughout
Central Asia as one of the champions of the faith. In his belief,
when the Creator pours the effulgence of His Holy Spirit upon the
creature, such a one himself becomes divine. So closely, indeed, is
he identified with the great Source of all good, that he finds the
power has been conferred upon him of sharing the regulation and
direction of other beings. With the created beings whom he
governs he is connected by a powerful bond of sympathy, so
strong, indeed, that in a mystical sense they are spoken of as his
limbs, as parts of his body; nor can they suffer and endure any-

thing that he must not endure and suffer as well, through a process of psychical sympathy.

One of the many mistaken objections to this portion of Sufi belief is that it implies that saintship is almost one and the same thing as deification. This is not so. At the basis of Sufi philosophy will be found the fundamental axiom that no mortal can be as a god. The union of the creature with God is not an apotheosis of man, but a return of a portion of the Divine Spirit to its original fount and nucleus. The result of the union of man and God is annihilation of the merely human part of man and the withdrawal of his spiritual part to that place whence it emanated. On the annihilation of self, man realises that his own real and imperishable ego is one with the essence of God. In this union, so great is the influence of the Eternal Spirit that man's human judgment – that which we might describe as his logical faculty, his understanding – is entirely quenched and destroyed by it; 'even as error passeth away on the appearance of truth', in like manner his ability to discriminate between the perishable and the imperishable is rendered negligible. This feeling of oneness with deity it was which urged the sage Mansur Hallaj to ejaculate in a fit of ecstasy, 'I am Truth'; meaning thereby, 'I am God'. But in the eyes of the orthodox this statement appeared blasphemous, and in making it Mansur forfeited his life – so little are those who grope in the purlieus and courts of the outer temple able to appreciate the wisdom and the speech of those who dwell in the inner sanctuaries.

The presentation of the idea of the origin of evil – the question of dualism – has been the cause of much learned contention among erudite Sufis. Many have argued that evil cannot exist in face of the fact that God is wholly good and all things are from Him. One Sufi poet has said:

> The writer of our destiny is a fair and truthful writer,
> And never did He write that which is evil.

Evil is, therefore, a thing entirely human, due to the frailty of man, to the perversion of the human will and the circumstances by which humanity is surrounded – the material environment which man believes to be real, and which serves to distort his vision. It has no part in the being of God. It follows that all the so-called spiritual powers of evil, those principalities of the air and demons of the abyss, the existence of which so many religious philosophies admit, and even expressly urge, are nothing but figments of the human mind, misled by the phantasmagoria, the unrealities, by which man is surrounded.

Underlying the gorgeous imagery and lofty mysticism of Sufi poetry, then, whether it be that of Persia or of the Middle East, there dwells a deep significance of hidden instruction, which he who seeks may find – shall find, if he be eager enough, ardent enough. In vain we search elsewhere for a system so satisfying to the soul, so full – when all is understood – of the higher, the more spiritual reasoning. We will not find it in the teachings of ancient Athens, in the wonderful philosophy of old Egypt, or in that child of both, the Neo-Platonism of Alexandria. To these sources the expression of Sufism undoubtedly owes much, as we have seen. But it has refined them, has excogitated for itself a manner of thought beside which they seem almost elementary, and a symbolism and mystic teaching of much greater scope and loftiness. As I have indicated, there can be little doubt that it powerfully affected European mysticism, especially through Paracelsus and Boehme. It is, indeed, the true allegory of the inner life – its erotic imagery, its glorification of the grape, are but veils which seek to hide the great truths of existence, as the language of alchemy sought to preserve its discoveries from the vulgar. Sufi poetry speaks of a love which is not carnal, and of an inebriation produced by no material vine. These are the ecstasies and transports of divine affection. If it be mysterious, shall the bread of life be given to fools, shall pearls be cast before swine? No! Let the wise seek till they find. That is the last word of all mysticism, Oriental and Occidental – meditation upon it is the one true way to exaltation.

NOTES

1 The Ismaeli faith, according to Sufi authorities, has had no Sufi content for the past three centuries, though some of its Chiefs had from time to time sought Sufi recognition.
2 Although, of course, the vanity and consequent desire to oppose others often found in scholars and not overcome will produce the very reverse of the Sufi.

Sufism and the Indian Philosophies

SIRDAR IKBAL ALI SHAH*

The very great strides which have been made in modern Western psychology towards an understanding of the human mind, together with the tireless researches of Western scholars in the field of Orientalism have created within the last few decades a most important situation in the field of cultural research and understanding. In the first place, modern psychology in the West, which has been feeling its way through practical experiment towards establishing itself as a recognised science, has come to resemble more and more in shape if not in terminology, the Oriental teachings about the potentialities of the human mind. Professor Rom Landau, in a recent book on the Spanish-Arabian philosopher Ibn el-Arabi, mentions that Freudian interpretations of dream-symbolism were known to the ancient sages of the East. Again, Professor Jung, the founder of the other major school of psychology, the school of analytical psychology, was of the opinion that modern – that is, Western – pioneers in the study of the human mind had not attained the maturity of the thinkers of the East.

'Analytical psychology,' he says, in his most important book *Modern Man in Search of a Soul* (London, 1959 edition, page 62) – 'is no longer bound to the consulting-room of the doctor; its chains have been severed. We might say that it transcends itself, now advances to fill that void which hitherto has marked the psychic insufficiency of Western culture as compared with that of the

*Previously published in *Indo-Asian Culture* 10 (1962) 419-425, revised.

East. We Occidentals had learnt to tame and subject the psyche, but we knew nothing about its methodical development and its functions. Our civilisation is still young, and we, therefore, required all the devices of the animal-tamer to make the defiant barbarian and the savage in us in some measure tractable. But when we reach a higher cultural level, we must forego compulsion and turn to self-development.'

Well, Western psychology has forsaken the clinic and come back to self-development: to philosophy as it is understood in the East; as something which can develop mankind and make man – and woman – realise the higher destiny of the individual and of the community. In this respect we differ from the partial thinkers who have in all times passed for philosophers. I refer to the logicians, speculative theologians and traders in words who have sought, always in the end unsuccessfully, to teach that man can arrive at objective truth through juggling with words, or through using reason as opposed to his inborn ability to distinguish truth and reality.

'Know thyself', which the psychologists postulate as the first essential, has always been a part of Indian as of Sufi philosophy: whether used in the Sanskrit term of *Jnana*, knowledge; or the Arabic phrase *Man arafa nafsahu, arafa Rabbahu*. It is through the path of self-knowledge that ultimate truth and real reality is reached.

Before we go any further, we have to make a clear distinction between the inner philosophy of the Sufis as well as of the Indian schools and the philosophy of religion. The difference, briefly, is this: in all forms of ordinary organisational religion, there are certain beliefs and certain practices which, taken together, are considered to be sufficient to imply that the practitioner is a believer in that religion. But the members of the initiatory schools go very much further than this. First, they say, you must know what religion really is. Then you will know whether you believe in it or not. Buddha's teaching was clearly calculated to make the disciple conscious of himself first; so that subsequently he would be able to banish 'self'. It is obvious that in order to banish a thing, you must first recognise it. In order to recognise it, you must develop within yourself the ability to assess it.

There is no golden key to enlightenment. Both the Sufi and the Indian schools teach that man must be capable of receiving a teaching before he can be taught. There can be no attaining any enlightenment until the individual is ready for it. It is to produce these favourable conditions for understanding that, in both the Indian and the Sufi systems, there is the institution of the human guide or teacher, whose first task is to prepare the disciple for the knowledge of himself, so that he is able to become enlightened.

The Sufi path of development is not a process or a philosophy foreign to India. Some of the greatest of Sufi teachers lived and taught in India; and many of them are buried in India. Sufism, in one sense, came to India; so did the Aryan invaders. Sufism, again, is not regarded by its practitioners as something which originated at a specific place in space, or at a point in time. 'Before there were vines on this earth,' the great Master Jalaluddin Rumi reminds us, 'the Sufis drank the wine of Wisdom, the spiritual wine of knowledge.' Another master says: 'Sufism is too sublime to have had an origin.' This was Hujwiry, the author of the Sufi classic *Kashf al Mahjub*, who was buried on Indian soil and is revered by people of all faiths as a great teacher under the honorific of Dara Ganj Bakhsh.

The philosophical stream from which the common root of Sufism and Indian philosophies stemmed may conveniently be termed *tarika*: a way of travelling, and also a method of doing a thing. To divide it and categorise it as 'Yoga' and 'Sufism' is useful only in a limited, and not in an ultimate, sense. In such books as the *Cultural History of India*, Sufism is claimed to have inspired the founder of the Sikh religion, Rabindranath Tagore, Kabir and scores of others. Again, a superficial belief is that Sufism was itself originally influenced by Vedantism. The division is in the eye of the beholder. When there is a mighty river which branches into smaller streams, these streams may be called separate rivers. But equally they may all be fed by the melting snows of some colossal mountain which is the goal of the search.

The organisation, procedure, methods and ideas of the followers of the truth, as of the followers of any objective reality, must be very similar, and there is an end to it. That there is cultural interchange between the followers of truth is inevitable, desirable and necessary. To make this contact the main object of one's attention is absurd. The buyer of 'halwa' is interested in what it tastes like and not where its ingredients came from and how. Even this parallel is inadequate, for to us the origin of sugar is sweetness and there, as I have said, is an end to it.

In Western countries, books on Oriental religion and philosophy, many of them of a more or less 'occult' nature, are appearing in increasing numbers. A second major aggregation of books is concerned with psychology. Western man is facing the crisis of trying to replace his failing religious values with a personality which shall give meaning and purpose to his life. Personality, that much misused word, is derived from the Latin word *persona* which signifies 'A Mask'; a mask worn during a stage play, with the intention of conveying to the audience something of the character portrayed by the actor. In the East the personality is very far from a mask. It is the external view of what actually is inside the man. The objective of practical philosophy of the Sufi and Indian schools is an inner transformation.

The diffusion of this sense of the integrated personality during the period from the Middle Ages until the present day has been a joint undertaking of the Sufi and Indian schools of philosophical thought and action. This task, the methodology and results of which are abundantly plain in recorded material, has been carried out in an atmosphere of struggle. What has this struggle been?

Western philosophy, upon which depend many of the lines of thinking of the past two centuries, is built partly upon Greek and Roman philosophy. In the form in which this philosophy reached the West, the odds were heavily weighted in favour of pure speculation and juggling with words. In the process of transmission of the knowledge of the ancients to the West, a very curious thing happened. In the teachings of Pythagoras and Plato, there is indeed a concentration upon the intellect. But it is only this one portion which appears in books. Equating the teachings of the Western classical world with those of the East will show that the intellectual exercises which pass for philosophy are only a part of the picture. The important part – the actual practice of self-cultivation – has been left out. It survives in the Sufi and Indian systems.

Take the classic syllogism of logic: 'Man is a liar. I am a man. Therefore, I am a liar. Therefore, when I say "Man is a liar" I am lying. Therefore, man is not a liar.'

The fallacy is, of course, that the statement 'Man is a liar' does not need to apply to every situation. This is all very well – as far as it goes. But it does not go far enough. The purpose of introducing such ideas into the mind, practised by all initiatory schools is not to exercise your wits but to point to the limitations of language. Man cannot, in the final analysis, rely upon words in order to arrive at truth.

So the books of the Greeks were not fully understood. They are still not understood, and people play with them; like the child who has a book of problems and no answers. The philosophy which we share, the practical wedded to the theoretical, is something of greater completion than the speculative or rhetorical which has passed for philosophy in the West.

People like Aldous Huxley in America are now feeling their way towards an understanding of experiential philosophy, as opposed to verbal juggling. Their books seem rather negative, tentative and incomplete. But the movement has started. They turn their attention, interestingly enough, towards two main fields for further support of their feeling that there is something within man which awaits realisation and is the ultimate source of truth – Sufism and Indian philosophy. Zen Buddhism, now in vogue in the West, is an offshoot of Buddhism – in other words, the Chinese (*Ch'an*) and Japanese form of a school of Indian thought. There is a movement in the West which looks towards the Vedantic ways of thought, for the same reason. The influence of the Sufis upon every branch of Western thought has been immense and continuous. Nietsche of Germany quotes Hafiz as the one who really knows and experiences. Goethe's work is soaked in Sufism. And even the Christian Saint John of the Cross has been found by Professor Palacios to have taken his ideas and many of his quotations direct from the Illuminist School (The Ishraquiyya) of the Sufis, as represented by Ibn Arabi and today the Shadhiliyya of North Africa.

However, philosophical movements in the West which are based upon Eastern models rapidly turn away from the main theme; that of self-realisation. There is only one reason for this. No school of human study can survive entirely by means of theory or the printed page. The continuous and repeated refreshment of Indian and Sufi teaching has come about and been maintained only because there has been a perennial succession of teachers, masters, those who knew how to carry the disciple from one stage to the next in this mission of self-realisation.

I have purposely avoided invoking the technical terms and dogmas which from time to time coalesce around teaching schools and make them appear different from other schools. I have done this deliberately, because the essence of initiatory knowledge, for the Indian schools and the Sufis alike, has always been their common denominator: the search for truth through a blending of theory and practice. I have set myself the task of explaining what the mediocre scholastics have made a dreary and footnote-loaded task, by means of ideas and references which are easily grasped by all. For if there is to be any reality in self-development, that reality must ultimately be a simplicity, not a multiplicity. As one of the sages has put it, 'Unity underlies all multiplicity'. Your attention is only confused by a thousand coloured sweets, if what you are trying to understand is sugar, and not the sweets individually. This sense of unity, and the final unification of experience, is central to the two initiatory schools of which Yoga and Sufism are expressions.

What of methodology? How do we go about the applying of the teaching of self-realisation and unification? We cannot measure in terms of human advantage the effect upon countless millions of people of a succession of teachers of the self-development schools throughout the milennia. The general effect has been there to which we may ascribe that 'difference', that ascendancy, which the East has over the West in terms of the power of the human spirit, the composure of the personality. And we disregard it at our peril, because it is the very basis of our lives.

The second characteristic is that of tolerance. Indian society today is possible only because of it. In its political and social expression it takes the form of secularism. But the secularism of India is rooted not in modern Western concepts of materialism or atheism, but in the immemorial concept that the next man has as much right to his inner experiences as I. We should never mistake this important source of tolerance, however much it may superficially resemble any other form of tolerance.

The man who wishes to enter the path of self-realisation must practise these virtues in himself first, before he can accept them from others as his right. Hence the methodology of the Sufi and Indian schools insists, each perhaps in its own way, upon tolerance of others and also upon individual composure of mind. How is composure attained?

Composure is necessary because the unregenerate mind is, in fact, not one mind, or 'self'. It is composed of a number of confused, often conflicting 'selves'. These must first be focussed, integrated, centralised, stabilised. Only when this is done can the mind work as one entity, capable of tackling the larger job of producing the Ideal Man: the man who lies hidden or rather incipient within us all. This is where the teacher comes into the picture. He is the guide who will enable the Seeker to find his way in life. There are false teachers, just as there are bad goldsmiths. But inner cognition plus careful observation tells all but the foolish which is the master for him.

Far from being old-fashioned, anachronistic, mumbo-jumbo, the discoveries of the ancient schools which are represented in the work of the Sufis today, are the result of enlightened, progressive investigation into the human mind. Metaphysical elaborations, meaningless accretions, have surrounded a great deal of Sufi preaching, and confused, misrepresented even, the truths of these inner schools. But nothing can destroy their essential validity.

VISITS TO SUFI CENTRES
Some Recent Research Papers on Sufis and Sufism

by
Djaleddin Ansari and Others

Basic Teachings of the Sufis

DJALEDDIN ANSARI

A famous contemporary writer has said: 'For the Sufi, Sufism is more of a science than a "trip"' – the Sufis realise that the Sufi Way is far too important to be something to be enjoyed or endured. It is something to be learnt.

The world is full of people who read Sufi books, or meet supposed Sufis and as a result imagine that they are Sufis, too. There are also so many scholars, journalists and earnest enquirers asking whether this pantomime really is Sufism, that ordinary spectators easily become puzzled. When dealing with the basic teachings of the Sufis, therefore, we have to note that the primary one (if it can be put in this way) is that nobody can learn to be a Sufi without being taught by a real Sufi. Is this so very surprising? Perhaps we might see what can happen with, say, Christianity, if adopted in a random and selective manner:

> Things got out of hand when the three McCuin sisters had a bible-reading session. They stripped, to get back to the Garden of Eden, smeared themselves with mustard and stole a van. The naked girls were arrested and Doshaline McCuin, 30, said from jail in Lansing, Michigan:
> 'We were high on the Holy Spirit.'[1]

Now, you note that not only was this a matter of individual (if intrepid) do-it-yourself religion. It also spread so that it infected three people. There have been cases where such sentiments have spread even further, eventually involving millions. And, even further, note that this mutual-excitement process is described by one of the participants not for what it is – a way of obtaining stimuli – but is regarded as being 'high on the Holy Spirit'. This is exactly what happens with some people who attach themselves to the Sufis, or to anything else which they can use for self-stimulation. It is not to be mistaken for Sufi activity, any more than the above anecdote reflects Christianity.

Another basic teaching of the Sufis is that, wherever there is a legitimate Sufi teacher, there will also be sincere and severe opposition to him. It must be admitted that history shows this to be true. Not a single one of the admitted Sufi great masters has failed to be plagued by critics and opponents. In the past they have generally (as with Europe in the Middle Ages) specialised in accusing the Sufis of heresy and opposition to religion.

The Sufis themselves have devised a counter to this continuing opposition, something which is often confused with a spiritual exercise. This is the often-quoted 'Path of Reproach' (*Rah-e-Malamat*). Centuries before the Zen masters in Japan found that you could disarm an opponent by using his strength against him, the Sufis did the same thing with words and appearances. It fitted in well with their contention that so-called 'reality' is in any case comparative, subjective. This is how it works: Someone vilifies a Sufi. He answers: 'Everything that you say against me is true, and it does not even go far enough. In fact, in the nature of things, you can only have an incomplete idea of how bad I am. I am the one who knows all the secret failings and shortcomings in me, and it is I therefore who am an expert on my iniquity.'

Nobody has yet thought out a counter to that one. I visited one Sufi group in the Holy City of Mecca, centre of students from all over the Islamic world. Here they were studying the works and sayings of Idries Shah, the notable Afghan spiritual guide. I said: 'Some people in the West, and several people I have met in the East, do not like Sayed Idries's work...' The Sheikh who was in charge of the meeting immediately answered: 'That is a little too late – rather like a wave saying: "I don't like Noah's Ark". The Ark is built, it works, it is designed to defy the waves. It succeeds. What the "wave" says may be interesting; it may be expected. But significant? No.'[2]

The basic teachings of the Sufis are not only frequently very surprising in that they contain elements which are not to be found in systems which depend upon indoctrination or upon the recruitment of 'game-players', emotionalists: they also find expression in areas which are completely unrecognisable as spiritual by shallower observers. Let us put it in this way, compressing somewhat the words of a Sufi teacher whom I met in Syria, and who would have nothing to do with the widely-advertised 'Sufis' of that country:

'Since externals (beard, rosary, litanies, begging-bowls, special meditation-rooms, constant meetings and reliance upon miraculous tales are examples) are what attract people to Sufis and other mystics, it follows that anyone who concentrates upon having and dealing in such things can establish himself in the eyes of the unregenerate as a Sufi. Conversely, someone who knows the essence of Sufi experience and how to engender it cannot become established, and will be considered a fraud.'

Following this clue led me through several years of investigations, and revealed a most astonishing (to me) state of affairs. When I visited a country and showed interest in its Sufis, I became aware that a certain amount of interest was being taken in me by people who were neither agents of the police nor what could be identified as Sufis. If I became friendly or assiduous in my interest with the supposed Sufis, these others melted away. If, however, I shunned the supposed Sufis and continued to look for people who could give me insights without 'externals', these people came closer. Eventually, I was able to find the real Sufis who stood behind the facade of imitators and imposters.

As one of these genuine Sufis said to me:

'We have to be sure that you are sincere. We have to keep an eye on you to see if the robes and beards and the emotional excitement, *zikr* (repetitions of holy formulas) are enough for you. If they are, we have to leave you alone, because in such a case you would have found what you sought: not the Sufis, but a source of comfort and sense of importance.'

I asked him:

'Are there, then, no genuine organisation of Sufis, or true Sufi masters, working in public and looking like what the superficialist imagines a man of religion to resemble?'

He said: 'Oh, yes, indeed. But these few can easily be tested for genuineness. The trouble is that the disciple will never test the master.'

'Why will he not test him?'

'Because he does not know how. If he is pre-sold on the desire to attach himself to someone, he will not want to find out that he is wrong. As an example, the other day I asked someone who believes that he is a Sufic aspirant why he was following a certain "master" who is certainly a deluded psychopath. He said: "He is obviously only testing me by practising the 'Path of Blame'".

'Now, in fact, the test is not at the level of the "Path of Blame". Leave that aside for the moment. Never start with looking at the Path of Blame. That is there, anyway, for the profane, to deflect them. Look, instead, at whether the "master" . . .

1 Can explain what he is doing by reference to the Classics.
2 Refuses to follow a single classical teacher alone.
3 Can operate outside of the ritualistic, without "gadgets".
4 Refuses to mystify you, and has no magical aura.
5 Produces no atmosphere of "power" around him. As the ancients have rightly said: "The fraud makes people believe that he is a man of power. The true Sufi spends much time appearing very normal."
6 Can work "in the world" and make what seem like worldly activities successful, as Khaja Ahrar did. He was a self-made millionaire, but none could say that he was not the supreme adept of the age.

'These are some of the qualifications and characteristics of the real Sufi teacher, whether he is a visible one or not.'

When I returned to Europe after that journey in the East, I made contact with a great many people whom no one would even suspect of being Sufis, or spiritual people at all. I could now recognise them because I had learned the basic teachings which cover so much more ground than the morbid and often vacuous nonsense of those whom the world takes for religious people, especially as Sufis.

Such people are so strongly represented in the West that, in little over a week, I noticed the following Sufis (without the reputation) appearing on television or writing or being interviewed in the newspapers:

one conductor of classical music; three businessmen; five industrialists; three writers; one singer; two politicians; one Christian priest, and several others.

Of course, the most basic teaching of all among the Sufis is that the teaching itself is produced by the teacher as a consequence of his own experience. As soon as he has had the ultimate experience, he can see from that viewpoint how to bring it to others. He has become a teacher. Now, if in order to bring it to others he has to do or to say things which do not seem to be spiritual or even relevant to those who cannot in any case judge, he will always find a way to bring the teaching to those who are open to understanding. He cannot, of course, reach everyone, and especially out of reach are those who come to him not for teaching but for something which they respond to emotionally.

It is such a teacher (the only genuine one) who will know what is and what is not relevant from the vast body of accumulated Sufic lore. Most of it of course is only the empty cans of the nutrition that it formerly contained. I came across an interesting example of this from a Sufi teacher whom I appoached to seek an explanation why certain ideas and practices endured for centuries.

I hazarded the opinion that, for a practice or belief to have lasted for centuries, it must have had – must surely continue to have – some value to the culture, or the individual, or some useful effect on the minds of the people.

'Well,' he said, 'I was recently in India, in a very old palace, in the jungle. Much of it had fallen down, and other parts had been undermined by exotic growths. But, here and there, I could see exquisite examples of artistry in the moulded stucco-work, amazingly well preserved.

'Why did these pieces, as distinct from others, survive? Why did other parts crumble to dust? No "function" is being performed by the intact ones that was not inherent in the parts which had vanished. Again, much of the lime in the deteriorated parts was serving as fertiliser. . . .'

This, then, is the true Sufi speaking. The imitator will try to preserve everything. Was it not Idries Shah who says somewhere that 'We must make a distinction between the constructive, the nutritive and the museum-keeper'?

Because basic teachings of the Sufis do not in fact attract – it is the non-basic, the herd, the chants, the emotion which do – the real Sufi must organise himself so as to:

1 Attract those who have gone beyond basics as generally understood.

2 Make his contact with other people on a completely different basis. Khaja Ahrar, already mentioned, not only made a colossal fortune, he operated a number of organisations in commerce, agriculture and learning, which attracted people by virtue of their success and inner energy. Then, at a later date, people would find, by contact, that there was something else within such structures. And they were then able to perceive that here was something of the spirit, of beauty, of value, and of the divine. It does not happen, except rarely, the other way about.

If you go into one of the bookshops which specialise in oriental or spiritual writings, you will nowadays be confronted by a positive barrage of books about and by Sufis. Most people have absolutely no notion of how to research this material. Familiarity with basic teachings of the living tradition, however, enables one to sort out the true from the false fairly quickly. In the first place, 'true' and 'false' here do not refer to intention, only to capacity. That is to say, we have to recognise that most of the writers are not so much 'mad or bad' as sad. Scholars and self-appointed specialists tend to search for things which attract them and represent these as Sufism. They also develop a quite un-Sufi fervour or hostility towards those writings which do not square with their opinions. Hence you can cut out all writings which contain polemic or personal attacks. You can, again, leave aside all the strictly 'symbolic' or 'artistic' attempts at representing Sufism as expressed largely or cogently through these means. Symbols and artistry in Sufism are instruments, not part of artistry or language or even communication. Then, again, you can avoid profitably all the materials which dwell on a single classical figure and his writings or doings, since these would in any case soon pall – or else condition you into a mere worshipper of that individual. See what is left, and you will probably have the real Sufi materials.

Basic Sufi teachings, however, warn against premature stabilisation of opinion. 'For every truth you find there is another and more profound one beyond: one which may seem to contradict the first.' This is a warning not to rely on written materials, however important, without a living source of information and instruction.

In this connection, the following dialogue seemed of the very greatest importance to me, when I heard it in a Sufi circle in Algeria:

'How do I know a real teacher?'

'People who ask this question will not find the answer while they are thinking in this vein.'

'What is the way to find the answer?'

'To try to perceive inwardly the essence, the reality, the truth and inner being, of the teacher and the teaching, in all things, not just in the assumed teaching function or appearance; no matter where or who this teacher is – it is almost to be predicted that you will find it where you do not expect it.'

'What if I make a mistake?'

'You will certainly make a mistake if you lack sincerity.'

'What is a sign of lack of sincerity?'

'The first sign is that you want to find someone who is acceptable, or something which pleases you, rather than that you want to find Truth, whatever that may be, wherever and whenever it might be.'

NOTES

1 Evening News (London) April 24 1980, page 9.
2 The astonishing support for Idries Shah in the academic, religious and literary (as well as spiritual) areas of the East as well as the West is well sampled in a vast array of articles, monographs and books. As one instance, the following is indispensible: Williams, Prof.L.F.R. – *Sufi Studies: East & West*, New York (Dutton) 1973 and London (The Octagon Press), a collection of some of these papers.

The Dinner-Meeting and Other Topics

ABDUL-WAHAB TIRMIZI, 'TIRYAQI'

Tradition has it that, in very ancient times, Sufi teachers would spread a cloth by a roadside, perhaps at a crossroads, and lay out whatever food people had given them to entertain travellers. These dinner-table offerings, naturally enough, became the occasions for rest and listening to the words of the Sufis. Some of the most famous *chaikhanas* [teahouses] and caravanserais are said to have originated in this way.

This habit of offering hospitality has been carried through to modern times and, while the nutritional importance of the food may decline in countries where the people are already well-fed, the special nature of the teaching which is carried out at the dinner-meeting has yet to be replaced.

For those who are unaware of the highly structured and yet carefully calculated behaviour of the Sufi master at a dinner-meeting (and this includes the majority of the Eastern people who have attended them, as well as Westerners) the whole transaction may look like nothing other than a jovial host entertaining guests. The major factor, which ordinarily escapes attendees, is that the dinner-meeting above all is one at which indirect teaching takes place. Let us take an example, which may be duplicated, more or less in any of a dozen such functions across the world.

The teacher will usually begin his talk after all have fed. During the actual eating, he will perhaps talk to the few guests who have been invited because they have individual matters to discuss. These disposed of, the audience sits back to hear what topic has been chosen, and to profit from its unfolding. Any resemblance

between the Sufi meeting of this kind and the conventional religious meeting has to be noted. In the latter, a text or theme is
taken and treated in religious and sometimes didactic terms. The
emotions and the logical mind are both engaged. In the Sufi
meeting, any topic whatever may be chosen, the intention being to
bring to the consciousness of the individuals a way of thinking and
a means of looking at things which is not available in their
ordinary experience.

The teacher may often range over all kinds of topics – Rumi's
table-talk is a good example of this in that it deals with local
culture and problems. But there is a startling difference between
the Sufi instructional meeting and any other kind of which we
have any record. With the Sufis, if you find yourself applying the
ideas expressed to yourself, you generally realise that you are
being subjective: you can, in other words, find moral exhortations
or formulae for running your life anywhere. Hence we can immediately make a distinction between the Sufi teaching and di-
dacticism. Equally, those seeking general principles soon realise
how conditioned or pedantic they are. The Sufi will often pursue a
course of thought and then switch over to the opposite seeming
opinion, simply to show you how fallacious or incomplete a single
way of thought may be. It is impossible to escape the feeling
that these people, in applying this expertise with such cogency
and artistry, are doing something which cannot be found elsewhere.

Many people, of course, attend such meetings and do not profit
from them in the way outlined above, But, especially in recent
times, those who have been in touch, even by the written word,
with Sufi activity, can find in the accounts of the actions and
words of Sufi masters a wholly sufficient grounding enabling them
to profit from any dinner-meeting to which they are lucky enough
to be invited. The test of whether one has profited or whether one
still needs some concentrated study of the published paradigms of
this kind of event is whether one's horizons have been widened by
following a new or unusual point of view given by a Sufi.

Some people have held that the mere fact of attending such
meetings develops in the individual capacities which result, at the

appropriate time, in illumination. There is a certain story about this, repeated in dervish circles.

There was once a dervish who found himself at the gates of Heaven, following a long line of people. When his turn came to enter the Gates, he paused, to be identified and tested. The Angel in charge said, 'What is your name?' The man gave it. Then he asked the Angel: 'Do I come in because of your having my name on a list?' 'No,' said the Angel, 'you come in because you answer in the manner acquired by the pupils of such-and-such a Master.' 'But,' asked the perplexed man, 'as I am not illuminated, how is it that I can enter Heaven at all?' 'This is possible,' said the Angel, 'because once the vegetable has been put in a pot and parboiled, there is no great problem in finishing the process.'

Sheikh Hamdun of Damascus summarised the matter for me in the following words:

'The purpose of Sufi study and development of "being" is, among other things, the establishment and maintenance of a way of thinking and perception which prevents the recurrence of primitive thought and action (including the predominance of the reward/punishment mechanism and indoctrination) instead of merely having secondary aspirations, as with all other institutions, however fundamental, or even vital, these may be.'

Making Sense of Sufi Literature, Experts, Paradox

ANDREW C.C. ELLIS

Before I went to the Middle East on an extended visit, to seek for answers to certain problems which I had extracted from a close study of publications on the Sufis and Sufism, I made it my business to meet as many predecessors – previous travellers and students – as possible.

They were a remarkable assorted collection of people: this I decided through looking at them from the viewpoint of a trained sociologist with an interest in psychology. It is not to say, however, that many of them found each other to be so 'different'. They tended, on the whole, to view one another through the eyes of the committed: was the other person displaying similar pre-occupations, had he (or she) visited the same people; of whom did they approve and of whom did they disapprove?

These attitudes, it seemed to me, left something to be desired. That something was, that if we were to be able to extract useful materials from the immense body of literature and current Sufi action, it would be necessary to suspend opinion and (to adopt a frequent Sufi admonition) see facts. In the event, I was to see that there was a remarkable consensus among Eastern Sufis in this matter. They almost always made a point of stressing that the people whom I had met (even though claiming impressive credentials as 'disciples of so-and-so') were to be regarded as 'failures for the moment'. This is the phrase which indicates someone who, in his spiritual studies, has got only to the point of seeking friends and enemies, following limited categories, looking for certainty and 'not the way to find certainty'.

I had noted something similar in groups studying Sufism in the West. Many made no progress precisely because they were too anxious to progress. Also, they were looking for social support or endorsement of their beliefs and other things which are not the fare at the Sufi table at all.

On the other hand, there were distinct signs that Sufi ideas and knowledge was penetrating into the West, and that this was being done in a way which betokened a powerful understanding and considerable ability, located somewhere and directing the effort.

My visit to the East (to the Arab, Turkic and Iranic areas, as well as to the Indian subcontinent) was because I found, in the West, representatives of a Sufism which I could glimpse only dimly through the documents and commentaries presented to us by the orientalists, the specialists. It was even less visible in the words and behaviour of a great number of supposed 'Sufis' who flourish in the West and hotly denounce the kind of Sufi teaching to which I have alluded, and which alone seems really interesting. The other, unfortunately, is only a rehashing of a sort of half-baked religiosity, of which there is probably quite enough in the West already. Nothing in it is new, nothing is in any way superior to the monkery of the Christian Middle Ages.

Amusingly enough, I (and other observers) had noted that it was the essentially sincere but as essentially misguided enthusiasts who were in fact quasi-monks in the old and distorted mould who most appealed to the traditional – old-fashioned – religious thinkers of the West. It was poets and scientists, businessmen and housewives, high achievers and ordinary people, who were interested in what some of us had come to regard as an important and intriguing display of real knowledge from the East. The others, the 'specialists' in religion and orientalism, could not or would not see it.

I was afforded facilities to visit and live with Eastern Sufis under definite conditions. In the first place, I was not to 'journalise' the materials. I was not to look at the outward face of things and make any play in any publication of local cultural matters, since these would not apply to me, as a representative of another culture. I was not to engage in political, economic or religious activity of any kind; apart from observing the rites of whatever might be my own religion. I was not to identify individuals and places. I accepted all these limitations not only with resignation but with relief. After all, when you read much sociology, you realise that you are in fact reading polemic. When you read so much anthropology or travel literature, you can see that you are being treated to opinion or self-display. I was more than contented to go, to see, to feel, and to collect facts.

I was also hardly less delighted to find, on my return with my materials, that the approach was welcomed by academic colleagues. So I cannot say that I have been a martyred worker, misunderstood and unsung.

The paper by Abdul-Wahab Tirmizi ('The Dinner-Meeting and other Topics') excellently well provides an introduction to the sort of material for which I was searching. His account, which I find accurate in every particular, may be called a classic example of how something (the dinner-meeting) can be on view and available to all, but can easily be swept aside as something of no consequence. Again and again, in the Middle East, I saw Western invitees and scholars wearily 'waiting for the dinner-talk to be over' so that they could ask about rituals, about personal preoccupations, about anything under the sun except the substance of the meeting itself, attention to which would have rendered their questions unnecessary!

But there is more – were there not, I would have to let Tirmizi's remarkable paper stand for my entire experience.

A study of major standard Sufi documents (cf. Hujwiri's *Revelation* and Attar's *Recapitulation*) shows that a very important part of Sufi teaching centres around examinations of the behaviour, words and activities of Sufi masters. These have almost always been mistaken for hagiographies, pious external propaganda, of the kind which was used in the Middle Ages to impress monks and laymen alike. The clue to their esoteric importance, however, even for the unwarned, is that we also find that Sufi teachers themselves, when retailing this information, act as if they were themselves uninformed observers. In other words, they have distanced themselves from the material, and are presenting it almost (but not quite) through the eyes of the student. It thus can have a powerful teaching effect, just as when a good teacher in any more profane subject adopts the stance of the learner, but brings to the selection, impact and projection of his materials the expertise which his knowledge makes possible.

The materials, therefore, are not hagiographies, and we find them in use, in a dynamic way which would surely completely bewilder an orientalist or other scholar innocent of this specialised usage, in living Sufi groups. If, however, the materials are simply read out by self-appointed students or teachers, and do not form a part of the measured projection of a legitimate Sufi school, they will operate only on the lower level, producing low-level results, mere consumers of wonders.

This remarkable application of the 'secret protects itself' principle by the Sufis is one of the most impressive new factors which we in the West have to learn.

The books are not, as we have noted, hagiographies; but, further than that, today's Sufis are actually revealing in so many words that their 'histories', and 'collected anecdotes' or 'travels' are in fact teaching documents which can be understood only by those who will forego the pleasures of wonderment and sentimentality. They are, in short, a part of a very highly sophisticated study system. As one Sufi put it to me, when I asked how we were supposed to be able to tumble to this fact, 'After all, if you style yourself an engineer and gaze in wonderment at the admittedly impressive symmetry of gears and ratchets, and if you construct a whole metier around this, and if you come to us asking to be shown more wonderfully balanced ball-bearings – how are we, if we are engineers, to break into the realm which you have closed off in your minds, the realm where these things actually operate for a purpose, work as mechanisms?' I had no answer, and I fancy that other scholars have none, either.

And yet, it must be conceded, that the Sufis have been trying 'to make engineers of us'. For this reason, indeed, they have since the 1960s – about 20 years – given admittedly limited but nonetheless valuable access to facilities which they operate in several centres where these things are well understood. Certain suitable travellers have been selected and teachers of the genuine lore have encouraged them to familiarise themselves with the 'gears and bearings' of the system. They have, too, allowed a certain amount of publication of these materials.

So here we come across yet another Sufi paradox, which is baffling only, as the Sufis never cease to remind us, because we have blanked out what they have said. The paradox involves the fact that a book by a non-Sufi (for instance the late Professor Arberry's *Sufism*) which is alleged (and believed) to convey what Sufis teach, cannot in any sense be a teaching-book. Yet, on the other hand, a book by a Sufi or sponsored by a real Sufi source (one such is undoubtedly O.M. Burke's *Among the Dervishes*) *is* a book from which one can learn, though looking like – and operating also as – a travel book with great entertainment content.

The above knowledge has led, of course, to a profound re-examination of books by and on Sufis and Sufism, which are available in so many languages, notably English. It also allows for the republication of texts and commentaries and all kinds of other materials (such as *A Dervish Textbook* and the collection *The World of the Sufi*) recently issued by the Octagon Press; because, with new instruments of study supplied by new knowledge of ancient processes, really useful instructional materials can be extracted from them by people who understand the way in which they work. It may be noted that Dr. R.E. Ornstein has supplied one way in which this material may be approached, in relation to brain-function; Professor L. Lewin has already published hints along this line,[1] and there are other materials to be seen from time to time in specialist journals and monographs.

Familiarity with the above-named materials and approaches explains how R.L. Thomson[2] has been able to relate the Sufi contribution to contemporary science.

By implication, of course, other current materials by run-of-the-mill specialists, orientalist scholars, those interested in religion and esotericists, are seen to be inadequate and skating upon the surface, however profound they purport to be. There is little wonder that some otherwise respectable and well-established conventional authorities with excellent apparent credentials so easily join the jealous 'mad monks' of the Sufic lunatic fringe in attacking this approach, which Shah has done so much to serve with his remarkable books.[3] What is, however, gratifying, and surprising in its generosity, is the fact that so many scholars[4] have shown themselves able to adapt to the new knowledge which, in fact, negates so much of their work.

NOTES

1 Lewin, L., Hon.D.Sc., Feature Book Review, *International Philosophical Quarterly*, Vol VX No 3 pp 353/64, Fordham University, Sept. 1975.
2 Thomson, R.L., D.Sc., Psychology & Science from the Ancient East, *The Brook Postgraduate Gazette*, pp 7ff, London Vol 2 No.1 March 1973.
3 Cf. the 8 reprint volumes of reviews and discussions of Shah's works (The Octagon Press, London).
4 See Prof. L.F.R. Williams, *Sufi Studies: East & West*, New York 1974 and London (The Octagon Press).

SOME FURTHER READING

Ornstein, R.E., Herron, J., and Swencionis, C.: 'Differential Right Hemisphere Involvement in Two Reading Tasks', *Psychophysiological Research*, Vol.16, No.4, pp 398 ff, 1979.
Deikman, A.J., 'Sufism and Psychiatry', in *The Journal of Nervous and Mental Disease*, Vol. 165, No. 5, pp 318 ff, 1977.
Ibid., 'Comments on the Gap Report on Mysticism', *idem*, Vol. 165, No. 3, pp 213 ff, 1977.

Aphorisms of a Sufi Teacher

HILMI ABBAS JAMIL

Cults and narrowly-based systems always attempt to reduce the range of thought and activity. People working within non-cultic systems, for instance educational ones, also tend to develop cultish, narrowed-down, attitudes. For example, they will tend to concentrate on only one or more aspects of the undertaking, the ones which please them most, and will at that point reduce their capacity for learning and progress.

Aphorisms, when they emanate from a source of knowledge and teaching, are not only entertaining and insightful: they widen the perspective, so that the individual can better see his or her previous limitations, and hence overcome them.

In current Sufi schools, a number of aphorisms are in use which clearly emphasise and illustrate this process. We shall take them one by one.

'*There is no such thing as "almost a Sufi"*', is the first. This is because *Sufi* stands for the product, the result, not the effort. The aphorism is intended to remind people that they cannot choose bits and pieces from Sufi practices or ideas and try to apply them without entering into a programme which is, after all, designed to develop a skill: the skill of being able to 'do, be and know'. The saying is also used as a test. People who think that it means that they should become obsessed with becoming Sufis are unsuitable for Sufi study while they remain in that state of mind or hold that opinion.

'*Imagination and intellectuality are the "Sufism" of the ignorant.*'
The phrase alludes to the two instruments automatically

reached for by people who want to approach something from a basis of ignorance. The imaginer, for instance, faced with a desire for riches, may fantasise how he might get them. The intellectually-oriented, faced with an artistic work, may try to analyse it. Each of these types can obtain something from his effort: but he will not obtain what is really resident in the object of his approach. The effort has been attenuated by the procedure used.

Similarly, any public library will provide you with books written on Sufism and Sufis which are packed with the imaginings or mental automatism of the writers. This is the 'Sufism of the ignorant', where ignorant means trying to portray something about which one really knows very little.

'Sufism is indeed teaching: but not all students are learners.'

Here we see the emphasis placed upon the fact that people who imagine that they are trying to learn may well be only trying to entertain themselves without knowing it. In all educational efforts there are such people: such as the 'perennial student', who is still 'studying' many years after he should have learnt. Learning how to learn is even more important than learning itself. Without the former, the latter may exist, but it is out of reach.

'People ask what Sufis are doing for the world. They would do better to wonder whether, without the Sufis, there would still be a world.'

This is an ideal context-expanding sentence. Whether or not the Sufis are responsible for making the world tolerable or maintaining its existence, people who query Sufi usefulness have rarely thought whether they could recognise a Sufic operation in the world if they met it. They have narrowed their range to a crude vision of a world where the Sufis should have removed all the things which the questioners find objectionable.

'You do not need the name, pedigree or knowledge of the eating habits of someone who is saving you from drowning.'

The need to approach all kinds of study only from relevant questions, and to suppress irrelevancies, is immediately apparent here. This aphorism needs little explanation; but it does need to be thought about. Very little training is offered by any extant society in the approach to learning needed to maximise its effect.

'When I first looked at my teacher, I saw a man. Later I saw no man: only knowledge.'

Again the approach from the outside. If you recall how people whom you have met struck you, you will tend to remember superficialities. The person was impressive, or disappointing; smiled or frowned, was rich or poor, old or young, pleasant or unpleasant. The teacher, on the other hand, is not a circus clown or baby-sitter. He or she is, for the student, a source of learning.

'Sufism does in twenty or thirty years what humanity will do in twenty or thirty thousand.'

This is intended to offer a suggestion of perspective, to overcome impatience. It is also meant to indicate that the Sufis are aiming for a maturation of all humanity, not for the development of a clique. The phrase is also used for diagnostic purposes. People who think that it is an example of haughty pretensions may be labelling themselves as something like paranoid.

'Metaphysics may drive people mad. This would be serious if everything else did not drive even more people mad. Sufism, in fact, drives many people sane.'

It is true that many people interesting themselves in spiritual matters are abnormal. So are many people interested in strawberry jam. In order to establish whether metaphysical interests are undesirable, surveys would have to be made. First, the number of mad people in other fields would have to be established. Then the number of mad metaphysicians who were mad before they became metaphysicians should be assessed. And, of course, the definition of madness should be carefully established. Not so long ago, people who thought that the earth was round were assumed to be mad. Nonsense is quite often something which people cannot credit, not something which is really impossible.

The British Astronomer Royal, according to Arthur C. Clarke in 1973, is stated to have said in about 1956: 'Space-travel is utter bilge'.

This is why the next aphorism in our selection has come into being:

'It is not learning which demolishes Sufis: it is stupidity.'

The Sufi enterprise is dedicated to asking the right questions. Sufis, when they teach, do not do so from doctrine or ignorance: they only teach what they know. This means that they organise their teachings to help to carry people from where they are to where the Sufi has already been. It is for this reason that they have the phrase:

'Sufis are people who will help you to ask the right question just as often as they provide the means to the right answer.'

This tendency to think of Sufis as people who repair the damage done to people by ignorance and assumptions about what can and cannot be done or experienced has caused some to say, sometimes approvingly, sometimes derisively, that Sufism is a hospital before it is anything else.

Commenting on this, a contemporary Sufi has asserted:

'If Sufism is a hospital, the ordinary world is a mortuary.'

Life in the ordinary world trains people to life and to work, to operate and to learn, only in certain ways directly connected with a small range of ambitions and desires. Some of this training helps to vitiate the higher ranges of perception, and people on the Sufi Path have to reclaim their sensitivity to subtler ranges of perception. He who tastes, knows, they say, following the great Sufi Jalaluddin Rumi. But to this we have to add the aphorism which states the present problem:

'Taste some things, and you lose the power to taste others.'

The experience of the Sufis, in fact, leads to an understanding of the human condition relating to what one can learn and achieve. Although obvious to those who know it, the resultant aphorism is, like all truths, hard to stomach for those who do not want to learn but may at the same time imagine that they do:

'The Sufi Way may be difficult – but what if other solutions are impossible?'

Three Forms of Knowledge According to the Naqshbandi ('Designers') School[1]

GUSTAV SCHNECK

The chaotic state of most people's conception of knowledge is seen in the fact that the word *knowledge* means all kinds of disparate things. There is the knowledge which comes from experience, the knowledge of a theory, knowledge of facts, and so on. One word, but several different conditions and substances being described.

The Sufi needs to make a distinction which other people may not feel necessary, because he is approaching the 'fine from the coarse', needs (like all specialists) more precise definitions than are needed at lower levels of understanding.

Approaching the question in the terms familiar to ordinary people, the Sufi description is of three 'kinds of knowledge' which have to be separated, and the difference has to be felt:

1 The description of something – as in the words used to convey the idea of a fruit;

2 The feeling of something, as when one can see, feel and smell a fruit;

3 The perceptive connection with something, as when one takes and tastes, eats and absorbs a fruit.

These three departments of cognition are described in more technical language as:

1 Certain knowledge (*Ilm-al-Yaqin*), which comes from the intellect, which tells us that there is a fruit;

2 Eye of certainty (*Ayn-al-Yaqin*), which is from the 'inner

eye', and operates like the senses but in relation to deeper things; the 'assessment of a fruit';

3 Perfect Truth (*Haqq-al-Yaqin*), which is the experience of 'union with Truth'.

The equivalence of these three areas in familiarly religious terms is:

1 Acceptance of divinity as a statement; (= intellect);
2 Feeling that there is divinity; (= emotion);
3 Perceiving divinity (= understanding: real experience).

According to the Naqshbandi path, the following four stages of aspiration have to be passed through in readjusting that part of themselves which has perceptive capacity:

1 Desiring things for oneself;
2 Desiring things for others;
3 Desiring what should be desired;
4 Being free from desire.

The purpose of the teacher is to guide the learner from one stage to the next. Greedy people remain at the stage of desiring things for themselves only, and cannot make the transition, in many cases, to wanting things for others. When they do reach this stage (which can happen with conventional idealists and the pious) they still have to detach from the desire to desire things for others in order to give themselves pleasure, for this is only a form of Stage One. This is the point at which the conventional moralist can only appeal for non-selfish service: he will generally not have the means to teach it, and hence most religious systems suffer from what they freely admit is vanity. Their constant battle against this, whether it has results or not, absorbs energy and lasts for whole lifetimes, as we know from the records left by saints and others fighting 'temptations' of all kinds.[2] The Third Stage, that of 'desiring what should be desired' comes when the previous barrier has been overcome. It signals the awakening of knowledge, because it is then understood that 'what should be desired' is more important than desiring itself. This paves the way for the Fourth Stage, when the individual is able to detach from desire itself.

Since he (or she) is now able to enter a non-desire state, the actions of a higher will ('Thy Will be done') may become manifest.

Certain spiritual systems, possessed of a tradition as to the overweening importance of this stage but evidently lacking the means to monitor and assist progress towards it, are characterised by striving to enter and stay in a 'non-desire' state. The result is a large number of people in a quietist condition. They have not reached the stage of ability to detach, but the state of the inability to do anything else, which, rather than spiritual, is possible to describe as a conditioning in apathy.

THIS CONDITION COMES ABOUT BECAUSE THE PREVIOUS STAGES HAVE NOT BEEN SUCCESSIVELY PASSED THROUGH.

NOTES

1 Formerly called *Silsilah-i-Khwajagan* (Succession of the Masters) ... it is probably the earliest of all mystic *Silsilahs* (Professor M. Habib, in *Muslim Revivalist Movements*, Agra 1965, p. ix).
2 Abstinence or generosity are not virtues if you enjoy them or enjoy suffering through them (Bahauddin Naqshband, First Teacher of the Naqshbandi Stream).

THE SUFIS OF TODAY

by
Seyyed F. Hossain

The Sufis of Today

SEYYED F. HOSSAIN

SUMMARY

The increase in information about the Sufis and their knowledge encourages cranks and shallow students as well as providing valuable materials for genuine study.

There are a very large number of imaginative emotionalists as well as numerous arid and over-intellectual scholars with prestige but without Sufic insight. Many of the former stampede for fragmentary information because it appeals to them. They fail to appreciate that Sufic study must be comprehensive and directed from its authoritative source: otherwise it is next to useless. The latter tend to concentrate upon fossil materials, unaware of the living element.

The longing for experience in religion among people, for instance of the Christian background, is at the root of a search for excitement: which is confused with spirituality because of a lack of the necessary distinction between these two important factors in most Western cultures as well as in other parts of the world.

The random adoption of selective parts of Sufi operation in the West is like a mirror image of the miming of Western technology among 'cargo cultists' in scientifically underdeveloped communities familiar to Western anthropologists. Because this somewhat shallow reaction occurs in what are otherwise developed societies, observers on the whole fail to analyse it correctly. They believe that such a mentality cannot exist in modern societies.

One major problem in the West until recently has been the absence of a single authoritative centre of Sufi studies. In the East, by contrast, both the legitimate teachers and the imitators have been discernible for centuries. As a consequence in the West (and in parts of the East where the tradition is no longer operative) anyone can imagine himself or herself to be carrying on Sufi learning, without effective supervision.

229

Imitation and self-imagined Sufis are characterised by:

1 An over-simplification of ideas and a narrow attitude towards literature; standardisation of exercises and studies;
2 Imitation of names, formulae, words and costumes; ritualism; absence of safeguards against conditioning;
3 Loss of the understanding that literature, organisations and other frameworks are instrumental and from time to time superseded; consequent adherence to externals and the ready adoption of fossil forms;
4 Lack of awareness of the uselessness of dilution and the mixing of specific curricula with extraneous ideas not indicated for that particular time, place and community;
5 Inability to observe the difference between social groups and learning ones; in extreme cases leading to placing the group or individual above the objective;
6 Attention-seeking not diagnosed as such; mistaken for genuine interest;
7 Difficulty in distinguishing the authentic Sufi enterprise from a false or imagined one.

Advantages of the present position

In spite of the drawbacks which inevitably attend the general release of unfamiliar knowledge, much valuable work has been done, by Idries Shah and others, to introduce the concept and to maintain the form, of the Sufi activity in thought and action best suited to the time, place and people. Even on the relatively shallow plane of literary, psychological and scientific affairs, these efforts have been widely appreciated.

Although the cults have proliferated, the large and coherent contribution of the legitimate Sufi stream has grown to such proportions that the gap between the Sufis and their (often unconscious) imitators has grown satisfactorily wide. This has increasingly meant that even relatively inexpert observers have been more and more able to distinguish the difference between them, paralleling the traditional experience of the East, where this gap has ensured the viability of the authentic tradition while leaving the imitators to their amusements: for whatever use these may be to them.

The contemporary existence of a central focus, *The Society for Sufi Studies*, means that competent work can continue for those who really want it.

THE SUFIS OF TODAY

It is nearly a decade and a half since Ted Hughes, writing in *The Listener*, described the Sufis as 'the biggest society of sensible men there has ever been on earth'. Studying widely in what has been published on this subject during this period and the hundred years or so preceding it, these words appear as a watershed. Here is a major scholar, writing in a literary magazine of the first importance, not an obscure quasi-religious journal. Here is a subject, in short, formerly to a great extent dealt with by cranks or frankly bemused academics (even the orientalist specialists have often said that Sufism confused them) brought into the mainstream of current thought, in a major medium, by a man with an immense audience. From this date onwards, an enormous interest in Sufi thought and action built up in the Western world, with some good – and inevitably a few adverse – consequences.[1]

Writer after writer since Hughes has stated how impossible it now is to look up the old, impoverished definitions of Sufism in reference works ('a mystical system among the Mohametans characterised by ecstatic exercises, a revolt against the formalism of Islam....')[2] and give them any credence. What had actually happened, to the delight of some and to the dismay of a few entrenched interests, was that the last great ancient psychological system was starting to find its place in the arena of present interest. Hughes himself went so far as to indicate the directions which would be followed by later researchers in disinterring Sufism's role in history: 'Many forlorn puzzles in the world, which seemed to suggest that some great spiritual age somewhere in the Middle East had long since died and left indecipherable relics and automatisms to trouble our nostalgia, suddenly came into organic life'.

While this momentous development was unfolding in Britain and the United States, I had been invited by Sheikh Imdad Hussein El-Qadiri, the Sufi historian, to travel through the Middle East, Central Asia, India and Pakistan. My brief was to consult the major Sufi authorities with a view to articulating our response to the avalanche of attention which we realised would

soon descend upon us. There was no doubt that those diluted
Sufic cults already operating in the West would receive a shot in
the arm from the above-quoted and subsequent revelations. As a
consequence, we would be meeting streams of seekers-after-truth
wishing to trace Sufism to its assumed local 'sources'. We also
knew that mimetic groupings, designed through error or downright imposture, would appear and would try to acquire involvement: what one respected but colloquially inclined
American professor had already termed in print 'a piece of the
action'. We knew that the rigid requirements of the authentic Sufi
voice would cause numbers of people to try to bypass the source of
authoritative exposition; and that, unless we were careful, the
superficial though articulate would produce one or more forms of
quasi-Sufism tailored to Western tastes but quite different from
the real thing. A fresh wave of interest would surround the pedestrian and often inaccurate works of some traditionalist scholars
who had written much on Sufism. They had hitherto, by default,
often been taken as authorities, and would not willingly yield their
position, however improper, since they naturally defended it like a
property interest.

And there was another likely consequence from the lid being
taken off Sufic private history, as Ted Hughes's article elsewhere
abundantly demonstrated: 'Among the scattered hypotheses of
amateur mystics, theosophists, and dabblers in the occult, one
often comes across references to "the secret doctrine", some mysterious brotherhood that is said to hold the keys to everything in
the West, outside Christianity, that touches the occult . . . all these
things originated among the Sufis, and represent degenerate,
strayed filterings of the doctrine. . . .' Although quite obviously
not intended as such, words like these could only cause further
uncertainty to people who had been unprofitably connected with
occult groupings – and they might run into the millions in the
West alone – and cause perhaps sizeable numbers of them to
embark upon an attempted investigation of the Sufis. Nobody can
prevent the quite laudable desire of men and women for knowledge: but people in the West who had no tradition of the kind of
specifics that are the Sufi specialization, who lacked a certain kind

of discipline or believed that it was not needed: who, on the other hand, would accept direction but only in a form or from a source that they themselves decided: all these were about to descend upon the purposeful and well-organised world of Sufi affairs.

It would not be long, either, before tireless researchers, devouring such books on Sufism as were available, would find that they were full of references to esoteric Christianity: indeed, many Sufis were in the past held to be secret Christians. In spite of Ted Hughes's disclaimer about 'outside Christianity', this time of doubt and re-thinking in Christian circles would undoubtedly add to the flood of searchers perhaps innumerable people seeking for the 'real truth of Christianity'. This could mean almost any number from a total of hundreds of millions of people in the Western world – and the consequent proliferation of Christian-Sufi cults.

I was chosen for my task by the Sufi Council because for almost twenty years (since 1945) I had specialised in investigating and assessing the potentiality of the so-called Sufi activities in the West, both experiential and academic. I was operating on the sociological level and not on one of direct ('telepathic') understanding solely because we had been unable to make any psychic contact with such people in the twentieth century West. To us, therefore, independent Sufi studies did not exist in Europe and America in our direct-perception sense. There were only amateur attempts to deal with the material on an intellectual or emotional, not a spiritual and higher-perceptive basis. At one end of the spectrum came the intensely cerebral theorising of the academics and their derivatives. At the other the circuses, with self-styled masters, funny clothes and even funnier rituals. Some of the cults, it is true, had been kind enough to term themselves 'a revival' of Sufi activity. But, whereas it is possible to revive, say, a fashion, it is not possible to revive Sufi activity unless one knows who and what to revive, when and where and how. We had found no trace of this knowledge among these self-styled Sufis.

Our prognostications as to the likely developments, hypertrophies and misunderstandings of Sufism could have been based on prescience: but they did not need to be. Sufi experience in the past, and anthropological investigations in the present, indicated sufficiently clearly on the rational plane that all 'new', or rein-troduced, activities undergo a deforming process in those circles which lack the basic knowledge and experience to prevent it. In the West this deformation is well recognised, is termed 'cargo-cultism', but is generally believed to be something which happens only in remote 'native' cultures. Actually, it happens everywhere. It is the penalty of ignorance. Idries Shah has called it 'heroic ignorance', but ignorance it remains.

Since we were faced with what was not a spiritual phenomenon in such expressions, but a social one, it was possible to deal with it only on the superficial level. Few things are more embarrassing, incidentally, than meeting leaders and members of 'Sufi' groups who lack the elementary communications capacity which we regard as inseparable from senior membership of a school. It is like being a linguist and meeting people who are styled as inter-preters, but who turn out not to be able to speak any second language at all. But, because of the contemporary taboo against being descriptive in case it appears critical, this side of things is not generally made known beyond our circles.

The result of our deliberations, carried on in India and Pakis-tan, in Afghanistan and Iran, Turkey and the Arab countries, was unequivocal. First, it was quite clear that in the West the only forms of 'Sufism' then well known were derivative or imitative ones. We have the same kind of thing in the East; but then we also have stable and authoritative Sufi establishments. The real Sufis – or, at least, their leaders – are well and widely known to the Press, the universities and other opinion leaders. The rest (some of them also being self-appointed 'Sufi experts' even in universities) are something of a tolerated joke. Some of the latter interact with their Western equivalents; but, in general, worthwhile people keep away from them. They fill the demand for a slightly weird or over-intellectualised expression on the part of people who for some reason cannot enter into the real Sufi world.

Our main problem was that the increasing links between the Eastern superficialists and their Western counterparts could become so strong and numerous that people in general might begin to confuse their activities with the genuine Sufi school. The bad, as Gresham's Law has it, might drive out the good.

The only way to make an easily-communicated distinction between 'them' and 'us' was soon agreed. We decided to make known, for the benefit of the West and the Eastern imitators and counterparts, the fact that real Sufic activity was not narrow-based like the spurious ones. That it was characterised by the use of the widest variety of methods and formulations. Like all cults, of course, the inadequate and shallow so-called Sufi groupings relied – and still depend – upon over-simplification and a narrow range of theories and practices, mostly copied from books or derived from quite inauthentic 'teachers'. They lack a living tradition in the true Sufi sense.

In addition to assuming 'Eastern' robes and names, some of these coteries employ merely one or two books, perhaps originally emanating from Sufi masters and intended for local use. Instead of seeing these as we do, and always have, as externals, they have often come to be regarded as a sort of perennial holy writ. Other groupings seek to link Sufism with one or two branches of meta-physics or ordinary religion, making a kind of inter-religious mish-mash which appeals to a wide range of people. Instead of getting to the root of things, they form a platform at a late stage of expression: the ritualistic. New cults tend to spring up and flour-ish or deteriorate; some of them more or less recognisable as derived from secondary Sufi materials and expressions, but gener-ally only taking advantage of the current interest.

Concurrently with our efforts to make known the truth about the ancient and also the contemporary facets of Sufism, we decided to encourage certain well-informed and competent Sufis to devote part of their time to the West, to monitor and represent the new developments which were to be expected there, of a healthier kind. From time to time local Eastern authorities lec-tured, wrote and broadcast in the East and West, so that the traditional voice of Sufism should remain represented on the public level for those who really wanted it rather than those who only sought emotional stimulus or circuses. Notably effective in this were the Sufi specialists Mahassini, Wasty, Yalman, Bokhari, Abbas and Qadiri[3] who contributed widely on this theme.

As time passed, of course, such was the interest in educational, literary and psychological circles in the East and West that volumes of collected papers began to appear, which now constitute a major source of authoritative and reliable verification of the real Sufi effort. These are being published widely in the West[4].

As predicted, of course, the cults and the confusions, the misunderstandings and the absurdities, have indeed grown in the West. They have also influenced some people in the East. Fortunately, in neither case has the distortion reached anything like the proportions caused by a similar process and so lamented by parallel authorities in the field of Hindu and Buddhist interest. What is particularly interesting about all this is to note that, in spite of the legitimate Sufi guidance and many materials now being freely offered in the West, there is a powerful demand from the alleged students for the spurious and 'amateur', because the latter is more attractive to those who want circus and not knowledge. The real Sufis of today are to be discerned from their flexibility and the range of their interests, just as their forebears were.

Before we further define the nature and action of real Sufis, there is the matter of those who oppose a clearer understanding of Sufi thought in its contemporary projection. Their motivation is almost always quite discernible. They include: the second-rate and 'threatened' academics, suffering from a sour-grapes syndrome, already referred to; the various stultified cults, which can neither learn nor collapse because of popular demand; sections of the sensationalist Press, which seek 'revelations'; and – not a negligible quantity – the rejected or disappointed who have tried to get into true Sufic groupings but have been dismissed or have not been admitted. In cases where one finds hostile comment about today's Sufism, it is always fruitful to check whether the opposition stems from one or other of such sources.

The nature and action of contemporary Sufism includes the literary and experiential learning-frame for its public projection and for some of its specific studies. The religious-cult and esoteric-school aspects, often in a very deteriorated form, are of course the most familiar sides of the recorded image of the Sufis. But this is only because, in the nature of things, these aspects have been more conspicuous and have received the greatest public support and hostility, and have generated more attraction value. A study of the classical literature shows that the more dramatic, the more attention-attracting, concomitants of Sufi (and perhaps other) schools are only a small part of the whole. It is also widely known to Sufis, but not to others, that Sufism has not only a vast constellation of methods, but also that its schools must adopt the working frame and the outward face which correspond with the nature and state of the culture in which they are operating. This not only accounts for the many ('baffling' of course) shapes of Sufism throughout the ages, but also for the current true Sufi dictum: 'We refuse to turn a perfectly good 20th Century man into a second-class replica of a 12th Century one!'

Idries Shah's reclaiming of this essential core of Sufi knowledge and versatility is one of the most 'classical' things about him. Although many of the 1500-odd tales, for example, which he has published, can be seen as therapeutic or other psychological encounters, psychotherapy is not the object nor the extent of Sufism. On the other hand, on the 'tail wagging the dog' thesis, the attraction of Sufism for those seeking mental stabilisation is probably due only to the fact that such people are to be found everywhere, such is the nature of their malaise. The Sufis – and everyone else – get their share of them. They will tend, however, to 'capture' any merely mimetic grouping and will in fact turn it into a personality-cult or social or would-be therapeutic operation. The distinction which is made by us today, between social and Sufic groups, is of the greatest possible importance in understanding both types: the false in order to avoid it, the Sufic in order to profit from it.

It is still regarded as a revolutionary concept (in spite of much modern sociological research and illustration of the fact) when we say that people connected with human groups, irrespective of their overt objectives, may be (1) mainly seeking attention or (2) responding to herd-instincts the price of which is to adopt the apparent aims of the group. Simple though this contention sounds – all important ones do seem simple, it seems – it is probably revolutionising contemporary thought in its working as an analyser of human systems. 'As an analytical tool,' one psychologist working in sociology recently remarked on this subject, 'this concept ranks for us today with the discovery that there was a chemistry lurking behind alchemy, making modern science possible.'

Sufism's further contention, that 'emotionality and spirituality are not, and cannot be, the same thing', is also widely seen as the reintroduction of an almost-forgotten principle of metaphysics, once very widely applied in the thought of the Middle East. Its loss due to the popularising of spiritual exercises – so-called – 'broke down the barriers between effective practice and wishful thinking', which had the same sort of effect as would be caused if, for instance, printing compositors were to start to believe that since all letters were indeed 'only letters', one could be used instead of another. 'It might amuse them,' says a major contemporary thinker, 'but what happens to the message?'

Sufism is the simplest and the most difficult thing in the world. It is the simplest because of its doctrine, which we may summarise:

> Man is cut off from perception of his real potential and of objective Reality because he is full of subjective imaginings and conditioning.

It is most difficult because:

> One of the consequences of the above situation is that man is almost unable, by himself, to overcome it, no matter how he tries. The secondary personality holds him in its thrall.

Methods have been devised, or, rather, devise themselves, and are used by those who know which one will work, and when. These people are sometimes known as teachers, because they have the overview which the others (known, sometimes, as the students) lack. Sufi study is never repetitive, never mechanical, because of the perception of the teacher as to what procedure will answer best in which case or cases. Mechanical systems differ from Sufism in this: they do not take account of the fact that the subjectivity of man will defeat any mechanical system: if you repeat 'I am mechanical' enough times, this repetition will automatise you, however sublime the intent. Besides, to treat everyone as if he or she were exactly the same as everyone else, in metaphysics as in anything else, is a sign of ignorance, not fairness, where it is not true.

In order to approach and to reduce the effect of the human conditioning factor, the Sufi master observes his disciple and prescribes the behaviour, studies and activities which correspond with needs. A Sufi teacher would regard the clamour for standardised exercises or practices demanded by many would-be students and many so-called teachers as bordering on the insane. As we have often noted in practice, almost the only similarity to our Sufi way of doing things which we find in the majority of the self-styled Sufic groupings which have grown up by themselves, is due to their having adopted our terminology. In no other way would any of us be able to recognise most of such social entities as spiritual, esoteric or religious. Even as psychological undertakings their only contribution could be to pretend to be spiritual. In the process, none would deny that they might achieve some therapeutic results: but that could be achieved more easily, and as Sufi activities there is no possibility of any yield.

A Sufi is not someone who is studying or believes in Sufism. A Sufi, according to Sufic tradition, is the end-product: the result of Sufi teaching. 'Sufi' used as it often is for a kind of seeker-after-truth, is a misuse of a technical term. Sufis, again, do not have 'leaders'. Sufis are all equal, by definition. A major difference between Sufi concepts and those of other persuasions which are allegedly in the same field is that the developed or realised man who emerges from Sufic study is of infinite variety. No two Sufis are alike in any way which can be measured by the non-Sufi. Those who carry out conventionalised exercises are known as dervishes, roughly equivalent to monkish seekers. For them, liturgy, say, may appear important. At the Sufi stage it is not. Most

Sufis go through the dervish stage, but they have to graduate beyond this, as many classical masters have frequently declared.

Another thing which has not been revealed loudly enough until recently by genuine Sufis for the imitators to register, is that Sufi studies may take almost any form. They are not confined to what people are likely to imagine they will be like. This concept, by the way, is so unfamiliar and yet beguiling that it is likely to be adopted by mimetics as soon as this report is published so, if you are interested and meet anyone who claims to be following it, find out by discreet enquiries if he got the idea here or whether he knew about it before! And remember, if he merely adopts it from an article, he is no Sufi, since the principle is rooted in experience, not in words.

The main problem with the projection of Sufi knowledge of general principles is undoubtedly great. A teaching which requires tremendous skill and great qualities, as a result of infinite patience and colossal effort, is unlikely to recommend itself to people who tend to believe that desire for truth is a good substitute for effort. The people of this latter type, we should honestly admit, are to be found very widely disseminated among those interested in esoteric matters, as elsewhere. In these days it is not considered acceptable or even authentic to point out requirements for learning which happen to be inseparable from Sufi knowledge. As an illustration we may note a passage in a book first published in 1961, where it refers to a Sufi teaching operation in Britain:

> At more than one point the youth thought that his mentor was more than half mad. He took him for long walks, telling him that one day he might tell him something of value, but that he would have to have patience. How much patience did he have? ... Listening to the way in which he tested him – for patience, tact, moral probity and sheer endurance – one felt that there could be few who would stand the pace: in Britain today, at any rate.[5]

Since we first decided to maintain the flow of information as to the contemporary existence of a conscious and legitimate source of Sufi teaching in the world, including the West, there has been a vast explosion of interest, both from the general public, from occultists and from the learned world. Each has tended to try to employ this information in its own way. What would be of greater value would be if the phenomenon were used not to support smaller preconceptions but in its own terms: as something perhaps worthy of more objective study. If there is one single thing worth saying for general information, it is this: Sufi activity is purposeful, well established and not in any sense experimental. Attempting to employ parts of it for shallower purposes than its own will yield only correspondingly disappointing results. If, in other words, it is used as a therapy, it will operate no better than any other subjective therapy, as with the placebo phenomenon. If it is used as a disguise for a power-group or social system, it will provide those things, but no more efficiently than any other incorrectly used outward decoration: it will not operate as Sufism. But it cannot be denied that where there is genuine aspiration towards truth, and when this aspiration is directed towards a source of it, there must be a correspondingly effective result.

Over the period from Idries Shah's first authoritative exposition (*The Sufis*, 1964) there has been, for the first time in the many centuries of Sufi research and publication, a clarification of what the Sufis have been doing and what they have not.

This process has been immensely facilitated by the acceptance by scholars and others of our revelation that what were formerly known in the absence of explanation as sacrosanct systems of the Sufis are in fact only fossils. Fossils, however, which make it possible to trace valuable information for those who want to verify the elements which lie beyond them: the fact of Sufi activity.

Two factors have helped in this process of 'separating the chemistry from the alchemy'. The first has been the coming forward of Sufi experts from the East to present people in the West and elsewhere with a unified voice as to what constitutes Sufism and that its authentic current voice is directed by Idries Shah. This has been necessary because people are accustomed to looking to a single institution as the central focus of any teaching or educational system. The second has been the work done by many experts and commentators, and the diffusion of the materials into general circulation.

Taking the second point first, we have seen the sale of more than a million copies of Idries Shah's books, in over a hundred editions, throughout the world. The critical acclaim and general public acceptance of the materials on various levels has been exceptionally strong.

In the specialist field, there have been numerous reviews and articles in the orientalist press and a great deal of enthusiasm from the religious and scientific world. That the Sufi materials have been hailed by psychologists as blazing new trails (although they are some of the oldest trails, in actuality) and by spiritual circles as profound documents of religious experience, means that at last the message that such branches of exposition are extrapolations from a central body of objective knowledge has now penetrated into more circles than ever before.

The following excerpts, reprints and comments from all over the world indicate, if anything does, that Sufi studies have at last broken out of the narrow confines within which lesser minds have for centuries attempted to limit them.

This does not mean that cultists will not continue to represent Sufi activity as a cult, or as exercises and emotional rituals. It does mean that such people will be less and less listened to; and the genuine activity will continue apace. What *New Society* has called: 'The alternative modes of learning, unfamiliar to the West'[6] are now on an entirely sound and effective footing.

REVIEWS AND COMMENTS ON SUFI AFFAIRS FROM A VARIETY OF COUNTRIES AND MEDIA

ADIL ASKARI *Sufi Studies: East and West*. Extract: 'It would have been a relatively easy task for Idries Shah to remain within the Eastern and devotional context of the traditional Islamic Sufi teaching role, surrounded by eager disciples and welding together the system's rich heritage, in much the same way that Jalaluddin Rumi himself did in his own time. He preferred to concentrate upon the publication, first, of typical materials in his field so that the world academic and informed lay public, in whatever discipline, could be made conversant with the relationship between ancient Sufi thought and the pressing concerns of today. *'Theoria to Theory'*, Vol.10, 1976, pp.249-254. Cambridge.

AFGHANISTAN NEWS Article on Idries Shah's *The Sufis*, emphasising the importance of the book and its authenticity, with a note on Shah's Afghan background. Vol.7, No.81, May 1964. Kabul, Afghanistan.

AMERICAN SCHOLAR, THE Review-article noting that scholars, unfamiliar with Sufi materials, finally accept them as valuable in their traditional fields. Vol. 39, No. 2, Spring 1970, USA.

ARAB WORLD, WHO'S WHO IN THE Family history and publications of Idries Shah (s.v. Shah) with affirmation of his mentorship of Sufi thought and documentation of his genealogy. 1971–72 Edition, page 1493, Beirut, Lebanon.

ARGENTINISCHE TAGEBLATT Report on Sufi Book Week, held in conjunction with UNESCO's World Book year, 25 November 1972, Buenos Aires.

DERVISH, BASHIR M. 'Idries Shah...' Programme of Shah's grandfather in Sufi development; spread of viable ideas to the West through a new method; backwardness of Middle Eastern projection of traditional ideas compared to the formula pioneered by Shah; the many Eastern authorities who accept Shah's role and importance: from Egypt to Mecca and Syria to India. *Islamic Culture*, Vol. L, No. 4, October 1976, Hyderabad, India.

GUARDIAN, THE 'Consider the Elephant' review-discussion of *The Dermis Probe*. Emphasises strong support for Sufic materials from eminent critics and the increasing use of the books in anthropology, sociology, medieval studies and work on Eastern literatures. 26 November 1970, London and Manchester.

MORENO, ARTHUR 'A Mind that has no Match' emphasises the synthesis of Eastern and Western wisdom in a Sufi frame which quotes a speeding-up of learning capacity where a three-week course in business management produced results which beat people with five years' study: and similarly technology and science. In *Blitz*, 9 March 1974, Bombay, India.

NEW YORK TIMES BOOK REVIEW, THE 'Books by Idries Shah'. Extensive article on the books and their background and influence. Refers to the use of the teaching story and its use among the Sufis. 7 May 1971, New York.

OBSERVER, THE 'Some kind of a Cake'. Review-discussion of *The Way of the Sufi*, *The Pleasantries of the Incredible Mulla Nasrudin* and *Reflections*. Refers to the new information brought to bear on, e.g., Romance literature; the atmosphere of the literature and the schools of the Sufis in the West today; the role of the Nasrudin stories in learning; the inner effect of the sayings in *Reflections*. 19 January 1969, London.

THOMSON, R.L. *Psychology and Science from the Ancient East*. In this scientific journal, the ancient and newer emphases of the Sufi activity are set side by side with contemporary thought. The author asks: 'What is the origin of this

material which can prefigure work which today needs sophisticated instru-
mentation to discern and test?' He quotes research into the various traditional
systems (such as the I-Ching, Zen, Yoga and Sufism) as concluding that 'of all
these it is the Sufi metaphor and method which not only correspond with the
new knowledge but are perhaps even ahead of current scientific work.' Vol.2,
No. 1, March 1973, London.

TIMES LITERARY SUPPLEMENT, THE Review of *Thinkers of the East*. On the
Sufi contribution to human thought and learning: 'Their instructional
methods, though contrary to canons unquestioned for centuries, are now seen
to anticipate, if not to extrapolate, the conclusions suggested by modern
psychological discoveries.' 7 May 1971, London.

VAN RENEN, D. 'Idries Shah' article on Shah's television programme ('One Pair
of Eyes'), on his life at home and ideas on various topics. *Argus*, 2 November
1972, Cape Town, South Africa.

WILLIAMS, PROF. L.F. RUSHBROOK Contribution on *The Magic Monastery*,
notes that the book illustrates 'the manner in which Sufi practice, with its
devastating criticism of purely academic learning and its continuing Socratic
search for truth at any cost, exercises a powerful appeal to many thoughtful
people in the West.' *Asian Affairs*, October, 1972, London (Journal of the
Royal Central Asian Society).

NOTES

1 Ted Hughes, in *The Listener*, October 29, 1964, reviewing Mircea Eliade's
Shamanism and Idries Shah's *The Sufis* (The Ocagon Press, London).

2 What, after all, does 'Mohammedan pantheistic mystic' (*Concise Oxford Dictionary*) mean? Presumably the same as 'Pantheistic Mohammedan mystic'
(*Chambers's Dictionary*).

3 Professor Z. El-Mahassini, in *Asda* (Beirut), July 1971; Professor Nayyar
Wasty, in *Jamhur* (Lahore, Pakistan) January 1973; Professor A. E. Yalman, in
Bayram (Istanbul) 22 August 1971; Dr. A. A. Bukhari, in *The Kabul Times*
(Afghanistan) 4 March 1973; His Excellency S. K. Abbas, in *Al-Sahafa*
(Khartoum, Sudan) 4 December 1972; Sheikh I. H. El-Qadiri, Introduction
to Shabistari's *The Secret Garden* (Johnson Pasha's translation) London 1969
(The Octagon Press) and New York, 1974.

4 Professor L. F. Rushbrook Williams (editor), *Sufi Studies East & West*, New
York 1973 and London 1974 (The Octagon Press); Professor L. Lewin,
(editor) *The Elephant in the Dark*, New York 1975; R. W. Davidson (editor)
Documents on Contemporary Dervish Communities, London 1966 (The Octagon
Press).

5 A. Daraul, *Secret Societies*, London 1961.

6 Lisa Alther in *New Society*: 15 June 1978, pp 610f.

IN A SUFI MONASTERY
and other papers

In a Sufi Monastery ...
Conversations with a Dervish

NAJIB SIDDIQI

What is the sensation of knowing things that other people do not know like?

It depends on the things and their real function, as well as your association with what these things seem to mean. For instance, if you dislike fungus and then discover that a form of it has antibiotic qualities, you may change your attitude to fungus or you may shun antibiotics. And I can give you another analogy, following upon this:

A man visits another world. He sees people there who are covered, some more than others, in fur. The more meritorious they are, the more fur they get. This upsets his preconceptions, which hold that fur is more primitive than nakedness. But he is able to understand when it is pointed out to him that the human love for fur is a hang-over from a distant memory of this state.

These people, too, practise physical and mental exercises which give them powers of survival during long interstellar journeys and to sharpen their receptive capacity to transmitted messages.

Further, they fear death, since what we call death is a sanction used by their controlling administration to punish wrongdoers. Its effect is to suspend their progress and make them start over again.

The man realises, but only just, that the 'yoga' postures and exercises, while of some use in the world, are designed for a very much more important cosmic purpose which cannot be discharged without other elements: for instance, the 'spacecraft' and technology from which they are extrapolated.

247

He comes to see, again, but this time somewhat dimly, that death is not what he was told it was.

So you see, I hope, how things can be different but how it is hard for us to understand them in reference to another form of being than our own.

And it is no use, and may be quite wrong, trying to adopt customs and ideas from another 'world', piecemeal. Like, say, killing yourself or trying to grow fur. Or even to try for spiritual gifts without knowing enough.

PEOPLE WHOM SUFIS DON'T ENCOURAGE . . .

Can you tell me what kind of approach would be disliked or rejected by Sufis?

This is a not untypical letter, which gives all the indications of an unpromising candidate who is trying to gain something for himself without the sense of *service*, or the requirements of the people whom he is trying to approach.

'I have not read your book, but I understand that you are an authority, so I will come straight to the point. I want to meet dervishes, to study them, and to benefit from what they have. Please let me know by return of post: (a) addresses of reliable teachers; (b) their communities where I may stay; (c) who gives training in dervish dancing that I could have; (d) where I could watch dervish activities, either before taking part or instead; (e) how I can tell who is genuine and will not exploit me.'

A copy of this letter was sent to me by the Sufi who received it. Attached was a copy of his answer: 'I am not able to answer any of your points except to say that, on their showing, no dervish or sufi would have you anywhere near him!'

CONTRARY TO POPULAR BELIEF

There are two kinds of popular belief:

1 Erroneous beliefs by individuals and groups, generally due to inadequate information, easily cured by exposure to the real facts purveyed by experts;

2 Erroneous beliefs, often held by experts and authorities of various kinds, and often enshrined in human organisations and institutions, which contemporary experience and to some extent investigation is showing to have influenced many of our ways of working and thinking in spite of being entirely or partly wrong. . . .

Because of both (1) and (2), it is quite certain that truth must be found before historical errors can be righted. . . .

Vanity and Imitation

FARES DE LOGRES

The importance of replacing vanity with a desire to learn is nowhere better illustrated than in the normal human tendency to try to learn without the basic training which can only be obtained from the people who are specialists, not mere proponents, in this area.

For centuries, and in every spiritual and other School, vanity has been considered an evil, something to be overcome. It is such a powerful thing that those who try to overcome it without the technical knowledge themselves thereby become victims of vanity. As has been said, the 'blind try to lead the blind'. The panoply with which supposed 'teachers' and allegedly 'good' people surround themselves are manifestations of that vanity: while any seeming ostentation in which a *real* specialist is to be found is no manifestation on vanity, since it does not touch him.

These simple truths are never tested by aspirants to higher knowledge, since they are debarred, through their own vanity, from being able to carry out the simple tests which would show them whether the man (or woman) with whom they are dealing is affected by pomp or indifferent to it.

It is for this reason that cryptic sayings have come into being. People no longer know what is meant by the words 'a real person will be found amid luxury, while a false one may be found glorying in poverty'. The appearance has driven out the reality.

In the West, religious teachers are to be found who revel in things of the flesh but imagine that they are untouched by these. In the East, people are to be found who are imagined to be austere

250

and therefore 'holy' just because they abstain from certain foods or adopt bodily contortions, or (as, too, in the West) they are able to intone certain sounds or carry out certain rituals.

Because there is some vague perception of these facts, again, some people have affected to maintain that there is therefore no reality and no value in spiritual pursuits. They, again, are misled by their immature desire for explanations at all costs. In this case the cost is too high: it is the cost of the truth.

Nowhere is vanity so well marked as in the supposedly diligent and virtuous observation of the norms and behaviour of tradition. Because a certain person did or said something, because a certain group of people followed a certain path, these things – when blindly followed or rationalised – are believed to confer sanctity, to be better than other things, to constitute 'a Way'. Few things are further from the truth. The truth, of course, is that vanity brings imitation. Imitation is not a way to truth.

Why is imitation not a way to truth? Simply because, where the truth is there, and someone knows the way to that truth, the 'way' is that way which is provided by that person. To carry yourself (or others) from one place to another is not performed by following the way which has been adopted by others, in different places, and under different circumstances. This is the great secret of the spiritual life: he who knows can do, and he who does not is unlikely to know if he is seen to be following something which was developed for a specific purpose.[1]

Humility, the reverse of vanity, is expressed by that person who is prepared to see that the way to reach an objective can only be that way which, traditionally, is beaten out by that person who knows the aim, and has the ability to beat out the Path.

It is for this reason that, throughout the centuries, there have been successions of real teachers. Always they indicate a path somewhat (or completely) different from what is expected by traditionalists. Almost always, for reasons of vanity, such teachers have been attacked and misunderstood. Only the absence of vanity on the part of the audience can be the key which opens this fact to the observer and would-be learner.

Then why does tradition (in its worst sense) endure?

Because the human being, in his ordinary role, will always seek that which flatters him. It is flattering to oneself to think that one is following the 'right path', that one is doing and thinking – and experiencing – those things which have been felt and thought and done by the great ones of the past. This may seem to be a simple fact. It is a great secret nevertheless.

NOTES

1 The Sheikh Idries Shah, in our times, is the first man to have pointed out this 'doctrine of supercessions' as he has termed it. It would be unnatural if many people did not feel threatened by it, and hence did not themselves adopt a threatening stance when faced by it.

Sufis Over Two Centuries

VALENTINO DE MEZQUITA, SR.

Jalaluddin Rumi (mid-13th Century) is marked by the *Mathnavi*, his great mystical work, which has reached every succeeding generation, prized for its content and its insights. In this way, Rumi ensured that his work would transcend the cult which was created by his followers, and centred around the mechanical and simplified performances of his 'dance' movements. He did well to leave the *Mathnavi*. His followers, over 700 years after his death, maintain the cult, gyrating in meaningless fashion, forgetting his strictures about the limitations of poetry and of the dance-form.

Just as Rumi had rescued from absurdity the concepts of parallel understanding and of symbolism, making them plain as psychological and spiritual frameworks, in the thirteenth century, Bahauddin Naqshband, in the fourteenth, swept away still further accretions. With him (his name means 'The Designer'), emphasis was placed on the thing, not the appearance. Hence he insisted in his followers wearing the ordinary clothes of the area in which they found themselves, banishing the cultishness of outlandish garb. He likewise instituted – or reintroduced – silent performances of exercises and the need for preparation to prepare: the solid basis for understanding, not the attractiveness of mysterious pronouncements.

From this century on, the Masters (Naqshbandis were alternatively known thus) determine the character and method of the impact of Sufi ideas on the rest of the world. Sufism was to retain its literary tradition through such classical poets as Saadi and Jami, of the late 15th Century; factors such as the importance of

253

humour and the need to be in the world as well as out of it, intermittently, were emphasised, to combat the cultishness which, again simplistically, caused imitators and fanatics to seize a single formula in a hopeless attempt to guarantee paradise.

It was this ability to distinguish the accretions from the essential, and to prescribe the necessary procedures rather than catering to amusement value which caused the Designers to be accepted as the only 'Order' whose teachers were authorised to initiate members for all the other orders of the Sufis; which thereby accepted that their outward differences were secondary.

What the Sufis do not want us to Know

EDWIN CLITHEROE

Sufis, like everyone in the 'communications business', whether they be religious, psychological or other, are at pains, it seems to me, to stress the importance of knowing, of knowledge.

That is just fine, we all want to know more. But the unusual paradox here is that there seems to be a distinct trace of a movement among the Sufis to want us not to know certain things.

I first approached Sufism to collect information about it, and to try to understand – to 'know' about its objects and methods.

I soon realised, however, that an outside student, however devout or academically learned, has about as much chance of doing this as a cannibal can grasp the aims and skills of a brain-surgeon. Visualise the difficulty our cannibalistic friend would have in approaching what the doctor was doing, why he was doing it, and what the outcome should be. . .

The cannibal – or the learned man – may feel sure that he can, given opportunities, grasp or experience, 'what it is all about'.

But each has to learn that his preparation, his own information stock, however adequate to his current culture's needs, may well be inadequate for the task.

SUFI SOLUTIONS TO THIS PROBLEM – AND THE SOLUTIONS' DECAY . . .

So the Sufis have to, seemingly always have had to, set up an intermediate ('Learning how to Learn', Idries Shah) phase. The cannibal, as it were, has to be diverted from his major interest and to be refocussed onto the medical art...

It is this phase which, eventually adopted and operated mechanically in subsequent and lesser hands, has left the strong traces which people imagine, wrongly, to be 'Sufism'. In such cases, the means has become the end, obscuring the aim and preventing success.

These means have included religious formalism, community enterprises, organisation, ranging from those of chivalry to commerce, and extending to literary and artistic expressions.

The indicator of Sufic potential in a would-be student is the extent to which he can either recognise the irrelevance of format, or approach a continuing source of the authentic tradition even if it has a very different face from the associative one to which he had become accustomed: but not too accustomed.

CONDITIONING AND CONVERSION

It is the Sufis, virtually alone, down the centuries, who have warned that emotional breakdown (leading to 'conversion syndrome') and indoctrination and conditioning produce devout or religious people and communities, but not necessarily any spiritual progress or even activity.

Those who feel that such a claim is unlikely to be true have only to read the devotional literature of many 'spiritual' persuasions in the light of current knowledge about mind-manipulation; and can check the matter for themselves.

It is only between 1950 and 1980 – an almost incredibly short period of time in terms of literary effect or the space needed to communicate general knowledge – that the facts known by, and published centuries ago, by the Sufis, have come to be known by the rest of us. And our cultures are not yet by any means adapted to these facts.

WHAT – AND WHY – DO THE SUFIS WANT US NOT TO KNOW?

The clue lies in the Sufi phrase, going back to ancient times, to the effect that 'The ignorant are better than those who do not use their knowledge'. Theoretical, or incomplete, knowledge has functions and characteristics which are unsuspected by those for whom 'knowledge' means narrow specialisation. Sufis assert that people should have a wide range of knowledge and experience, because, quite obviously they understand that a little knowledge is a dangerous thing. Those who follow a narrow line are more likely to think that they know more than they do. The Sufis want us not to know, too, things which disturb the developmental process because they can be given an untoward degree of importance in the wrong rhythm or succession of learning. 'It is not what you know, but when you know it; it is not how much you know, but how you can use it; it is not what you think that you know, but what you really do know.'

Those who find these statements mystifying have only to inspect the lives, the thoughts and the actions of people who claim to know a great deal, or who are believed to be knowledgeable, to understand what these words mean.

THREE MAJOR CONSIDERATIONS

A close scrutiny of the common factors in the enormous multiplicity of sayings, doings and lives of Sufi masters yields a piece of valuable information here. Three major considerations emerge:

FIRST, impatience prevents learning. At its worst, it causes a preoccupation with the thought 'Why am I not making any progress?', which effectively blocks that progress. It is for that reason that beginners are required to give up this attitude.

SECOND, preconceptions themselves (of which the above is one – 'I should be learning at a pace set by me and in a way perceived by me according to criteria accepted by me') increase the blocking effect.

THIRDLY, the splitting of attention, which is also found in preconceptions and in impatience, blocks learning.

It is only when a teacher succeeds in causing the learner to refocus and to avoid these three habit-patterns that learning can recommence.

The present writer has been allowed to observe the filtering and rejection of no less than 132,000 applications for Sufi teaching, extending over fifteen years, where the three manifestations just listed were the prime cause of the failure to progress. What had really happened was that the individuals in question actually preferred impatience, preconceptions and split attention to other modes of focus. A conspicuous form of all three hobbies was the approach as a cultist, or as a religious body, or as a source of emotional stimulus.

THREE COMMANDING PRINCIPLES

Distilled from the above-mentioned experiences, it is possible to isolate three very important casts of mind which enable a learner to approach and to benefit from Sufi knowledge:

1 Few ideas are wrong, but many people (including the devout and the 'ignorant specialists', very often, in the Sufi field) have so distorted ideas as to cripple their higher value for themselves. People imagine, too often, that they can take an idea and improve upon it. In fact, this cannot be done with a really fundamental idea. By re-experiencing the idea, and then getting to its roots, real progress is made.

2 Sufi insights and the Reality beyond are constantly, perenially and permanently in action in the affairs of this world. To try to make sense of human life, individual or collective, without understanding this element, is bound to lead to the kind of mess in which so many people so often find themselves.

3 In one sense, the beneficial effect of the real Sufis (not the self-appointed ones) in this world is immense. In another, the ultimate success of this effort requires a greater contribution from those who are sympathisers, even though they are less insightful than they might be.

The knowledge that the Sufis do, however, want us to have is that fixation on externals may give satisfactions which please, but these may well be barriers to progress.

One of the great classical Sufis, Tustari (died 896 AD) had a companion called Abdur Rahman ibn Ahmad. One day he claimed that when he washed his hands before prayer the water turned to silver and gold. Tustari said:

'Beware of what you do; for small boys are given toys to play with.'

This report (from Sarraj's *Kitab al-Luma*) is exceedingly worth pondering.

Religion as Repetition or Experience

HAFIZ JAMAL

People in the West often find it hard to understand the value of religious thought and action in the sense that people do in the East. This is because the Western kind of thought, which is now found throughout the world, operates on an 'either/or' basis, and a selective one at that.

'Either', so runs the unspoken doctrine by which this type of mind works, 'either we are dealing with religion or with non-religion. If with social groupings or psychology, it cannot be religious in the spiritual sense.' The either/or mind also tends to say: 'Religion is good and takes precedence over other subjects'; or, 'religion is irrelevant: other things take precedence'.

If these things were always brought out and dealt with as lucidly as that, there would not be as many confusions as there are. But what in fact happens is that you have to analyse a conversation, a lecture, an article and so on in order to determine what its unspoken assumptions are before you can see exactly what the people are really talking about.

This problem, oddly enough, seldom or never troubles the people who are carrying on the conversations, or writing or reading the articles, or listening to the lectures. It is because of this that it is easy to occasion surprise and sometimes annoyance, by pointing out the assumptions which underlie the thinking in such cases.

In various Eastern societies, on the contrary, the same kind of distinctions are not usually made. Religion, for most people in the

West whom one has studied for a quarter of a century, and whose books and other productions can be examined, is something of a rather homogeneous kind, in the sense that a religious person is ideally often supposed :

1 to be virtually incapable of doing something wrong;
2 always to be doing or thinking the same kind of things.

Naturally he will not necessarily recognise himself from this description, because there has been no noticeable effort made to convey it to him. In Eastern ways of thought, the emphasis of merit lies not in being incapable of doing something, but in being capable of doing it or not doing it. Although this idea would be claimed as theirs, too, by the people we are talking about, observation does not bear out the assertion that they really believe it or act according to it. Secondly, the religious activity in the East is more marked by the recognition of religion as something which has all kinds of phases. By this I mean that the religious requirement is that the individual and the group shall act according to circumstances and not according to mechanicality, or dogma as it is generally termed.

Illustrating the first case, we find that in the West people are praised for constant and unthinking service to certain beliefs: whether or not they are applicable to circumstances. While some lip-service is paid to the theme that people may do things which go against their nature and are yet 'good' things to do, this comes under the heading of 'struggling with temptation'.

The Eastern view of this is somewhat more sophisticated. It postulates a third kind of action: one which is performed not because the person cannot help doing it because he is indoctrinated, not because he knows it is good but would really prefer to do otherwise, but because he has an understanding that it is the correct thing to do.

It is this conception of the existence of this third, higher range in human awareness which has been suppressed in most Western thought familiar to us. It can therefore occasion little surprise that the belief-systems which generally obtain in the West are regarded by many in the East as assuming that the human being is to be stabilised at too low a level in the light of his capacities as known elsewhere.

Expanding upon the second case, we constantly find that religious thought and activities in Western-type communities are increasingly thought to be 'irrelevant' by people outside those circles. It is my belief that the much-lamented decrease in religious awareness in the West is due to this cause: to the gap between what could be done as a response to a situation and what people are attempting to do in order to follow a faithful path or 'party line'.

This latter form of conventionalism is, of course, what produces hypocrisy. Once you know what the community has been trained to regard as the words or apparent actions of a 'good person', all you have to do is to imitate these, whether they are having any 'good' effect or not.

This theme has, it is true, been extensively explored in Western fictional literature, when the struggles between what people have thought to be right and what others believe to be wrong have for many years been part of the stock-in-trade of imaginative writers. But we are almost always left with a question-mark. The exploration of this theme has not as yet, to any appreciable degree, led people to ask as to whether human conduct, in its needs among different people at different times, is not to be examined in phases. That is to say, the whole matter is regarded as a conundrum. People have assumed that there is a clash of wills, of doctrine, of attitude to life, and they have generally left it at that.

In the East the response to this situation has more often been the seeking of ways to understand not only what is supposed to be 'good', but when, where and how to do this good, to choose the 'right' course, on some basis more elevated than that of a community which has accepted certain things as always good and certain others as always bad. Further, one that has accepted that certain things have always to be done or thought by rote, or as priorities, without striving for the understanding of which things out of, perhaps, a wide range of possible 'good' things, applies to a particular case.

This kind of thinking, when I have mooted it in Western circles, has usually engendered the response that I am talking occultism or that it is a 'matter of common-sense' as to when, how, and so on, certain forms of goodness or rightness, certain thoughts or actions, are employed. Again, experience does not in fact show that people act in this way at all, even though they may imagine that they do.

There is a way into this kind of more sophisticated thinking, which does not require us to adopt 'Eastern' ways of thought. We only have to face up to relatively recent Western psychological discoveries and observations to see that if we happen to have a conditioned community, we have an individual and collective 'conscience', and that this 'conscience', this response as to what is good and what is bad and when one is to act in a certain direction, is subjective and implanted, not objective. It may, and frequently does, militate against the interests of other individuals and groups, and can be called 'religious' only in the anthropologists' sense that a religion of this kind is a social phenomenon.

People who have done any reading in Sufi literature may more easily recognise what I have been saying, for this point is often made there. One of the advantages of cleaving to this subject, even through the results of social scientists, is that it enables us (1) to postulate something higher in the way of a religious understanding; and (2) to recognise the deterioration when it invades originally superior spiritual groups. When the doctrine becomes inflexible, when practice and observance take precedence over the aim or understanding, we are faced with a deteriorated system. In these days, when a myriad of imitative cults are springing up and claiming, however temporarily, the attention of more or less sincere people, such a yardstick is very useful.

Outer and Inner Activity and Knowledge

HAFIZ JAMAL

All socio-religious formulations, systems of life based on precept and belief, have an outer and an inner aspect. Some people are so well satisfied with the outer aspect that they cannot – and often, for psychological balance, must not – imagine anything other than the literal and immediate. These people are sometimes called 'literalists', or 'fundamentalists', and both their behaviour and abundance are well understood (though often forgotten) in every human civilization. Their reluctance to examine ideas, behaviour or activities beyond their personal and peer-group experience is descriptive of their own mentality, not of that which is being examined. A horse says: 'Food is grass; there is no other food than grass. If there is, it is not good or necessary. What is wrong with those who want to complicate or upset life?' No doubt you will know at least one person who reasons similarly. He is, as we can easily see, describing himself and his preferences, not discovering what actually is there. There *is* food other than grass, whether everyone seeks it or not. Denying its existence places one not among an élite, but visibly among the bigots. The visibility is more or less great according to how analytically the victim is being viewed.

The statement of those who wish, as it were, to look for additional nutrition, is that the outward formulation is not only a solace and a means of support: it is potentially a way towards greater understanding, towards the inward. If, of course, it is regarded as the whole story, it may inhibit, not encourage, inner understanding. Yet the very fact that the outward, simplified, socio-religious formulation (the system or way of life as it is often called) can provide acceptable satisfactions for a large number and variety of people means that it also 'protects itself' by this very fact, from successive tampering by people of excessive subjectivity. Social stability for large numbers of people is possible and provides a haven and useful standards and satisfactions for these people. Those who fail to observe this valid function of the outward formulation often accuse such people of being shallow. It would be socially more satisfactory if they were to be pleased that it is so easy to suffice such numbers who, if they were in a ferment, would hardly be contributing to general human tranquillity.

Successful socio-religious systems or formulations are readily identified. They must contain a relatively small number of basic precepts which are of wide applicability; they should appeal to personal or group pride (even if overtly denying this); they must allow for extremes of intellectual and emotional stimulus to absorb the mental and physical demands of the spectrum of the participants.

The degree to which many intellectuals and emotionalists resist outside analysis of the systems to which they adhere, and the sophistication of their avoidance of such analysis, underline the validity of this contention.

The system, for these participants, is providing social and psychological support, as a splint supports a broken limb. Without it the individual would have to rethink the roles of his intellect and emotion, would have to decide to become an individual in the sense of aiming towards a life without the support of a herd of people or mass of ideas; would, in fact, have to contemplate decisions for which he has no preparation at all.

People who say that they believe that they can understand something by thinking it out or by experiencing it, in the field which we are discussing, are unlikely really to believe this. It is more probable, if one is to judge by performance, that these beliefs are interposed to preserve the status quo: to prevent understanding, since it is (often irrationally) feared that understanding might involve commitments which the powerfully intellect/emotion-based mind is unwilling to investigate.

Intellectual and emotional activity, in the minimum necessary proportions, however, may be employed to *provoke* understanding. They are not continuous with it.

Activities and experiences, as well as working hypotheses in this tradition, are so arranged as to help align oneself with the potentiality for understanding. The understanding is not standardised: it does not come to everyone in the same way, at the same time, even by means of the same formulas. This intricacy of operation is the rationale and the origin of the institution of the Teacher and Guide.

It may be said that all efforts in this tradition are designed to encourage the understanding by man of himself. This is not to say that importance is placed upon fleeting or partial understanding, or vague sense of semi-understanding. These latter are best to be described as no more than preliminary stirrings. To over-value them is generally to destroy their value for the individual who does so.

Conversation with a Sufi Master

AZIZA AL-AKBARI

Can you tell, from a letter, the next steps that a student should be taking, or the things which are holding that student up in spiritual progress?

Certainly, you can tell. The vast majority of letters are not of course concerned with spiritual things at all. They are generally full of opinions, assumptions and decisions which show clearly that the writer is seeking spirituality within a much lower-level context.

Could you be more specific on this?

Yes. Take this letter. The writer has decided to live a 'simple life'; has adopted all kinds of prayers and techniques, and writes to ask what should be added to all this to complete, as it were, his religious progress.

This means that people choose certain ideas and practices and then want to add to these, without realising that the very bases of their thinking may be at fault?

Precisely. This is very clear when you have a 'crank' letter, because you and I are perhaps agreed that obviously stupid procedures are not spiritual. But, when people are invoking practices and ideas which are generally considered pious or good in themselves, the blocking function of the obsession, or what we could call the idolatrous effect of over-valuing symbols or instruments, is not immediately apparent. To revert to your original question, anyone could immediately see what is holding up the student if it were only generally realised that secondary things: mere totems, useless conceptions, forms of amusement, are not in any sense spiritual. It is because of this insistence that secondary things are not primary that Sufis have been execrated by literalists.

An example of the problem?

The great woman Sufi, Rabia, carrying a lamp, saying that she wanted to 'Burn the Kaa'ba [holiest place of Islam] if it stood in the way of the worshipper's way to God'.

So secondary considerations become primary. How does this condition come about, in the first place?

Two tendencies, sometimes working together, cause this situation. The first is that all people have a yearning towards the Divine, as you may have read in Rumi's writings. This causes people to adopt anything that they imagine to be divine or of divine origin. They have forgotten that yearning alone is not enough. The second is that many people register, within them, the divine origin or connexion of certain ideas or practices. This leads them to suppose that these thoughts or actions must necessarily apply to them, or to everyone, or to all times. They have mistaken the container, with its 'scent of former content of musk', with 'the musk itself'.

But can it be true that anything in the world is of Divine connexion? Surely such things are of a totally 'other' nature?

On the contrary; because of the principle '*Al-mujazu qantarat al-Haqiqa*' [The Apparent is the Bridge to the Real] there are many things which conduct to the Real. This, indeed, is the purpose of the presence of the Sufi teacher and the nature of his work. It is the distinguishing of irrelevance from relevance which marks the Sufi enterprise.

So the apparently divergent projections of various Sufi groups and 'orders' mark the difference between different people and times, stressing what activities are relevant at what times, to guide people to Truth?

That is so. Equally, of course, this knowledge gives you the opportunity to discern, in so many self-styled 'Sufi' people and groups, the unfortunately imitative nature of their activities and ideas. They do not, of course, belong to the spiritual world, but to some kind of circus.

Would you call this kind of imitative person or grouping a false one?

I would prefer to call it 'useless for spiritual purposes'. 'False' may seem to some people to imply deliberate deception; whereas the falsity here often comes about because of sheer lack of information and of perceptivity.

Does this remark connect with Idries Shah's statement that 'there are even more false disciples than there are false teachers'?

Certainly. The fact, is of course, that where there is a demand from 'learners' for something which is offered by 'teachers' there is always an abundance of 'teachers' and 'learners' who are not in fact carrying on any real teaching or learning activity. This happens in all human communities.

Surely this means that there are two sorts of 'spiritual' activity: one which is only emotional and the other which is real? If this is so, it seems that people will feel that you are claiming everyone other than you to be wrong?

There are indeed two sorts; there may even be more than two. But it is not we, but the facts which indicate the existence of the two. Think of an analogy: suppose people performed fertility dances to ensure good crops and someone came along and said that fertility was not produced by dancing and also that something entirely different was responsible for good crops. Would you not then find many people who would think that this new suggestion was unacceptable and that the newcomer was claiming all kinds of qualities for himself or herself which were not inherent in the statement of fact?

So you are not going so far as to say that the proferring of this information entitles you to any special consideration or ascendancy for you or your personal or group organisation?

You are, I fear, confusing ascendancy of leadership – the socio-emotional activity, with function. This is best illustrated by using another analogy. Supposing I and perhaps my organisation were to come into a community where art or arithmetic were unknown or were faultily known. We would demonstrate these things, quite aside from any activity which also claimed to be the same or which claimed importance or ascendancy. People would then be able to study with us and there would be no need for leadership or ascendancy. What we demonstrated and contributed would be perceived and employed, and its function would be understood to be educational and operational. This, indeed, is the essential distinction between something learnt to be employed and something experienced to be enjoyed.

But should one not enjoy something which is employed? And why should people always learn things to be employed?

There is no reason why something which is employed should not be enjoyed. What is ineffective is when something is enjoyed and thought to be something more than, or other than, that which is enjoyed. Further, there is no reason why people should always learn things which have to be employed. The point is that there are things to be employed, and people should be allowed to know which are employable so that they may benefit from this employment.

What, then, is the real character of people who claim, or for whom it is claimed, that they are the greatest or most important exponent or representative of spirituality?

This is two questions. Taking them in order, the supposed Sufi who says or implies that he is supreme is no Sufi at all. As for the second question, people for whom things are claimed by others cannot be ranked or described by character, since the description originates with others, and the claiming describes the others, not the person being described.

How does one know whether a teacher or an organisation is fully authoritative?

It is not a matter of describing *how* one knows, as this cannot be described. It is a matter of stating that people always know.

Then why do they follow spurious or ineffective people and cults?

For the same reason that people buy false bargains offered by deceivers. The reason is that they know, inwardly, that the offer is false. Their own inner falsity answers, and they find their affinity.

But does this not mean that you are saying that nobody can be trapped by false things as every trapped person is himself dishonest?

No, it does not mean this at all.

Then what can it possibly mean?

Not only does it not mean what you imagine, but it demonstrably means that there is a true part and a false part to everyone. Whoever extends the false part will perceive through his or her own falsity, and will be able to perceive only the false.

How are people to extend the real part of themselves to the Real?

Those who do not have to ask, can do it. Those who do have to ask, are given instruction on the methods to overcome their own falsity by the Sufi School itself. Many people, of course, can learn this apart from through a Sufi school.

But how does anyone know when he or she can profit from contact with a Sufi School?

It is not a matter of 'how' since there is no 'how' which can be spoken in words. But the perception comes through that part of one which looks at one's own falsity. People are always trying to find sincerity. They should give equal attention to the perception of falsity, so that they may instantly shun it.

SOME RECENT RESEARCH PAPERS ON
SUFIS AND SUFISM

Brent, Peter: The Classical Masters
Pendlebury, David: Sanai and Sufism in the 20th Century West
Chand, Pandit Kishan: Yoga and the Sufis
Deikman, A.J., MD: Sufism and Psychiatry
Lewin, L., Hon. D.Sc.: Sufi Studies/East & West
  (All the above reprinted in *The World of the Sufi*, London, 1979 – The Octagon Press)

Shah, Idries: Christianity, Islam and the Sufis
Sanchez, Ismael: Christian Mysticism and the Sufis
El Qadiri, Sheikh Imdad Hussein: Sufi Thought
Foster, William: Sufi Studies Today
  (All the above reprinted in *The Elephant in the Dark*, ed. L. Lewin, New York, 1976)

Kolinski, Boris: How they see Us
Archer-Forbes, A.: Dervish Ritual
Fischer, Raoul: Social Mysticism
Samuelson, Arthur: The Festival of Dervishes
Faris, A.L.M.: The Sufi Way
Butterfield, A.C.: The Pattern of the Sufis
  (All the above reprinted in *The Diffusion of Sufi Ideas in the West*, ed. L. Lewin for Institute for Research on the Dissemination of Human Knowledge, Boulder, 1972.)

Shaw, Julian (Correspondent of The Times):Abshar Monastery
Brook-White, S., Dervish Assembly in the West
Burke, O.M.: Travels and Residence with Dervishes
Hallaji, J.: Study of Specialised Techniques in Central Asia
Daraul, A.: A Sufi Organisation in Britain
Martin, D.: Account of the Sarmoun Brotherhood
  (All the above reprinted in *Documents on Contemporary Dervish Communities*, ed. R.W.Davidson, London 1966 – The Octagon Press)

Abdullah, A.: The 'Pointing Finger' Teaching System
Aksu, G.: Preparation of the Student
Foster, William: Teaching Techniques
Grant, John: The Known and the Unknown in Studies
Khan-Urff, R.: Learning by Contact
Simac, R.: In a Naqshbandi Circle
  (All the above reprinted in Abdullah, A., et al., *New Research on Current Philosophical Systems*, London 1968 – The Octagon Press)